The Battle for Flanders

The Battle for Flanders

German Defeat on the Lys, 1918

Chris Baker

Pen & Sword
MILITARY

First published in Great Britain in 2011 by
PEN & SWORD MILITARY
An imprint of
Pen & Sword Books Ltd
47 Church Street
Barnsley
South Yorkshire
S70 2AS

ISBN 978-1-84884-298-4

A CIP catalogue record for this book is
available from the British Library.

Typeset by Concept, Huddersfield, West Yorkshire
Printed and bound in England by CPI UK

Pen & Sword Books Ltd incorporates the Imprints of Pen & Sword Aviation,
Pen & Sword Maritime, Pen & Sword Military, Wharncliffe Local History,
Pen & Sword Select, Pen & Sword Military Classics, Leo Cooper, Remember When,
Seaforth Publishing and Frontline Publishing

For a complete list of Pen & Sword titles please contact
PEN & SWORD BOOKS LIMITED
47 Church Street, Barnsley, South Yorkshire, S70 2AS, England
E-mail: enquiries@pen-and-sword.co.uk
Website: www.pen-and-sword.co.uk

Contents

List of Plates

French reinforcements passing through Caestre, 13 April 1918.

A 6-inch howitzer in action at a farm near Strazeele, 13 April 1918.

A German signal station established at Mont de l'Hospice, just outside Locre.

Lieutenant Archibald Gordon MacGregor RE, who halted a retirement at Siege Farm.

Elbow Farm, scene of the dawn raid by 20 Middlesex thwarted by the German attack. On the horizon is the dominating height of Kemmelberg.

The River Lawe at Locon today. View looking south.

Second Lieutenants Collin and Schofield, awarded the Victoria Cross for their actions at Givenchy on 9 April, are both buried at Vieille Chapelle Military Cemetery.

The battlefield near Festubert and Route A Keep: peaceful once again.

The Portuguese memorial in La Couture.

The River Lys at La Gorgue, looking west towards Merville and the area defended by 50 (Northumbrian) Division.

The German military cemetery at Sailly sur la Lys, close to their first bridge-head over the river at Bac St Maur.

Aval Wood, last resting-place of many who took part in the fighting around Caudescure.

On the Hogenacker Ridge, looking north towards Meteren. This important high ground was defended by the gunners of 33 Machine Gun Battalion and the infantry of 19 Brigade.

Memorial to 25 Division in the rebuilt town of Bailleul.

Once the Germans had reached this summit of the Ravelsberg they had perfect observation, making the continued occupation of Bailleul untenable.

From the Ravelsberg, the importance of the Flemish hills becomes clear. Kemmelberg is the summit on the right.

From Brulooze crossroads looking north to the wooded height of the Scherpenberg. Along this road the Alpine Corps advanced, but the Germans were eventually brought to a halt, marking an end to the Battles of the Lys.

The French army memorial on the summit of Kemmelberg.

Still remembered. A photograph left at the grave of Second Lieutenant George Rumball MC at Outtersteene Communal Cemetery Extension in 2009, perhaps by a member of George's family.

List of Maps

Introduction

My journey began in the mid-1980s. I had developed a growing interest in the British Army of the First World War and, as many people do, became immersed in books about the Somme and Ypres. Chatting to an acquaintance at work led to him bringing some family papers to show me. I did what I could in those pre-internet days to research the soldier they described, and it took me into territory completely unknown. The documents were about the death of 18-year-old Alfred Follows, lost for ever on the Lys on 12 April 1918. His story troubled me, especially when I discovered how many comrades from his battalion had died on that day and how few had known graves. Why was a lad from the Black Country of the Midlands in a unit that I recognised as the Barnsley Pals? What was going on near Doulieu that day? Where was Doulieu anyway? I decided to look more deeply into what had happened; I had never heard of the battle before and while it was not too far from Ypres the place-names were unfamiliar to me. Alfred Follows led me to the Lys.

On one of my first trips to see the Ypres battlefields for myself, a second set of questions entered my head. Working my way south down the rolling and attractive countryside of the Messines Ridge and on to Ploegsteert, I went on a detour to Kemmelberg. The familiar white stones and memorials of the British cemeteries dotted the entire area. On ascending the hill all I intended to do was to take in the view, which I already appreciated was of such strategic importance in this region, back across Messines to the towers of the Ypres Cloth Hall. Just over the summit, as the hill begins to fall away to the west – in what I still then regarded as a rear area – I came to an imposing French memorial, and further down the slope an ossuary containing the remains of more than 5,200 soldiers of France, of whom fewer than 60 are identified. They too fell in April 1918. What were they doing there and why were so many unidentified?

I still do not understand why this desperate fight in Flanders, later officially recognised as the Battles of the Lys, has received relatively little coverage. It is as important to the story of Ypres as any, yet in reading most histories of that terrible salient one could be forgiven for thinking that the fighting here ended when the Canadians slogged up the last yards to Passchendaele in early November 1917. The German attack on the Lys cost tens of thousands of military and civilian lives, caused panic and retreat, and came close to victory. Had the Germans pressed on just a little more, and the key railway junctions at Hazebrouck or the Poperinghe road had fallen into their hands, the British and Belgian forces holding Ypres and the line of the Yser would have been seriously endangered and potentially cut off. As it was, German pressure on the Lys was such that the ground won at Ypres at such tragic human cost in 1917 was voluntarily given up in April 1918, virtually without a shot being fired. The British had little choice; it was the only way that sufficient reserves could be found to stem the German attack. Once the Lys and the Flemish hills had fallen and the Germans held the railways, there was no other natural line of defence before Dunkirk and Calais. Steps were even taken to begin flooding a wide area to assist a desperate last stand.

The ultimate defeat of the German operation was an international effort: British, Portuguese, South African, Australian, New Zealand, Newfoundland, Guernsey, Canadian, French and Belgian troops all played their part. It is an extraordinary story and the men and their stories are worth remembering: that is why this book was written. In carrying out the research prior to writing, I have referred in the main to primary British sources, drawing on a mixture of secondary, official and regimental sources for the Portuguese, French, Belgian and German side of things. With more time, money and appropriate language skills, the battle from the viewpoint of the non-English speaking nations could be narrated in much more depth than I have managed: I look forward to seeing it and apologise in advance for any serious misinterpretations of the battle when seen through those different lenses.

In the desperation of battle, formations and units were often broken up, stuffed piecemeal into the line and ordered to hold to the last man. Quite separate actions went on in different parts of the battlefield at the same time. Taken together, this makes for a rather fragmented tale. Conscious of readability, I have generally tried to take the story of one part of the battle to a natural conclusion before examining another that may have overlapped it in time but took place in quite a different place. This does mean that the telling is not always in strict chronological order. The fighting on the Lys was a large action even at the outset, with the British force engaged being larger than that which had landed in France in 1914, but it sucked in more resources and grew to be a very substantial battle. Inevitably I have not mentioned every unit that took part, but concentrated on those where the fighting was at its most critical. I hope that the reader can forgive me for these characteristics.

I should also mention place-names. The area in which this battle took place is in Flanders, both French and Belgian. Since the First World War the Province of West Flanders in Belgium has officially adopted the Flemish language and many of the place-names that were expressed in French in 1918 are now changed. As a general convention I have used the contemporary names: Appendix II cross-references them to the modern spelling.

I would also like to share a thought that occurred to me on numerous occasions while writing the book and walking the ground. It has not proved to be easy to isolate the number of casualties of the battle, for the available statistics either covered all the fighting since 21 March or included that in areas outside the geographic area of Flanders. The Official Historian concludes that British losses during the battle amounted to 82,040, of whom 31,881 were missing (a proportion of these were later reported alive). His calculation of net loss is just over 76,000. Adding German, French and Belgian losses takes the total to well over 160,000 men. What unimaginable sorrow, pain and suffering this number represents. How easy it is to describe a battle, to draw one's finger across a map and say, 'this is where the Blankshires stood and died'. How pleasant to walk the fields and enjoy the views. How readily one can put words to high-explosive bombardments, attacks and counter-attacks, poison gas and machine-gun barrages. But how impossible it is to imagine the extremes of fear, cold and bewilderment that the men in the front lines must surely have felt. The hellish noise, the flashes and unearthly smells. Try to do so, as I have, while you read, and we can only wonder at how the First World War generation of all nations found the strength to carry out such exploits.

Finally I would like to thank the many institutions and individuals who have helped me along the way: the staffs of the National Archives, Imperial War Museum and British Library, all unfailingly helpful in person and in correspondence; the Reichsarchiv and Australian War Memorial, just as supportive at arm's length; pals at the online Great War Forum; staff and friends at the University of Birmingham Centre for First World War Studies, and in particular the inspirational Dr John Bourne; Brian Morris, my companion on many a battlefield trip; and those who have kindly allowed me to use photographs or personal material, including Captain William Nute (Old Birkonians), Brett Butterworth, Carlos Goulão, Anna Welti and Graham Thornton. My thanks to the Office of Public Sector Information for permission to use Crown Copyright material held at the National Archives; Major Hereward Wake Bt, for permission to access the collection of papers of his father Major-General Sir Hereward Wake Bt; Northamptonshire County Record Office Archivist Sarah Bridges and her staff; the Imperial War Museum and Australian War Memorial for permission to use photographs from their collections; and holders of other copyright information who have given their permission for me to use it. I have made every effort to contact known holders of all copyright material. My thanks too to Pen & Sword for being brave enough to be my first publisher, and especially to Rupert Harding for his patience and sound advice. And last but not least my wife Geraldine, who seems to have lost me for many months while I have been gone, physically or mentally, to those battlefields of more than ninety years ago. Without her support I could not have understood, let alone attempted to tell, the story.

Chapter 1

The Road to the Lys

Trench raids could never be called routine, but that codenamed 'Sammy's Slash' looked as straightforward as any. In the early hours of 9 April 1918 Second Lieutenant Alfred Hulls led his men of B Company of the 20 Middlesex Regiment into no-man's-land a few hundred yards to the left of La Boutillerie. They crept to within 50 yards of the German wire, under orders to wait until 4.45am when British artillery would lay down a barrage around the trenches in front of Bas Maisnil. The party planned to go into the enemy front line, kill as many Germans as they could and generally cause trouble, with the prime objective of gathering intelligence and taking prisoners. The night was quiet and a thick, cold mist had come down. With half an hour still to go before zero, the ground suddenly shook as thousands of guns opened fire and a deluge of poison gas and high explosives fell on the British lines behind the raiding party. Hulls' men thought at first that they had been detected and that the enemy had opened fire to stop their raid. Moments later the British guns responded, firing a protective barrage on pre-arranged positions in order to stem any German infantry attack. This included a barrage across no-man's-land. Half of Hulls' party were killed or wounded by their own artillery. Confused, Hulls decided that the craters just short of the enemy wire were no place to be and ordered the remnants of his group back to their own front line. Shortly after reaching the trench, a message came from his commanding officer that the enemy had broken through the Portuguese troops on the battalion's right and instructing Hulls to form a defensive flank in Tin Barn Avenue. He did so and took cover there until 6.30am when, sensing no lessening of the bombardment, he began to move further back to the dubious shelter of Elbow Farm, the billet of the support company. It was by now all too evident that the enemy shell-fire was not a local response to his raiding party but something very much bigger. Hulls did not understand. There had been no warning of a German attack and indeed he had been told that his unit had been sent into a cushy sector to recuperate from recent fighting elsewhere. He would not be alone in being taken completely by surprise at the start of the Battles of the Lys.

The development of the German strategic plan
In order to appreciate the German strategy that caused the Battles of the Lys to be fought, we need to go back in time to 21 October 1917, almost three months

into the British offensive now officially known as the Third Battle of Ypres. On that day a convoy of buses bumped and splashed along the roads of Flanders, taking the men of 10 Canadian Brigade from Le Nieppe through Cassel to Kruisstraat, the last place accessible to vehicles before shell-fire and ground conditions made the journey impossible. After a short period of rest and training the Canadians were on their way to take their place in the murderous front line of the Ypres salient. From Kruisstraat there was a short march through the ruins of Ypres and on to the dubious shelter of what little was left of Potijze beyond it. After a welcome mug of tea and the issuing of haversack rations, 50 Battalion was first to move off, under lowering skies and sodden by heavy rain, to relieve the men of 11 Australian Brigade at Levi Cottage. They were the vanguard of the entire Canadian Corps, sent to the salient to make the next, and it was hoped final, push for the Passchendaele Ridge. Over the next two days most of the units making up the four divisions of the corps filtered into place. The Canadians soon went into action and achieved all that was asked of them, pushing up through deep mud on to the higher ground at Crest Farm, through the powdered brick that was once Passchendaele and a little beyond it to marginally drier ground. Behind them, and back as far as Ypres itself, was a slough of several miles of utterly devastated and shell-swept ground, miserable conditions that stretched the soldiers of both sides to the very limits of their physical and mental endurance. By 11 November the Canadians had suffered 12,924 casualties. Nine days later the British Commander-in-Chief Field Marshal Sir Douglas Haig closed down the offensive; the same morning, a new attack began at Cambrai.

This ceaseless British battering against the German armies on the Western Front was beginning to have an effect. The offensives on the Somme in 1916 and at Arras, Messines and Passchendaele in 1917 had steadily worn down German resources at the front, while the naval blockade and economic warfare made for a deteriorating picture at home. Even as the Canadians were trudging up from Potijze, the German Fourth Army reported that its troops could not carry on much longer, such were the physical and psychological stresses on those defenders who survived. General Hermann von Kuhl (Chief of Staff to Crown Prince Rupprecht's Group of Armies) called Passchendaele 'the greatest martyrdom of the World War'. Despite this, the General Staff at the *Oberste Heeres Leitung* (OHL – General Headquarters) remained hopeful of retaking the initiative and breaking the Allies on the Western Front. There was now some urgency: a need for a quick and decisive result in France before the arrival of the Americans tipped the balance in favour of the Allies. General Erich Ludendorff (First Quartermaster-General) met with von Kuhl and Colonel von der Schulenberg (Chief of Staff to Crown Prince Wilhelm's Group of Armies) at Mons on 11 November. The situation on the Eastern

Front was now such that a move of huge forces to the west could be made, to the extent that the army would have 35 divisions and 1,000 heavy guns available for an offensive in the coming spring. Opinions were divided on the best course of action. Von Kuhl wanted to strike against the British in Flanders, his Group attacking from the Lille area towards Hazebrouck and Bailleul with the objective of cutting off the mass of the British Second Army holding Ypres. The vital Channel ports and key railway lines that fed all of the British armies might then also be threatened, with potentially war-winning results. Von der Schulenberg, supported by Lieutenant-Colonel George Wetzell (Head of Operations at OHL), held a different view, favouring an attack by Crown Prince Wilhelm's Group against the French, who were believed to be still fatally weakened by their efforts at Verdun in 1916 and on the Chemin des Dames in the spring of 1917. There were too many options and unknowns for a decision on the day, but Ludendorff concluded that a single offensive should be made, aimed at beating the British once and for all, and that it should take place as soon as possible. He saw some value in the Flanders attack but believed that the low-lying ground, waterlogged in winter and so prone to becoming a quagmire, would not allow an attack to be made early enough in the year, and time was of the essence. The discussion moved on to the possibility of an attack made on the drier ground of the St Quentin area, but no conclusion was reached. The Chiefs of Staff were ordered to study the alternatives, but an attack would be made. No reference was made to Kaiser Wilhelm II, the political leaders or the German nation in reaching this decision, which inexorably committed Germany to a climactic battle in France.

The balance of military power on the Western Front began to swing rapidly in Germany's direction during the remainder of 1917. Haig was obliged to send five divisions to Italy in the wake of a serious Italian defeat at Caporetto, thinning out his already dwindling force. The innovative and initially highly successful British strike at Cambrai on 20 November dwindled into defeat, recrimination and a high-level enquiry when the Germans counter-attacked with equally innovative tactics. It was on the very day that the massed British tanks and a surprise artillery bombardment were cutting through the defences at Cambrai that von Kuhl reported back to Ludendorff with regard to the spring offensive. Pressing for the Flanders operation, already codenamed 'St George', he believed the British would not expect an early attack there and that great opportunities would arise from an assault against the River Lys front between Festubert and Frélinghien. The St Quentin idea also had merit in that it could be made at any time and was also a weak front, but Kuhl pointed out that it would require much larger resources than would an attack in the north. Wetzell reported his thoughts on 12 December, by which time it was clear that Russia under Lenin's new Bolshevik government would no longer fight and therefore that considerably larger German forces might be brought to France. Wetzell put forward a different view, proposing not one single knock-out blow but a series of offensives. The ultimate goal would be the destruction and defeat of the British. His plan was to hold the French by attacks at Verdun, draw in British reserves from Flanders to contain an initial German attack from St Quentin, then within a fortnight strike the main blow in the Hazebrouck direction before rolling up the rest of the British line. It was a brilliant piece of strategic thinking, even though it would stretch German resources to the limit. Wetzell's plan called for courage, superb staff work and excellent logistics. On 27 December Ludendorff ordered the two Army Groups to make plans for a number of offensives: 'George' in Flanders with a secondary operation known as 'George 2' near Ypres, 'Michael' on both sides of St Quentin, flanking operations near Arras and south of the Oise, and further attacks at Verdun and on the Champagne front. The staffs were advised to aim for the offensive to begin as early as 10 March 1918.

The plan that emerged proposed 'George' as an attack in the direction of Hazebrouck, on a 12-mile front with the left flank resting on the La Bassée Canal. The associated 'George 2' would have three components: Operations *Hasenjagd* against the Messines Ridge south of Ypres, *Waldfest* against the line to the north of the salient, and *Flandern* at Dixmude. Ludendorff gave his decision on 21 January 1918. 'George' was too dependent on the weather to make it the primary offensive, and 'George 2' was dependent on 'George' succeeding. 'Michael' would thus have to be the main effort, supplemented by the flanking operations 'Mars' and 'Archangel'. 'George', or alternatively 'Roland' in the Champagne area, would then follow 'Michael' once the artillery and supply of what Ludendorff called the 'battering train' could be moved from St Quentin to the appropriate area. The detailed plan for 'George' needed to be ready by early April.

As the plans and objectives for the priority operation 'Michael' developed, the scale of the resources needed and the logistical and training effort required became clear. There simply would not be enough men, guns, ammunition or transport to be able to undertake Kuhl's version of 'George' in addition to 'Michael'. On 10 February Ludendorff advised Rupprecht to scale back the operation. By the time 'Michael' was launched on 21 March, *Waldfest* and *Flandern* had been shelved.

The St Quentin offensive began with spectacular success, advancing further, covering more ground, taking more prisoners and creating more destruction of the British Fifth and to a lesser extent Third Armies than had been envisaged. By 24 March the German Fourth and Sixth Armies, which would undertake the 'George' operations in Flanders, were ordered to continue preparations, albeit on a reduced scale. As it became clear that the opportunity opening up on

German offensives March-April 1918
Principal operations and front line prior to attack on Lys

North Sea

Nieuport

Belgian Army
King Albert

4th Army
von Arnim

Second Army
Plumer

Ypres

6th Army
von Quast

Hazebrouck

Georgette

First Army
Horne

Lille

17th Army
von Below

Third Army
Byng

Arras

Mars

Cambrai

2nd Army
von der Marwitz

Amiens

St Quentin

18th Army
von Hutier

Michael

Fifth Army
Gough

Army Group
Crown Prince Rupprecht

Compiegne

Soissons

Front line reached
by Michael operations
by 4 April

Reims

Front line before
Michael operations
began on 21 March

Paris

March
1918

Planned for
April

Approximate scale

0

km

80

N

the Somme front was greater than foreseen, planners at OHL calculated that only ten divisions could be added to the Sixth Army for 'George'. It was presumably von Kuhl's staff that revised the codename for the scaled-back operations to 'Georgette'.

By 26 March 1918, after five days of 'Michael', German thoughts were increasingly turning to what to do next. The flexibility of Ludendorff's plan, based on Wetzell's concept of multiple offensives but with a singular lack of a defined strategic goal, gave plenty of room for choice. Wetzell pressed for 'Georgette' to be launched but the logisticians advised that it would take ten days or more to shift the point of attack to Flanders and align the necessary material resources to it. It was too long: the initiative would be lost. 'Mars' was launched on 28 March, only to prove a costly failure against the staunch defence of the British Third Army in front of Arras. So finally 'Georgette' was on. Orders for the numerous moves and regroupings were given, and the roads and railways feeding the Lys area from Lille and all the way back to Germany itself hummed with the movements of a million men. Rupprecht's forces received their operational orders on 3 April: the Sixth Army, commanded by General Ferdinand von Quast, and so ably administered by von Kuhl, would attack on 9 April 1918. The Fourth Army received confirmation on 8 April that it would also attack the day after the Sixth Army, undertaking the operation that had begun as *Hasenjagd*.

The development of British strategy
Even as the men of the Canadian Corps fought their way on 6 November 1917 through the brick and mud pools that marked the site of the village of Passchendaele, an objective for which the Commander-in-Chief Field Marshal Sir Douglas Haig had been striving since July, there was deep disquiet in London about the conduct of the war on the Western Front. The British Expeditionary Force, by some measure the largest organisation ever created by Britain, had been hammering away at the Germans in an almost unbroken series of offensives since July 1916. With the exception of the short and successful attack at Messines in June 1917, all had turned into ghastly, long, attritional battles that served only to inflict enormous losses in men and material on both sides. The casualty lists appalled many, not least Prime Minister David Lloyd George: 694,000 British dead, wounded or missing in 1916, another 894,000 in 1917. He assigned the losses not to staunch and sophisticated German defence but to the 'reckless prodigality' of the British high command.[1] There were increasingly clear signs of war weariness among both the men at the front and civilians at home. The bitter débâcle of Cambrai, coming on the heels of a promising start, confirmed serious doubts in some quarters regarding British strategy, command, intelligence and the relationship with the Allies. It

simply could not, in Lloyd George's view, go on this way. With his fine politician's sense of which way the wind was blowing, he took the opportunity to press for military changes. Some of Haig's key staff officers were removed but the Prime Minister did not go so far as to sack either Haig himself or the Chief of the Imperial General Staff, General Sir William Robertson. With the Prime Minister and the army high command at loggerheads, what followed became a series of manoeuvres and compromises by politicians and generals alike that engendered distrust and exposed the army to great risk, at the very time when the enemy was plotting its destruction.

Paris too was alive with discontent. There had been much discussion among French politicians and military leaders on the need for change, brought to a head during the crisis in Italy in the wake of Caporetto. Sir Sidney Clive, head of the British Mission at French General Headquarters, found Micheler, Debeney, Pellé and other generals all very anxious for a unification of command in the form of an Allied Commander-in-Chief, a *Generalissimo*. The Allies were simply not working together and were squandering their resources. Despite the compelling logic of command unification, Lloyd George shied away from it, believing such a move to be politically unpalatable, and the French Prime Minister Paul Painlevé did not press the point. Lloyd George would have recalled that his last attempt to place Haig under French command in 1917 had led to rancour and embarrassment. The Prime Minister would even go so far as to say in the House of Commons that he was 'utterly opposed' to a unified command.[2] He concocted an alternative plan – the Inter-Allied Supreme War Council (SWC) – and implemented it just days before Ludendorff's fateful strategy meeting at Mons.

Although it was formally agreed between the British, French, American and Italian governments at Rapallo on 7 November 1917, the formation of the SWC was already a *fait accompli*. Lloyd George had lobbied Painlevé before the meeting of the British War Cabinet on the morning of 2 November and gained agreement to his idea. Egged on by the voluble Francophile Lieutenant-General Sir Henry Wilson, whom he preferred as an informal adviser and sounding-board to the blunt Robertson, Lloyd George drew up the outline of a new organisation that would in his view provide fresh thinking and make coalition warfare work. The SWC was conceived as, and remained, a political and not a military body, although its focus was the military prosecution of the war. Only Britain, France, Italy and the United States would be represented on the council. The final Rapallo agreement described its functions:

> with a view to better coordination of military action on the Western
> Front, a Supreme War Council is created, composed of the Prime
> Minister and a member of the Government of each of the Great

Powers whose armies are fighting on that front ... [it] has for its mission to watch over the general conduct of the war. It prepares recommendations for the decision of the Governments, and keeps itself informed of their execution and reports thereon to the respective Governments.[3]

Furthermore, its object was 'to secure such an adjustment and coordination of national policies as will make possible the execution of a single coordinated strategical plan of Allied operations'.[4] It was to be 'an instrument for arriving at a common policy, not for carrying it out'. After more than three years of war, the Allies would finally have a mechanism for plotting Germany's defeat. The members of each government would be advised by a group of military advisers, one from each of the powers. The War Cabinet, encouraged by Painlevé's reported backing, duly ratified the proposal. Some believed it to be the most momentous decision of the war. Behind the scenes, arrangements began to fall into place. Immediately after the Cabinet, Secretary Sir Maurice Hankey wrote to Lord Derby, the Secretary of State for War, confirming the decision to make Henry Wilson the British military representative to the SWC and to promote him to full general before he accompanied Lloyd George to Rapallo.

Once Painlevé was on his side and the War Cabinet had approved the proposals, Lloyd George knew he would have a clear run at the Rapallo Conference. He told Haig as much when they met in Paris on 4 November. Clive noted on the same day, 'Amazed to find Henry Wilson at the [Hotel] Crillon, saying that all is settled.' The appointment of Wilson caused much angst in the British military hierarchy, partly due to quite proper considerations of clarity and who was responsible for what, and partly because his brash personal style was not universally admired. Continuity between SWC meetings would be achieved by frequent liaison visits by the ministers and the existence of a permanent staff, the most important elements of which were the 'competent military authorities' known as Permanent Military Representatives (PMR), one from each of the four powers.[5] The function of the PMRs would be to act as technical advisers to the politicians on the Council. Plans jointly drawn up by the four PMRs were to be submitted to the Council and, once agreed, would be taken back to the respective national War Cabinets for executive action through the normal governmental and military channels. Conversely, the Council could refer subjects to the PMRs for review and recommendation.

The British Army Council was flustered by the introduction of the new Council, upon which it had not been consulted. There was already a military adviser to the British government, and that was Robertson as Chief of the Imperial General Staff. It protested that under existing Letters Patent, and to avoid the clear risk of 'duality of counsel and the attendant evils of delay and ill-defined responsibility', the British Military Representative must be subject to Army Council authority. The War Cabinet agreed but added in undisguised tone, 'it should be understood that [the PMR] ... will have unfettered discretion as to the advice he offers'.[6] Lloyd George had got his way: there would be fresh British military thinking through Wilson, and it would be heard. Robertson and Haig had been outmanoeuvred.[7]

The new organisation was, to some, an 'unimpeachable ideal'.[8] More cautious observers recognised that the SWC was burdened with international and personal conflicts and was an inherently risky development at a time when the Allies could afford to take few risks. They recognised at the outset that the new structure 'will require the most careful and thorough working out if it is not to produce friction and overlapping'.[9] *The Times*, staunchly behind Haig and Robertson, thundered, 'The risk at the moment is that it is regarded by certain amateur strategists as an opportunity for disparaging all that the Allies have achieved in the past.'[10] The 'amateur strategists' were not named in this article but the newspaper's owner Lord Northcliffe would have had in mind Lloyd George, Wilson and some of the oddments that were appointed to the British staff, such as Member of Parliament Leo Amery. But such cautionary voices were barely heard among the trumpeting that marked the Council's establishment in the plush offices set up at Versailles. Henry Wilson and General Ferdinand Foch, named as the French PMR, now took centre stage. Unlike Wilson, Foch was not outside the normal command hierarchy. Much work was also done by his deputy General Maxime Weygand, who represented Foch's views to the letter.

Although its formal task was stated to be to unify strategy 'with a view to better coordination of military action on the Western Front', the definition of the Council's scope was loose and allowed the amateur strategists full rein. Within weeks of its establishment, the SWC had discussed and made resolutions on matters of grand strategy, as well as on military operations and even details of tactics. Wilson and his staff had barely consulted with Haig or Robertson, but – perhaps unsurprisingly - they were not given much assistance when they did.

Lloyd George had announced the formation of the Council by saying that 'Stitching is not strategy'.[11] After the messy business of shoring up the Italian front by piecemeal transfers of British and French forces to that theatre, both Wilson and Foch were determined that the overriding priority was to regard the entire Allied force and the whole fighting front as one. Wilson remarked: 'My own view is, and has been for at least two years, that we must treat the whole war as a war of one front ... If we don't work the picture as a whole we shall be beat.'[12]

The logic was that with the application of pooled intelligence, interchangeability and mobility of forces and systematic cooperation, the Allies' collective advantages would be brought to bear. Caporetto and all the costly and unsuccessful prior attempts at winning the war, essentially carried out on a national basis, would not be repeated. The first Joint Note submitted by the PMRs proposed that the entire Allied line 'from the North Sea to the Adriatic' should be considered as a 'definite and coordinated system of defence', and that steps should be taken to maximise the use of mechanical means, including the improvement of lateral rail and sea links, to make it effective.[13] This statement pointed the way to Joint Note 12, 'The 1918 campaign', which was issued on 21 January 1918 and approved at the Third Session of the Council. The Note was based on intensive analysis by the staff of the fighting strengths and dispositions of both sides, their reserves and abilities to sustain fighting, and the situation in terms of politics and morale.[14]

The 1918 campaign plan, expressed without a trace of pessimism, acknowledged that there had been a fundamental change in strategic circumstances as a result of the collapse of the Eastern Front. In the face of a rapidly growing but temporary manpower advantage for Germany, it required the Allies to stand on the defensive on the Western Front and in Italy, safe in the knowledge that, with appropriate maintenance of strength and correct dispositions, the enemy could not secure an outright victory. A German attack in France was considered to be highly probable, although the exact place and timing remained as yet uncertain. The plan admitted that the Allies could not win either, at least until the Americans were there in great numbers. Although it called for the military to be alert to opportunities to counter-attack, the plan did not require any of the armies to plan for an offensive except in the Middle East. Lloyd George, always keen on attacking the Turks rather than the Germans, naturally applauded; Robertson advised against the scheme and Haig would have too but alleged that he had not been consulted.[15]

The idea of the single strategic front made sense except that there was still more than one man in command of the various Allied forces. France and Flanders had two men in command, Italy another, Salonika a fourth. If the logic extended to Palestine and Mesopotamia, the situation was even more fragmented. General Henri-Philippe Pétain, Commander-in-Chief of the French Armies, wanted to split the entire front from the North Sea to the Adriatic into two sectors, one under himself and the other under Haig. Clive was swayed by his argument, noting 'I like this plan; it achieves a twin command, which is a step towards unity, and gets to some extent out of our national shackles', which he thought the principal barrier to cooperative action. However, by the time the Germans struck against Haig's armies with 'Michael', no steps had been taken to change the command structure.

Wilson and Foch's second concept was that the national armies would place a proportion of their forces into a central strategic reserve, which could be deployed where it was most needed, whether it was Ypres, Arras, the Somme, Champagne, Verdun or Italy. This was expressed in the PMRs' Joint Note 23, issued on 25 January. The members of the SWC ratified the proposal and went further, stipulating that the size and composition of the reserve, where it was placed and when and how it would counter-attack, would be the decision not of the commanders-in-chief but of the PMRs, now to be called the Executive War Board. Haig and Pétain nodded sagely and simply refused to give up any of their armies to the reserve; Haig suggested that the divisions he had given to Italy might be treated as such. Both men were jealously guarding their own resources, and each would have jumped at the chance to control the other's.

On 2 March 1918 Haig reported that he had come to a private agreement with Pétain, in the event of a sustained enemy attack:

> For such a purpose or to meet any emergency on the Franco-British front, I have arranged as a preliminary measure with the Commander-in-Chief of the French Armies for all preparations to be made for the rapid despatch of six to eight British divisions with a proportionate amount of artillery and subsidiary services to his assistance. General Pétain has made similar arrangements for relief or intervention of French troops on the British front.[16]

With the General Reserve unworkable and the PMRs stymied, Haig and Pétain returned to considerations of how they would defend against an increasingly likely German offensive. Any chance of a strategic Allied approach to defeating the enemy's offensive had now vanished, and the focus switched to local operations and tactics. As Foch would later ask, 'which of the two commanders would dare to part with the reserves he had promised' when the enemy attacked?[17]

The state of the British armies in France
The Adjutant-General's strength return showed that there were 1,949,000 British and Commonwealth troops in France and Flanders on 5 January 1918. While this figure was 303,000 higher than the equivalent at the start of 1917, there had been a fundamental shift in the mix during the year. The 1918 numbers were swelled by an increase in non-combatant and labour troops, as a result of the constant clamour for more men to carry out manual work behind the lines, a process facilitated by the large numbers of returned wounded and men classed as below fighting grade who were made available to do such work. The total of fighting troops had declined by almost 95,000, representing a reduction of 8 per cent, despite conscription having been introduced in 1916.

The Dominions continued to find ways to build up their contingents, and the fighting manpower of their units had increased by more than 12,000; the problem lay in the frittering away of British fighting grade troops, and this core element of Haig's armies had fallen by 10 per cent in the year.[18]

The allocation of Britain's already overstretched manpower was a most complex question, which government committees and staffs studied in great depth. The needs of industrial production, shipping and the various armed forces needed to be appropriately balanced. A Cabinet Committee decided that the priority for manpower, driven by the primary need to sustain the war economies of the Allied nations, at least until such time as the Americans changed the balance, should be 1. the fighting needs of the Navy and Air Force; 2. shipbuilding; 3. tank and aeroplane production; 4. food production and timber felling. The army did not take any priority for allocation of men, but would have to hold on until the effect of prioritisation of manufacture of the tools for armoured and aerial warfare filtered through.

Alongside the 62 under-strength infantry divisions facing the Germans on the main front in France, the British army was by now also providing four divisions in Salonika, ten in Egypt and Palestine, one in Mesopotamia, and three on garrison duties in India. Eight divisions plus 13 cyclist battalions were being kept in England for training purposes and to fight off an enemy assault should one come. Haig was ordered to send five of his divisions from France to Italy in early November 1917.

On 3 November 1917 the War Office informed Haig that they would not be able to replace expected losses in 1918. The current shortfall against the on-paper establishment of infantry units of 75,000 men would be at least 379,000 by 31 October 1918, and as other theatres also needed men it could be as high as 439,000. Conversely, 110,000 men could be made available for the artillery, tanks, Machine Gun Corps and Royal Flying Corps. Haig's GHQ staff calculated that the infantry would be 40 per cent below establishment on 31 March 1918. He advised the War Office that unless more troops were forthcoming, he would have to break up five corps and 15 of his 57 infantry divisions to bring the remaining formations back up to strength. Inevitably the length of line he could hold would have to be shortened. The Cabinet Committee on manpower disagreed and proposed an alternative, suggesting that the shortfall could be remedied through a reduction from 12 infantry battalions to 9 in every British division. This would enable Haig to bring his units up to strength and provide a reserve. Each of the three infantry brigades in a division would then have three battalions rather than four. The ten Canadian, Australian and New Zealand divisions were not to be restructured in this way. The military members of the Army Council protested against this move – which affected every infantry regiment and cut through an organisational structure for which every officer had been trained – but to no avail. Their plea that this proposal represented 'an unreasonably grave risk of losing the war and sacrificing to no purpose the British Army on the Western Front' fell on deaf ears. The army moved to the 9-battalion structure in February 1918 and was still coming to terms with its effects when the enemy struck with 'Michael' and 'Georgette'.

A French study of the strengths of the opposing forces, submitted to the SWC in late January 1918, revealed a serious imbalance on the Western Front even without taking into account the enormous casualty lists that could be expected if and when the enemy attacked. Germany was currently estimated to have 170 divisions in France, a total of 2.9 million men, of whom 1.45 million were 'rifles' (that is, combatants). They also had some 8,000 field guns and 5,000 heavy artillery weapons. They would be able to add to this strength another 30 divisions, 450,000 combatants, 1,500 field and 950 heavy guns by May 1918. Compared to this, the Allies had 167 divisions (just 30 of them British), 3.06 million men (1.266 million of them British), of whom 1.45 million were rifles (580,000 British) with 8,852 field guns (3,770 British) and 6,558 (1,670 British) heavier pieces. The French and British were believed to have no possibility of adding to this total except by withdrawing men from elsewhere. Pétain told Haig and Robertson, when they met with Foch at Compiègne on 24 January, that he would have to reduce his divisions by 20 during the year even without a battle being fought. If attacked, he intended giving up ground in order to avoid casualties, and had already given his armies instructions to select locations where this could be done. All agreed that orders should be given to bring back as many troops and guns from Italy as could be afforded, not least to reduce the burden on the railways.[19]

GHQ planners believed that heavy fighting would force the British to reduce their forces to a total of 30 divisions. This was based on the assumption that in a full-strength German offensive, losses could not be expected to be fewer than 500,000 men. France, being in a similar condition, would be down to 92 divisions. Germany would be able to maintain around 170. The only hope of closing the gap lay with the Americans, who were forecast to be able to add by September 17 divisions, 435,000 combatants, 816 field guns and 408 heavy guns. By then, something like parity of forces would be achieved – but nine months seemed an awfully long way ahead.

At the same time that GHQ was wrestling with the effects of manpower shortages, the length of front held by the British armies was extended. Lloyd George first agreed in principle to extend the line occupied by the British at the Anglo-French Boulogne Conference in September 1917. He then asked Haig to consider this and report. Haig did so on 8 October, insisting that in view of the dubious ability of the French army to resist a German attack all other British fronts should be placed on the defensive; all remaining forces should be concentrated on the Western Front and take an offensive stance; the 62 British divisions now in France should be brought up to full strength; and the occupied line should not be extended. He was applying the well-known military maxim of concentration of force at the decisive point.

At a meeting of the War Cabinet three days later, Lloyd George sidelined Haig's report and himself outlined various strategies for the war, paying special attention to operations against the Turks. He invited Wilson and Sir John French (who had been removed from command in 1915 and continued to harbour ill-feeling towards Haig and Robertson) to offer their opinions. Both men played along with Lloyd George and advised a course of action that would require the establishment of a politico-military Allied body to advise on these matters; as we have seen, this soon came into being.

Wilson met Foch with Lloyd George on 9 October and recommended that the British should take over more of the line. Pétain specifically asked the British to relieve his Sixth Army down as far as Barisis, which meant putting six more divisions in the front line. Haig said he would do his best, but he knew that this move was the end of Allied aspirations for the continuation of the Passchendaele offensive. On 3 December 1917 Haig ordered all of his army commanders to organise their zones for defensive purposes.

Although at this time the French army held more than three times as much of the Western Front as the British, it was the British sector that was geographically the most critical. Most of the French line was quiet, with Pétain having placed the army in a passive defensive role since the mutinies of April 1917. Since mid-year it had been the British army that took the fight to the enemy and in consequence the German army had moved nearly half of its total force to face the BEF.

In Joint Note 10, dated 10 January 1918, the PMRs suggested that while the British line should be extended, the precise boundary should be determined by the respective commanders-in-chief, who should also plan to extend their lines in the event of an enemy attack depleting the other's reserves. In other words, if Haig was in trouble, Pétain would extend to the north, and vice versa.[20]

Haig's immediate dilemma was how to find the forces needed to hold the longer line. The space between the front line in Flanders and the all-important Channel ports was very narrow, and it was full of vital lines of communication. Any serious withdrawal in this area, forced by enemy action, would have dire consequences for the ability of the British – and hence the Allies – to continue to wage war on the Western Front. Haig had little room for manoeuvre in terms of reducing the force in Flanders. To the south, where the extension was planned, this was not so. A withdrawal of, say, 40 miles would not have real strategic consequences and such a move was clearly on Pétain's mind. The line could then be held with relatively fewer men, as long as some insurance was there in the form of reserves that could be moved quickly to the area should the Germans attack and break through.

Lieutenant-General Hubert Gough's Fifth Army was to hold the extended portion of the line:

> by the end of November we were able to make a good guess that our destination was the French front on the right of Third Army. Up to this date this had been a quiet sector and held by two French corps only; but though quiet at the moment, it was a considerable addition to the British front – about 28 miles – to which Haig very naturally objected and against which he strongly protested … the enemy [here] was very active in making raids and took a prisoner or two from us regularly … and this was the first sign which came to my notice that our front was likely to be the one selected for attack by the Germans.[21]

By 14 December 1917 Pétain was pressing for the relief of his Sixth Army and a further extension of the British line. The next day the War Office cabled Haig to say that Georges Clemenceau, the new French Prime Minister (who took office in November), had threatened to resign if the British did not extend as far as Berry-au-Bac, a further 37 miles beyond Barisis. Haig reluctantly arranged with Pétain to extend to a short distance beyond the River Oise. The extension of the line began on 10 January 1918, with Fifth Army being given the unenviable task of preparing to be attacked.

The British High Command was given a reasonable prediction of German intentions as early as 29 January 1918. Among the many innovations brought by Wilson to the British staff appointed to Versailles was an arrangement whereby there would be a specific study of enemy strengths, policies and strategies. Headed by the experienced Brigadier-General Sir Hereward Wake, the 'E' (Enemy) group was asked to think as far as possible as a German staff officer would. Typical of Wilson's humorous touch, Wake's team were encouraged to wear their caps back to front, to remind themselves that they were now the enemy. For the first time in the war, a serious analytical study was made of German intentions and their ability to execute them, including evaluation through war gaming. Wake and his opposite number in the 'A' (Allied) group, Brigadier-General Herbert Studd, were invited to demonstrate their conclusions to Lloyd George and Lord Alfred Milner, a member of the War Cabinet. The analysis was powerful indeed: Wake forecast that the Germans would have up to a hundred divisions ready for an offensive by 1 April, and that they would attack the British right flank on a 35-mile front centred just north of St Quentin. The British and French armies would have been driven apart within days. Pushing on through Amiens, the enemy would then roll up the British front in the direction of the Channel coast. Studd, looking at this from the viewpoint of a British commander-in-chief, admitted that his front would be driven in by as much as 17 or 18 miles, but stated that the enemy could be held before Amiens if a large enough reserve could be assembled. That reserve would have to be Allied, rather than just British. According to Leo Amery, Lloyd George was 'spellbound'. When the story was repeated for Haig the next day he received it with indifference, if not incomprehension: 'Frankly bored and contemptuous, he twiddled his moustache impatiently, and then frankly ignored it in order to con a paper of his own . . . I grew hot more than once as Studd pointedly explained the precautions he would take, but Haig never realised that he was being taught his business as Commander-in-Chief.'[22]

Insightful as it was, even Wake's analysis did not guess at the full extent of Wetzell's breathtaking plan, perhaps due to doubts as to whether the feats of logistics and command flexibility that such multiple offensives would require could possibly be delivered. The Allies certainly could not have successfully undertaken such a strategy at this time and there was no compelling reason to believe that the enemy could either. While there was no love lost between them, the SWC and GHQ staffs agreed at least that a major strike was coming and that it would be against the Arras–St Quentin front. All agreed too, that an attack against the Lys Valley could be written off on the basis that the ground would be too wet for major operations, possibly until June.

A new doctrine of defence
Much has been written about German innovation and the development of new artillery and infantry tactics for the offensive; they would come as a big surprise to the British armies in France, which had not faced a major German assault since the very different days of 1915.[23] There was barely a man in the front-line units that had not experienced the enemy's apparently endless ability to counter-attack whenever British gains were made, but this was not remotely the same as being attacked by a hundred fresh and trained divisions. Faced with such a prospect, in the knowledge that manpower would be thin, the planners at GHQ issued a new set of guidelines on 14 December 1917. Their 'Memorandum on defensive measures' outlined the adoption of the defensive principles that had been applied so successfully by the enemy. The front would no longer be protected by a number of continuous trench lines, but would consist of deep defensive zones, 'with the main resistance being made on ground favourable to us'. The Germans would have to negotiate intensive cross-fire

from well sited, sheltered and barbed-wire-protected strong-points, held by tenacious troops. Should the enemy penetrate the first zones and beat off local counter-attacks, strong reserves would strike with a major counter-attack and ideally go on not only to recover the ground but to inflict defeat. Adoption of the scheme placed enormous burdens on the British armies. The concept was unfamiliar and demanded a great deal of consideration and training of officers and men alike; it also required the construction of an entirely new system of defences – and as in December 1917 it was not yet understood where the Germans would attack, this meant that the entire British front had to be developed in this way, at the same time that the existing trenches needed to be manned and on the alert. The principle of elastic defence was an appropriate one and already proven in warfare, but its practical application proved to be a stretch too far for Haig's troops. Neither men nor defences would be fully ready when Ludendorff unleashed 'Michael' and 'George'.

The Germans attack: Operations 'Michael' and 'Mars'
At 4.40am on 21 March 1918 no fewer than 6,473 guns of the German artillery opened fire, launching a bombardment of unprecedented weight and violence against the front of the British Fifth and Third Armies between La Fère and the River Sensée. From that moment and for several days, aside from Pétain's constant worry that this was a feint and that the real attack was about to come against his troops in the Champagne, all Allied eyes were on the Somme. There is not a word about the Lys, and little on the possibility of a second German attack, in the papers of the many meetings and conferences held at this time.

By the end of the first day German infantry had penetrated the British front at all points, had broken into the Battle Zone in three areas and had passed beyond it in the area between Tergnier and Grand Seraucourt. The way was open for an enemy advance across the Somme in the direction of Amiens, and north of the Somme towards Doullens. The legacy of numerical inferiority, an overstretched front, under-trained and tired troops and the too-late adoption of a little-understood defensive doctrine all contributed to the inability of the British armies to do more than slow the German advance. More than a hundred thousand British troops were captured or became casualties in the onslaught; whole units virtually disappeared. It was now a question of whether sufficient reserves could be moved to the area in time, and whether they could hold the line.

The local reserves held by Fifth Army and its respective corps and divisions were fed quickly into the battle. Pétain began to release reserve divisions to Haig from the early hours of 22 March; by the day's end he had sent three divisions to the Crozat Canal. Haig also began to move whatever reserves he thought could be spared. By 23 March the German advance was proceeding at such a rate that it was becoming necessary to thin out the line in other sectors. At 7.00pm that day Lieutenant-General Herbert Plumer, now back from Italy and once again in command of Second Army at Ypres, said he could hold his line with eight divisions, thus enabling 3 and 4 Australian Divisions and 5 Australian Division less its artillery to be sent south. Plumer could also release 23 Division if the Belgians would agree to extend their line, but he 'did not wish to leave the Passchendaele Ridge, as it would create a hornet's nest and give the enemy to think that our whole line was shaken'.[24]

Despite giving initial assistance, Pétain was reluctant to hand over his reserves to Haig. The gentlemen's agreement made by the commanders-in-chief did not survive the German hammer blows on the forge of the Somme. Still expecting a German attack in the Champagne, and with orders from his government to protect Paris at all costs, on 24 March Pétain informed Haig that he had ordered General Fayolle, whose forces were adjacent to the British Fifth Army on the Somme, to withdraw towards Paris – rather than keeping in touch with the British – should the enemy attack develop. It is hardly to be expected that Haig would remember this as being precisely what Wake and Studd had forecast. Shocked by Pétain's demeanour and the disastrous potential of his instructions to Fayolle, Haig 'hurried back to my headquarters at Beaurepaire chateau to report the serious change in French strategy to the CIGS and Secretary of State for War [Milner], and ask them to come to France'. Within two days the Allies took the long-overdue decision to appoint Foch as a coordinating Generalissimo, effectively in command of the Allied armies, although it was not until a further agreement was made at Beauvais on 3 April that Foch was placed in strategic command.[25]

One of Henry Wilson's less endearing habits was the endless repetition, to anyone who would listen, of the key points of his latest idea or belief. Foch shared this habit. From the moment that Foch assumed control, Haig and the GHQ staff soon became familiar with three of his favourite expressions: 'Never withdraw'; 'Never relieve tired troops while the battle lasts'; and 'One does what one can'. Foch never tired of stressing these maxims and Weygand faithfully represented them. They became an unchallengeable dictum and lay behind all of Foch's advice and orders to the British. It took a while for the fundamental logic to sink in to the men in khaki, and at times of maximum stress during the remainder of the German offensives they often perplexed and frustrated the British staff. These three simple phrases dictated the course of the Allied defence on the Somme and on the Lys.

> What was to be done? We could not afford to lose a yard of ground, and, above all, it was necessary to maintain liaison with the Allies. To

do that, the first thing to do was to hold the enemy and to stand fast. There was only one method of doing this, to reorganise, cost what it might, in the positions which we held and with our feeble resources. Only after that could we think of reliefs. Then we must also counter-attack in order to break down offensives. ... But even this is insufficient; we must conquer, that is to say, attack. To do that, we must have reserves. After that, to build them up.[26]

On 28 March the flanking operation 'Mars' was launched against the British Third Army, in one of the most strongly held and well defended sectors of the line. Although it wrested some ground between Arleux and Mercatel from British occupation, the German attack failed with heavy losses. With Allied reserves now beginning to shore up the Somme front, it was clear to OHL that the operations had all but run their course. Although Rupprecht was all for renewing the 'Mars' attack once he had received fresh reserves, Ludendorff demurred. He would now press on with 'Georgette', and orders were given to implement the planned movement of forces to the Lys front.

On 4 April Hereward Wake submitted a fresh appreciation of the situation. The German advance to date had lengthened the front by 35 miles. Some 200 German divisions had now been identified in France, of which 53 were in the front line on the battle front, with 85 holding the line elsewhere and 62 in reserve. The 176 Allied divisions were deployed with 33 on the battle front, 78 elsewhere and 65 in reserve. Of those in reserve, 40 German and 36 Allied divisions (5 British and 31 French) were fresh, fit and ready for action. It was getting very close to the point where the British army was fully engaged, with no further reserves to come. In this situation, it was critical that the forces were in the right place. But where would the Germans strike next? Wake considered Ludendorff's alternatives in the British-held sectors. He discounted the likelihood of attack against the southern stretch from Barisis to the River Luce (south of Amiens) as French reserves had arrived and were strong there; from the Luce to Albert (on the Somme) was more attractive owing to the proximity to Amiens, but again there were French reserves in place; the sector from Albert to the River Scarpe at Arras was most strongly held by the British. Conversely, the sector from Arras to the La Bassée Canal was less strongly held, and although it included the tactical difficulty of Vimy Ridge, it was attractive due to the presence of the Bruay coalfields, which lay within reach of a short advance. This area also had an excellent network of railways by which the front could be supplied. The stretch from La Bassée Canal to the coast was held by tired British troops, the Portuguese Corps and the Belgians, but was still considered to be difficult in poor weather; the artillery defences were good and the immediate effects of a German advance not so grave for the

Allies. The latest intelligence reports suggested an enemy move south of the Somme. Wake summarised by predicting a possible attack astride the Somme, with some holding actions to pin down French reserves and the main effort falling between Arras and La Bassée. As things turned out, this was not an unreasonable view but Ludendorff's *schwerpunkt* was in front of Lille rather than Lens.[27]

The resources of the Royal Air Force in Flanders – the new service having been established on 1 April – were not committed to the destruction of the apparent German build-up in Flanders as it was not believed to indicate a main thrust, although some bombing was undertaken of the German railway network, notably in the areas around Don and Haubourdin.

Haig continued to press Foch for reserves. It is unlikely that he had seen Wake's summary but the GHQ staff had come to a similar conclusion. He wrote on the morning of 6 April that Ludendorff 'appears to be preparing a force of 25 to 35 divisions to deliver a heavy blow on the Béthune–Arras front'. Foch and Weygand discussed Haig's message with his staff officer Major-General John Davidson, who suggested three ways in which the French could assist and take pressure off the British: they could either mount a counter-attack, relieve four British divisions south of the Somme or push four divisions of reserves behind the British around St Pol-sur-Ternoise. The Frenchmen flatly refused. Foch met with Haig later in the day, and just after 11.00pm a frustrated Haig sent a message to Wilson:

> I placed my views, which are identical with yours, before Foch today. He declines to take over any part of our line, which I consider the only possible solution. He proposes to put a small French reserve west of Amiens. This cannot in my opinion intervene effectively at [the] decisive point. Foch most friendly but immovable. Can you come here tomorrow or shall I send a staff officer to London.

The upshot was that there would be no French reserves remotely near the Lys front when the enemy struck three days later.[28]

The British armies in France were, however, the sudden recipients of many tens of thousands of fresh troops. In the crisis of late March the government revised the law regarding the age at which men could be sent for service overseas, reducing it from 19 to 18½ as long as the soldier had had six months training. At a stroke this released for service the 'A4' men, known as such after their medical categorisation which marked them as fit in all respects other than age. The Channel troopships were filled to bursting with these young men, and NCOs across the front found themselves dealing with large and wholly un-expected drafts. In addition, many older, unfit and less capable men had been combed out of whichever comfortable base, barrack or store they had been occupying and were now facing the prospect of immediate action. Many would be in the front line on the Lys within days of arrival.

Despite this doubtful influx, Haig persisted. Having received information from a captured German aviator that the enemy was massing in the Tournai–Douai–Cambrai area, on 8 April Haig asked Foch, via General de Laguiche, to relieve six British divisions in the Ypres area, in order to provide a reserve. Foch refused.[29]

Chapter 2

The Lys Sector and
Preparations for Battle

The Flemish town of Bailleul lies centrally within the area of ground wrested from the British army by the Germans in April 1918. Exactly a mile to the east of the town is a hill, barely 250 feet high, known as the Ravelsberg. It offers a unique, almost 360 degree, view, in which the vital features of the battlefield can all be seen. To the south lies the valley of the River Lys, flat as a billiard table for many miles. Here there are none of the vast and open fields that characterise the Somme, but a pleasant patchwork of woods, farms and villages, each identifiable by its church spire. The many hedgerows line innumerable drainage ditches, small rivers and canals. Estaires, a town of light industries on the banks of the Lys, stands out for its silos and chimneys. The far southern horizon 20 miles away is marked by the heights of the Vimy and Lorette Ridges, with industrial Béthune and the spoilheaps of the Bruay coalfield just in front of them. To the west is Hazebrouck, with its vital railway junctions; a forested area just to the south of it and the lonely hill of Cassel are the only landmarks in an otherwise flat and nondescript land that stretches all the way to the Channel coast. Dunkirk is just 26 miles distant, Calais 40.

North of Bailleul the land becomes more rolling, the fields larger. On the horizon, and just 5 miles distant across the border into Belgium, stands the dominant wooded hill of Kemmelberg, the highest point of a ridge that stretches westwards and includes the peaks of Scherpenberg, Mont Rouge, Mont Noir and Mont des Cats. Kemmelberg is just over 500 feet high, the other peaks much the same. In this generally flat area the Flemish hills are always there, just over your shoulder, always looking down at you and providing a natural line of defence. With the exception of the waterways and to some extent the Forest of Nieppe, there are no other geographic features that offer such military advantages in this area. East of Bailleul the landscape changes again. Armentières, with the Lys snaking around the north of it, almost merges into the industrial conurbation of Lille, grown hugely since the First World War. North of Armentières the ground begins to rise to another gentle ridge, hidden from the Ravelsberg by Kemmelberg, which stretches almost as far as Ypres and is known as the Messines Ridge.

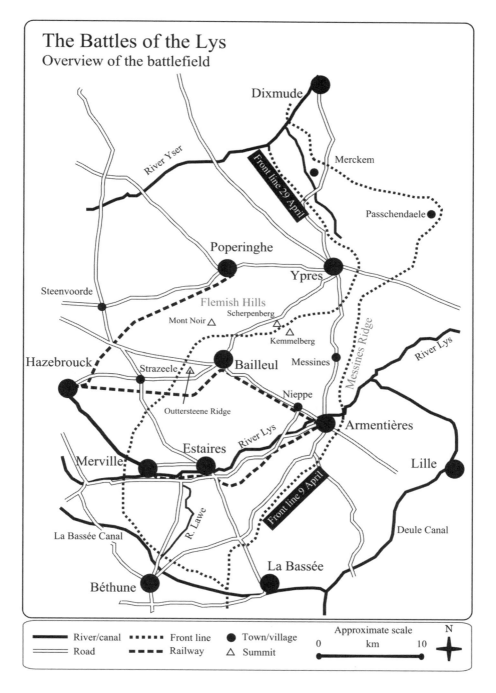

The Battles of the Lys
Overview of the battlefield

Dixmude

Merckem

River Yser

Front line 29 April

Passchendaele

Poperinghe

Ypres

Steenvoorde

Flemish Hills

Scherpenberg

Mont Noir △

△
△
Kemmelberg

Messines Ridge

River Lys

Hazebrouck

Strazeele △

Bailleul

Messines

Outtersteene Ridge

Nieppe

Armentières

River Lys

Estaires

Lille

Merville

River Lys

Front line 9 April

R. Lawe

Deule Canal

La Bassée Canal

La Bassée

Béthune

▬▬▬ River/canal	••••• Front line	● Town/village
═══ Road	▬ ▬ Railway	△ Summit

Approximate scale

N

0   km   10

The key tactical objectives of a German attack in the area were the railway junction at Hazebrouck, the Cassel–Poperinghe–Ypres road and the heights of the Flemish hills. Achievement of the first two of these would choke the British supply line to the Ypres front and affect supplies to the key Béthune sector too. Seizing the heights would render the continued British occupation of the Messines Ridge and the southern half of the Ypres Salient most difficult. All three would almost certainly force a British withdrawal from Ypres towards the coast, and quite possibly dislocate the British organisation in Flanders to such an extent that a further German advance would allow the British – and the Belgian army holding the last strip of ground by the coast – to be comprehensively defeated. A breakthrough in the southern part of the attack front, along the La Bassée Canal, also opened up possibilities of a flanking movement around the north of Béthune and into the vital coal-mining area.

The British front line between Ploegsteert (north of Armentières) and the La Bassée Canal had remained largely unchanged in this sector since the initial German offensive had been brought to a halt in November 1914. The 'trenches' here were more commonly breastworks, defences built up by the use of sandbags and other suitable materials, because the high water table meant that any attempt to dig usually resulted in the hole quickly filling with water. Effort and ingenuity on the part of the Royal Engineers had improved the drainage of the area over the years, and this, coupled with the exceptionally dry spring of 1918, meant the ground was nowhere near as boggy and difficult as it had been in previous years, although it was still hard going.

As reserves finally arrived on the Somme, Haig could afford to take his tired and depleted divisions out of the line there, but with so few fresh divisions at his disposal he did not have the luxury of sending them rearwards for an extended period of recuperation. There was little choice but to send them to hold the normally sleepy sector between Ploegsteert and Givenchy. There had been no fighting of any magnitude in the area since 1915, when the First Army had begun to learn the costly realities of trench assault, dashing itself against the strongly held German line at Neuve Chapelle, Aubers and Festubert; little had been gained but heavy casualties were incurred. After the Battle of Loos in September and October 1915, just to the south across the La Bassée Canal from Givenchy, the Lys front had been quiet. Both sides improved their defences and used the sector to familiarise newly arrived units with trench warfare. There were frequent raids and minor operations, but on the whole the Lys remained a backwater while great offensives took place elsewhere. Despite growing signs of an enemy build-up, sending the exhausted divisions to the Lys was Haig's least risky option.

The accumulation of German strength for 'Georgette' was rapid and impressive, representing a prodigious feat of staff work and logistics. No fewer than 195 German field batteries and 230 heavy/super heavy batteries of artillery were amassed: four times or more greater than the number of Allied guns in the same area. As far as the British were concerned, the German artillery on the Lys was unnaturally quiet, refusing to be drawn and expose its positions. XV Corps, for example, reported that enemy heavy artillery was curiously inactive from 30 March onwards and that trench–mortars had only fired during localised raids, following what had appeared to be a major build-up in early March. It was even thought that the activity in early March had been the result of batteries firing off their ammunition before leaving the area.[30] The Germans carried out no trench raids and British patrols failed to make any contact, for the enemy had temporarily withdrawn from the outposts and saps of the front line. This was ominous, for the same tactic had been played out before 'Michael'.[31]

Orders filtered down to the enormous assault force quietly assembled in Flanders. Von Quast's Sixth Army, south of Armentières, was now swelled to 28 divisions, which would push forwards in the direction of Hazebrouck after making a decisive attack on the perceived weak spot, the thin line held by the Portuguese Corps. All units were impressed with the need to cross the Lys quickly before British reserves could assemble in force. The Fourth Army of von Arnim, taking the line up from Armentières to the coast, had 33 divisions and would join the attack on the second day. There is no obvious rationale for this phased timing. What was clear was that this would be a conventional attack, albeit using both Brüchmuller's tactical innovations in the use of artillery and the infantry's fast-moving *stosstruppen* (stormtroopers), trained to seek out and exploit weaknesses in the enemy's defences.[32] These tactics had already prised open the Fifth Army on the Somme and were difficult to counter, although the British had since circulated so many memoranda that commanders knew precisely what to expect. But by no means were the German forces available for 'Georgette' all comprised of these fit, well trained and well armed assault units; more than half were ordinary 'trench' divisions.

The German armies would also attack without the benefit of armour, although its use had been planned to a small extent. The large A7V *Sturmpanzer-Kraftwagen* tanks proved to be far too heavy for the Flanders mud, and the ten captured British tanks assigned to II Bavarian Corps failed to deploy.[33] The assault troops filtered quietly into the front-line trenches as the whole Lys Valley became blanketed in fog during the night of 8/9 April. Behind them the gunners completed stacking up the tens of thousands of shells, and took the chance of a final cigarette before hell was let loose on the English and their oldest allies, the Portuguese.

Chapter 3

The First Day

The destruction of the Portuguese Corps

Although Germany had declared war on Portugal on 9 March 1916, it was not until 4 April 1917 that Portuguese troops first moved into the line in France and it was only on 10 July of that year that a Portuguese division took full responsibility for a sector of the front. By that time some 59,000 officers and men had made the lengthy sea and rail journey via Lisbon and Brest and concentrated in the area of Thérouanne and Aire-sur-la-Lys in Flanders. The Portuguese force had been organised into two groups, the *Corpo Expedicionário Portuguese* (CEP) under command of General Tamagnini de Abreu e Silva, and the heavy artillery of the *Corpo de Artilharia Pesada Independente* (CAPI). The CEP comprised two divisions and from 5 November 1917 came under command of the British First Army. Around fifty Portuguese-speaking British officers were provided for liaison purposes.

Despite the initial commitment, things were never going well for the CEP. Support at home for the war with Germany was mixed, and after the December 1917 revolution led by Sidónio Pais, formerly Portugal's republican ambassador in Berlin between 1912 and 1916, the fortunes of the men in France spiralled quickly downwards. A number of factors were at play, but predominant among them was the impossibility of leave for the 'other ranks' while certain officers could return to Portugal; after the December revolution many officers went home and never came back. The food was poor, reinforcement drafts did not come, and morale dwindled as the CEP suffered casualties amounting to more than 5,000 men in day-to-day trench warfare before April 1918. There is evidence of men, certainly those with connections, arranging various subterfuges to get them out of the trenches and home. Matters were not helped by the Portuguese units having to hold a miserable, waterlogged area through a bitterly cold winter, on a front renowned for its boredom and lack of activity. Some chose to give themselves up to the enemy rather than stay put: Rupprecht noted on 30 January 1918 that 30 Portuguese had come across no-man's-land that day alone.

As early as July 1917 General Gomes da Costa, whom Haking believed to be an 'upright and honourable soldier', had complained that his 1 Portuguese Division was not capable of holding the line it was given. He pointed out that several units were commanded by militia officers and that some officers had already been in the line without a break for over a fortnight. There was also a shortage of artillery and transport, with inevitable breakdowns in ammunition supply. But the main issue was a worsening shortage of men. By April 1918 some battalions of the 2 Portuguese Division – which Costa took over from General Simas Machado on 6 April – had as few as 13 officers from an establishment of 37, and others were down to as few as 577 men of a planned 1,083. Not a man among them had experienced anything remotely like the German attack that was about to hit them. Few had even fired a rifle in anger.

The Portuguese front ran across a flat area, studded with farms and villages and crossed by numerous ditches and streams. The forward defences comprised three positions, known as the A, B and C Lines, which together provided a system over half a mile deep. A was the front line, which was continuous and interspersed with small posts, not all of which were shellproof. Behind A were communication trenches connecting it with the rear, further posts, dug-outs and support trenches. This was essentially the line as it had been since the end of the Battle of Neuve Chapelle as long ago as March 1915; it ran to the east side of Richebourg l'Avoue, Port Arthur, Neuve Chapelle, the Moated Grange, Chapigny Farm, Fauquissart and around the top of the German salient known as the Sugar Loaf, which had caused so much trouble for the 61 (2 South Midland) and 5 Australian Divisions in their attack on Fromelles on 19 July 1916. The B Line, running broadly parallel to the front line, but some 400 yards behind it, was meant to be the main line of resistance. More strongly fortified, it ran from what was known as the Old British Line east of Festubert up to the west side of the ruins of Neuve Chapelle. The C Line comprised a number of strongly wired posts situated some 500 to 800 yards behind B, connected by communication trenches but without continuous breastworks or barbed-wire defences in-between.

At a distance behind the front lay two further defensive positions, known as the Village Line and the Corps Line. The Village Line, which ran northwards from Festubert and the Cailloux Keeps to Richebourg St Vaast, Croix Barbée, Pont du Hem and to the south side of Laventie, was considered to be the front of the Battle Zone. The Corps Line came up from the Tuning Fork locality west of Festubert to La Couture, Huit Maisons, Bout Deville, Riez Bailleul, Le Drumez and on to the north of Laventie. Both consisted of a number of disconnected but strong defensive posts and localities, well wired, with concrete defences and fields of fire that allowed one to cover another. Behind these the crossings over the Rivers Lawe and Lys at Vieille Chapelle, Fosse, Marais, Pont Riqueul, La Gorgue and Estaires had reasonably strong defences. Although there had been some earlier construction, virtually all of these works had been built since the adoption of the zone defence doctrine in early 1918.

The distance from the front line at Fauquissart to the Lys bridges at Estaires is 4 miles.

By the end of 8 April, the Portuguese were holding 10,000 yards of front between La Quinque Rue (north of Festubert) and Picantin. With just 16 badly under-strength battalions in the area, this was by far the most thinly manned part of the British front in Flanders. Three brigades of Costa's division held the front system. On the extreme right the Ferme du Bois sector was held by 5 Brigade, headquartered at Cense du Raux Farm near Le Touret. In the central Neuve Chapelle sector was 6 Brigade, with its headquarters at Huit Maisons, while 4 (do Minho) Brigade was on the left in the Fauquissart sector, headquartered at Laventie. Each brigade placed two battalions in the front line, with one in close support and one in reserve. In addition, 3 Brigade was in deeper reserve near La Gorgue, having been relieved by 6 Brigade on 8 April. Haking had agreed that since the Portuguese division only had sufficient troops to man the A and B Lines, the reserves behind them, holding the Village and Corps Lines, would be British.

A vast force of no fewer than four German divisions lined up to attack the Portuguese, with another three in reserve ready to move forwards to reinforce and exploit the expected breakthrough. On their left the 1 and 8 Bavarian Reserve Divisions of *General der Kavallerie* Friedrich von Bernhardi's LV Corps, with 8 Division in reserve, assembled facing the front between Festubert and Neuve Chapelle. To the north of them, the Prussian 35 and 42 Divisions of XIX Corps under *General der Infanterie* Adolph von Carlowitz had 10 Ersatz Division in reserve and extended up to the north of Rouges Bancs (north-west of Fromelles). 35 Division was known to contain a large number of Poles and was of dubious fighting quality. 81 Reserve Division, which had been holding the front facing the Portuguese, quietly slipped away and took up a further reserve position. It is noteworthy that most of these formations had not recently arrived from the East but were hardened to battle on the Western Front: of those in the assault positions, only 42 Division was new, having arrived in December after the fighting at Riga; 10 Ersatz Division had also come from the East in January but had only gone to Galicia in October 1917 after seeing action at Passchendaele. All were fresh, although morale appears to have been mixed.[34]

The British XI Corps took command of the area on 6 April. Haking soon met Costa and the Portuguese brigade commanders and told them that if they were attacked they were to arrange to make a stand on the B Line; they indicated that they understood. Costa said he was short of establishment by 399 officers and over 7,000 men; after the battle he revised his numbers to 139 and 5,972, but even so it was clear to Haking that the Portuguese force was tired, too few and too thinly stretched. Arrangements were made to reorganise the position, but achieved little except to disorganise it just before the Germans attacked. Plans were also made to reorganise the CEP so it would have four full brigades in the line rather than six depleted ones, to provide an opportunity for rest and training, but these plans were not implemented. According to Haking, 'one battalion [7], which was going to be withdrawn [in this scheme] and was then ordered back to the line, mutinied ... though many excellent schemes existed in paper, they were rarely appreciated or mastered by subordinate commanders, such as brigade and battalion commanders, and still less by company and platoon commanders'. The fact that the relief of a battalion, a normal enough procedure that should have been worked out without any hitch, caused uncertainty and even mutiny speaks volumes for the quality of staff work and command in the CEP. Haking ordered the 51 (Highland) Division to relieve the Portuguese on 7/8 April but the newly arrived Highlanders were exhausted after their mauling on the Somme. They were still assimilating large drafts of 18-year-old conscripts and had not even had a chance to test their new replacement guns. The order was duly postponed for 48 hours – and in the event was never carried out.

The annihilation of Costa's division began punctually at 4.15am on 9 April, 2 hours before dawn in thick fog on a cold, raw morning. The batteries of the Sixth Army opened as one, laying down a terrifying bombardment on the posts, gun positions, crossroads, headquarters and villages behind the lines. A deluge of high explosive and poison gas destroyed strong-points, killed men and horses and shattered the nerves of many. With no wind, the gas was concentrated and hung in depressions and shell-holes. By sheer bad luck the first heavy shell to fall on Lestrem destroyed much of Costa's headquarters in the Chateau de la Cigale. All divisional communications were soon cut off, leaving the staff helpless. While the German artillery concentrated on the areas behind the lines, trench-mortar batteries fired on the A and B Lines. Major Horatio Berney-Ficklin, on the staff of 152 Brigade and taken prisoner on 12 April, recalled his thoughts as he passed through the old Portuguese front as a prisoner-of-war: 'The concentration of German trench-mortars was terrific. I should estimate one every two or three yards, and the trench system in this area had been obliterated. This was the only place at which I saw any considerable number of Portuguese dead.'[35]

Costa realised at once from the violence of the bombardment that it preceded an infantry attack. His first instinct was to order 3 Brigade from its reserve position at La Gorgue to reinforce the Village Line. Unable to do so by phone, he sent his ADC, Lieutenant João Herculano de Moura, who rode on horseback through the shell-swept area, taking an hour to get the order

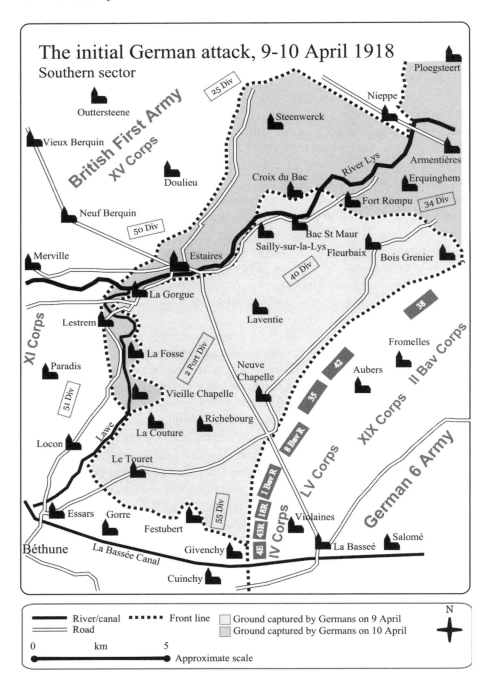

The initial German attack, 9-10 April 1918
Southern sector

British First Army
XV Corps
XI Corps

Ploegsteert
Nieppe
Outtersteene
Steenwerck
25 Div
Vieux Berquin
River Lys
Armentières
Croix du Bac
Erquinghem
Doulieu
Fort Rompu
34 Div
Neuf Berquin
Bac St Maur
Sailly-sur-la-Lys
50 Div
Fleurbaix
Bois Grenier
Merville
Estaires
40 Div
La Gorgue
38
Lestrem
Laventie
La Fosse
Fromelles
2 Port Div
Paradis
Neuve
Chapelle
Aubers
42
II Bav Corps
51 Div
Vieille Chapelle
35
8 Bav R
XIX Corps
Richebourg
La Couture
Locon
German 6 Army
Le Touret
1 Bav R
LV Corps
Essars   Gorre
18R
Violaines
Salomé
Festubert
55 Div
43R
IV Corps
Béthune
La Bassée Canal
Givenchy
4B
La Basseé
Cuinchy
Lawe

— River/canal   ▪▪▪▪ Front line   ☐ Ground captured by Germans on 9 April
═ Road   ☐ Ground captured by Germans on 10 April

N

0   km   5
Approximate scale

through. At 4.50am Lieutenant-Colonel Guy Glover, the key British liaison officer at Costa's HQ, managed to contact XI and XV Corps by phone. The latter was still of the opinion that the shell-fire was only the precedent to a heavy raid; Haking was quicker off the mark, ordering the XI Corps reserves forwards to their allotted positions.

Although the main German infantry attack did not begin until 8.45am, much of the Portuguese front-line system was already in German hands. Parties of infantry had entered the A Line under cover of the bombardment at around 7.00am, and mayhem ensued as the defence withered. According to one German officer, 'they ran away faster than we could run towards them'.[36] Others said they flocked back 'in companies'.[37] British units on both flanks began to report seeing Portuguese troops flooding away from the front as early as 7.30am, and by 8.15am the Portuguese gun batteries reported that their infantrymen were withdrawing through them. Most of the Portuguese-held B Line was in German hands by 9.00am, and an hour later the majority of those fleeing had even crossed the Corps Line and were jamming the river bridges and the roads through Estaires and beyond. At 1.40pm the hapless Costa reported that his whole division of 394 officers and 13,252 men was now lost or scattered. No fewer than 6,585 officers and men fell into enemy captivity during the day, most of them taken in the forward system as the German infantry overwhelmed it, caught helplessly in the trenches, posts and dug-outs. Of those that got away, Horne later reported:

> These Portuguese troops were not retiring. They were in flight; many without arms, some with their boots off, some half dressed. Their officers do not appear to have attempted to rally them, even after passing through the British lines. In some cases, they actually resisted attempts by British officers to rally and reorganise: at this time, the enemy was not in close pursuit, and it should have been possible to reorganise them. Portuguese troops in rear defences, when they found those from the front were not stopping in the rear defences, also withdrew.[38]

The precipitate flight of thousands of Portuguese troops was witnessed by many, and their tales soon became the stuff of legend: of men stealing bicycles to get away a bit faster; of armaments abandoned; of men seen riding three to a mule. Brigadier-General Arthur Beckwith, moving up to Le Cornet Malo at the head of his 153 Brigade, 'saw many episodes which did not redound to their credit and could find no place in a sober and diplomatic account'.[39] There were stories, too, of British officers and men threatening and shooting their Portuguese allies in order to halt their flight. While much of this can be dismissed as unreliable bravado and hearsay, Lieutenant-Colonel Arthur

Stephenson, commanding 15 Royal Scots of 34 Division, privately admitted on paper that he had ordered his men to open fire. He had seen the

> full measure of the results of the breakdown of the Portuguese Division which was on our right and having seen them running like hares (and, incidentally, having seen them shot down like hares by my own men, on my orders, to try to stop the rot) . . . I watched their rout from the roof of a house at Erquinghem and am convinced that had they held their ground we need not have been pushed back across the Lys.[40]

Others were more phlegmatic. Lieutenant-Colonel Humphreys, commanding 8 Royal Scots, recalled:

> I happened to be at the 153 Brigade HQ when a young subaltern in charge of the Area Employment Companies came to make a report to the General. He thought the time had arrived when his clerks and other details should be armed, and he came in to say that he had encountered a battalion of our oldest Allies in full retreat. He had taken their rifles from them and given them to his own command. 'But I gave them a receipt and hope I did right, Sir,' he said to the General.[41]

The sheer scale and speed of the Portuguese capitulation makes a coherent view of the battle difficult to compile. No messages came; corps and the other divisions received little or no information from the Portuguese area. Haking did not receive definite news of the loss of the front lines until around 10.00am and of the general retirement until 11.30am, although it was obvious that something terrible was happening. Nevertheless, it is clear that despite the confusion on the CEP front, there were places and moments when units and individuals did not simply give in but fought back, sometimes with great tenacity despite the cost in lives.

On the German left, where 1 Bavarian Reserve Division faced 5 Brigade, the advance was swift. The front system was held by the Portuguese 10 Battalion (raised in Bragança), with 4 Battalion (Faro) in support. The latter was effectively destroyed, losing 533 of 679 officers and men on the day. Elements of 10 Battalion appear to have put up more of a fight but found themselves attacked on the right flank and from behind, as the assault units probed a gap opening up between the Portuguese and British 55 (West Lancashire) Division. Battalion HQ was lost as early as 6.50am. Meanwhile, 13 Battalion (Vila Real) began the day in reserve in the Corps Line at La Couture. Most of it moved up to the forward system where it suffered heavy losses, but 4 Company remained at La Couture – fortunately, as things turned out. The HQ of 5 Brigade at

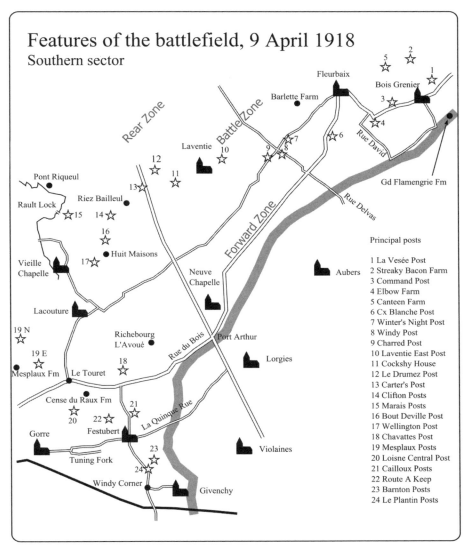

Features of the battlefield, 9 April 1918
Southern sector

Fleurbaix

Bois Grenier

Barlette Farm

Rear Zone

Battle Zone

Rue David

Laventie

Gd Flamengrie Fm

Pont Riqueul

12

11

Riez Bailleul

Rault Lock

15

14

16

Rue Delvas

Forward Zone

Huit Maisons

Vieille Chapelle

17

Neuve Chapelle

Aubers

Lacouture

19 N

Richebourg L'Avoué

Rue du Bois

Port Arthur

Lorgies

19 E

18

Mesplaux Fm

Le Touret

Cense du Raux Fm

21

La Quinque Rue

20

22

Gorre

Festubert

23

Violaines

Tuning Fork

24

Windy Corner

Givenchy

Principal posts

1 La Vesée Post
2 Streaky Bacon Farm
3 Command Post
4 Elbow Farm
5 Canteen Farm
6 Cx Blanche Post
7 Winter's Night Post
8 Windy Post
9 Charred Post
10 Laventie East Post
11 Cockshy House
12 Le Drumez Post
13 Carter's Post
14 Clifton Posts
15 Marais Posts
16 Bout Deville Post
17 Wellington Post
18 Chavattes Post
19 Mesplaux Posts
20 Loisne Central Post
21 Cailloux Posts
22 Route A Keep
23 Barnton Posts
24 Le Plantin Posts

Village ☆ Post ═══ Road ▬▬ River/canal

● Farm or other defended locality   Front trench system

Approximate scale

0   km   4

N

Cense du Raux Farm fell to Bavarian infantry at around 1.00pm, with the commander Colonel Manuel Martins among those captured.

The 8 Bavarian Reserve Division encountered little resistance from 5 Brigade's 17 Battalion (Beja) which had been holding the front line near Richebourg, and not much more from 6 Brigade's supporting 11 Battalion (Évora). 6 Brigade's HQ at Huit Maisons was struck by a shell at 6.30am, causing a fire which was fortunately extinguished after half an hour but disrupted command at a vital time. All phone lines were cut, and in an attempt to gain information cyclists were dispatched to the front. None returned. The brigade's 1 and 2 Battalions (both Lisbon), in the front lines on either side of Neuve Chapelle, were simply overwhelmed by the German 35 Division.

The German 42 Division attacking on the Fauquissart front initially encountered much stiffer opposition from the 4 (do Minho) Brigade. Both 20 Battalion (Guimarães) and 8 Battalion (Braga), fighting mainly in the B Line, suffered losses of more than 500 men in holding up the attack, although by 7.30am they too were falling back on Picantin. The reserve 3 Battalion (Viano do Castelo) and 29 Battalion (Braga) also performed creditably when they came into action as the Germans advanced towards Laventie, but suffered the loss of 60 per cent or more of their effectives in doing so.

The 64 field guns of the divisional batteries and the two brigades of corps heavy artillery, themselves under fire, opened up in the dark and fog, firing on pre-agreed SOS positions soon after the German bombardment began. The few messages that were received from the hard-pressed units at the front took so long to get through that it was not until 10.15am that a report reached 1 Battery of 2 Group that the enemy was in Fauquissart and they should shorten the range. This was at least an hour too late for any meaningful support to be given to the Portuguese infantry. Some batteries received orders to cease fire, but these messages were so dubious that they were ignored, in the belief that they had been issued by enemy soldiers who had overrun the forward signals positions. Second Lieutenant Costa Cabral of 1 Battery, 5 Group, on hearing that the enemy was at Chavatte Post just 300 yards from his guns, took a number of men to attack it and was never heard of again. By 11.00am those batteries still firing were beginning to report that they were running out of ammunition. Some, like the 1 Battery of 6 Group, disappeared to a man as the enemy infantry pressed forwards. The Portuguese artillerymen 'behaved with great gallantry and stuck to their guns until the last,' according to one observer.[42]

By noon, with the exception of some detachments now fighting at or moving rearwards into the Village Line, the Portuguese front had been broken and the CEP effectively destroyed as a component of the Allied forces. Around 11.30am Haking ordered Costa to hold the River Lawe crossings and to rally fugitives west of the river; the order got through at 1.40pm, by which time what little was left of 2 Portuguese Divisional HQ had moved to Calonne. By now, Costa had no division to command. It never returned to action.

Despite its undoubted success in breaking the Portuguese defences, the German attack had not yet broken through to the Lys, for it still faced the Village and Corps Lines. Already the advance was falling behind the expectation that it would reach and cross the river in a single bound. Hampered by the thick fog that hung around in some places until early afternoon, the gas that forced attackers and defenders alike to wear masks for many hours, the heavy nature of the ground and British artillery fire on the few decent roads, the pace at which guns and materiel could be moved forwards was already lagging behind the infantry. Pioneer groups tasked with constructing the many small bridges required came under fire, the transport struggled to bring up the planks and ironwork, guns got stuck and too few field batteries could get forwards quickly enough to exploit the early victory. Later in the day the tired infantry would find that no field kitchens had reached them and there was no hot food to be had. And while the centre divisions pressed on as best they could to the Village Line, a serious problem had developed on the left, at Givenchy.

'Bustle': the defence of Givenchy
The extreme left of the German attack faced Givenchy, which by 1918 was little more than a rubble-strewn area near the bank of the La Bassée Canal. The village stood on a knoll, only a few feet higher than the surrounding countryside but offering great advantages of observation in this otherwise flat region. Three divisions of General von Kraevel's IV Corps were assembled to attack the garrison, the Territorial 55 (West Lancashire) Division. On the canal bank and facing the village was 4 Ersatz Division, which had moved to this front from Galicia in January and taken up position on 5 April; next to it was 43 Reserve Division, which had left Russia in early February; and on its right was 18 Reserve Division, which had been on the Ypres front but moved to the Lys area just before the attack and was considered by British intelligence to be of dubious value. All had been informed that the men of 55 (West Lancashire) Division were tired and fit only for holding the line. Six more German divisions were in reserve behind the three assault formations: 44 Reserve and 16 Reserve Divisions were in immediate support, with 12 Reserve, 48 Reserve, 240 and 216 Divisions behind them.

Givenchy had been in the front line since late 1914. Over the years the area had become riddled with trenches, posts, tunnels and mine workings. To the east and north-east of the village itself was a crater field half a mile long and some of it impassable, the result of intensive underground warfare in 1915 and 1916. Avoiding a frontal attack across the crater field, 4 Ersatz Division

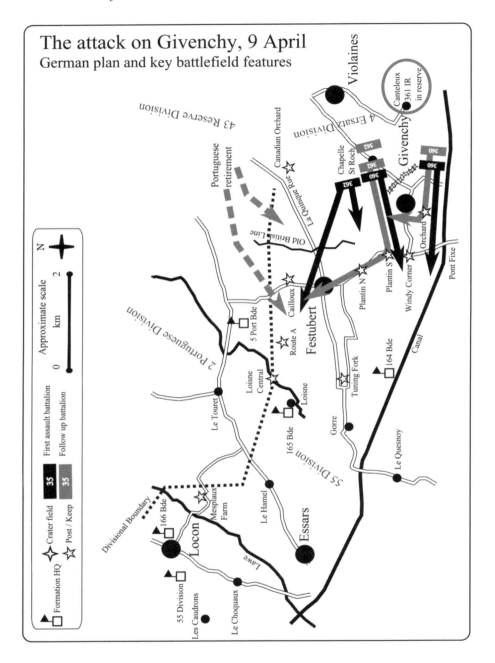

The attack on Givenchy, 9 April
German plan and key battlefield features

planned to strike out on either side of it with two converging forces. To the north of the village two battalions (one each from 360 and 362 Infantry Regiments) would advance towards Le Plantin, followed by two battalions from 362 Infantry Regiment, which would turn northwards near Le Plantin South Post to roll up the British line from the rear. The southern force, consisting of two battalions from 360 Infantry Regiment, would attack along the canal bank south of Givenchy, advancing on Pont Fixe and Windy Corner, with elements turning north to attack the village from behind as they passed.

The men of 55 (West Lancashire) Division had arrived in the Givenchy area in mid-February and by 9 April held 4,000 yards of front from the canal bank to where La Quinque Rue crossed the line just north of Canadian Orchard near Festubert. This meant that its ratio of battalions per yard of front was 40 per cent greater than that of the thinly stretched Portuguese. However, the division had something of a cloud over its head, having been centrally involved in the defeat by the German counter-attack at Cambrai. The division assimilated large drafts after that battle and also received men from units broken up in the February restructuring: for example, the 1/4 Royal Lancaster Regiment received a large draft of officers and men from the regiment's disbanded 7 Battalion. The divisional commander Major-General Hugh Jeudwine had been hauled up, rather unfairly, as part of the Cambrai Court of Enquiry and vowed that he would never be placed in a similar position. His personal drive played a significant part in the preparations for defending Givenchy. On 7 March 23 men of the 1/5 South Lancashire Regiment holding posts at Barnton Island were surprised by a night raid and taken prisoner. A local Court of Enquiry listed the contributory factors to their capture: many of the men were new, the posts were not properly officered, there was a lack of fighting spirit, rifles were not used, and divisional orders to strengthen the wire defences had not been carried out. Jeudwine exploded. He left his subordinate Brigadier-General Reginald Kentish and the battalion commander Lieutenant-Colonel McCarthy O'Leary in no doubt regarding their future responsibilities, and the entire division stepped up its readiness for any German attack.[43]

Haking and Jeudwine received GHQ instructions regarding the new zonal approach to defences, but would have no truck with them. In the knowledge that no ground could be given up in the Givenchy area without losing the knoll, and facing an insufficiency of reserve counter-attack troops upon which the zone system depended, they decided to stand on one line only, a 'Line of Resistance' that would under no circumstances be lost. A conference was held with the brigade commanders to determine exactly where the Line should be. In front of Givenchy it had to be the existing front, while to the north it switched back to the so-called Village Line, which ran in front of Le Plantin and Festubert. Every possible effort was to be made to strengthen the barbed-wire defences and key strong-points along the line. Each platoon would be either a garrison unit, holding a position, or in close reserve ready to counter-attack. Everything was to be worked out in detail, and repeatedly rehearsed. Jeudwine and his three Brigadiers-General, Clifton Stockwell (164 Brigade), Lionel Boyd-Moss (165) and Reginald Kentish (166), drove the division hard.

By April confidence was high. The physical condition of the troops was good and with few casualties having been sustained since coming into the area, officers and men knew each other. All had had repeated practice at manning the defences, and all knew the role of their unit and of those alongside. Methods for counter-attack were tested; in the event of the enemy breaking through, such counter-attacks would work around the flanks, taking full advantage of the intimate knowledge of the ground gained over many weeks of occupation. Rifle training was stepped up too. Artilleryman John Brind was a Brigadier-General on the staff of XI Corps:

> I remember going round the Givenchy trenches with Stockwell a few days before the attack. Stockwell constantly stopped and would ask a man,
>> 'What would you do if you saw the Bosches coming over there?'
>> 'Shoot, Sir, shoot like hell.'
>> 'And if they got into that little bit of trench there in front?'
>> 'Up and at 'em, sir!'[44]

Although he had great confidence in his men, Jeudwine anticipated problems on his left flank in the event of a German attack on the Portuguese, and made suitable arrangements. One of these was to extend I Corps, south of the canal, right up to it so that all of 166 Brigade could be in place as a reserve. Every unit and every man knew the code word that would order the move to battle stations: 'Bustle'.[45]

The days prior to the German attack were quiet, although a suspicion began to grow that something was about to happen. Patrols encountered no enemy soldiers in the nights leading up to 9 April, but the troops could hear exceptionally heavy traffic moving behind the German lines. Some men of the division speculated that the enemy was moving his guns south to Cambrai. Photographic reconnaissance showed little but it was noticed that piles of road metal and bridging planks had been collected by the roadsides and streams.[46]

Heavy shell-fire fell on the divisional front from 4.15am on 9 April; as with all other sectors, the front line escaped the worst while the gun positions, roads, dumps, reserve posts and headquarters were plastered with high explosive and soaked with gas. Jeudwine's headquarters at Les Caudrons was unscathed; it had recently moved from Locon, which took the fire that was meant for him. Previous periods of heavy shell-fire on Locon had forced Jeudwine to move,

and wisely the deep-buried signals cables, so critical to divisional communications, had been routed around the village. Despite the weight of shells falling
in the area and the destruction of many telephone stations and wires, signals
communications were maintained and in retrospect proved to be a crucial
factor in the division's defence.

It soon became clear that the shell-fire was not simply a ruse or a raid, but
a sustained bombardment similar to that which had preceded the 'Michael'
attack. Reports came in that the enemy was using Phosgene rather than
Mustard gas. This suggested it preceded an infantry attack. The divisional and
corps artillery was ordered to open fire on pre-arranged 'counter preparation'
lines, particularly the enemy's main Canteleux Trench. As arranged, the
reserve units moved on receiving 'Bustle'. The 2/5 Lancashire Fusiliers, the
support battalion of 165 Brigade, headquartered at Gorre brewery and with an
advanced HQ at Pont Fixe, got the word at 5.15am, as did O'Leary's 1/5 South
Lancashires of 166 Brigade at Essars, although others reported receiving the
order as early as 4.45am. The battalions of 166 Brigade moved to their pre-
rehearsed northern flank positions at the Loisne and Tuning Fork posts to
provide cover for the left of the Line of Resistance at Festubert, while the
reserves of 164 and 165 Brigades also took up their respective positions.
They advanced in thick fog and wearing gas respirators, and casualties were
soon incurred as shells continued to fall all around, and a platoon of the
1/6 Liverpool Regiment was wiped out by heavy shell-fire as it moved up
towards Route A Keep. Many groups of men were forced to take shelter or find
ways around the fire. No. 355093 Sergeant James Briggs of Z Company,
1/10 Liverpool Regiment (Liverpool Scottish), awoke in his billet at Mesplaux
Farm and was soon on his way to the north Tuning Fork posts:

> The CO gave the word to get to his Bustle position tout suite so off
> we go, I am afraid with wind vertical. The gunfire was at this point
> awful – the whole front was ablaze with the flashes of the Hun's
> artillery. We hadn't got more than 200 yards along the road before
> the two scouts which the OC Company had pushed forwards
> reported that to get along that road was suicide. About turn was
> given so back we go past the farm again to go on out towards Le
> Hamel. Getting across there was bad going owing to the mist, the
> Loisne stream and several successive belts of wire which ran across
> towards Locon. To make things worse the whiff of gas was getting
> stronger each pace so of course we had to don our masks which do
> not tend to make marching go all clover. On we pushed, great HE
> shells and gas as well dropping all around us up to Loisne Chateau.
> Here we picked up spades and picks and then plodded on. How we

platoons (we split up here and marched at 100-yard intervals) missed getting wiped out between Loisne Chateau and the Tuning Fork Line goodness only knows.[47]

By 7.00am the division's defensive flank was in position, even as the German infantry completed their assembly prior to the assault. But not even Jeudwine had guessed at how completely and rapidly the Portuguese defence would collapse, and how exposed the division's extreme left would become. At around this time a message came through from Captain Frank Edwards, whose C Company of the 1/5 Liverpool Regiment was holding the forward outposts in front of Festubert near Canadian Orchard, reporting that an enemy infantry attack was developing; this was the last that anyone heard from him or most of the 140 men of his company. The battalion's Intelligence Officer, Lieutenant John Pennington, staggered in from patrol, wounded in the hand and reporting the extraordinary news that the Portuguese had evacuated and he had seen German troops. By 7.30am Captain Michael Meade, commanding B Company in the Old British Line, on whose immediate left was the Portuguese 10 Battalion, was signalling that their infantry were pouring back through his trenches and saying that the outpost line had gone. This was the most information that the division received about the Portuguese, for not a signal was received from them that day. Remnants of the outposts held by 1/7 Battalion also fell back to the Old British Line. Meade's second-in-command, Lieutenant Edmond Clark, recalled:

Suddenly the bombardment lifted and the Germans came at us in great numbers out of the mist. There was a cry all along the line, 'They're here! They're here!' Every rifleman used his weapon to the best of his ability, the bombers put down a splendid barrage and the machine gunners supported our front with enfilade fire. We kept the enemy at bay, causing heavy casualties in his ranks, when suddenly Lieutenant Sanders came running up to report that the enemy had broken through on our left and were working round behind us.[48]

Meade's detachment erected blocks in the trenches and fought on. They are believed to have kept up a defence despite being surrounded, under fire from a machine-gun post and with dwindling numbers of men, until about 1.00pm.[49]

Reports vary as to the timing of the commencement of the main German infantry attack but it appears to have been around 8.45am. Figures appeared through the gloom; some penetrated the front at a few points but in other places were held off by determined resistance. Shouts of 'cease fire' were heard but not trusted, and German infantry seen negotiating the wire defences were mown down whenever they were spotted. There were signs of the attackers being surprised by the unexpected resistance and their advance struggled to keep up with the creeping barrage laid in front of them, but sheer numbers and firepower soon began to tell. Once again, as at St Quentin, survivors would report on the speed with which light machine guns were brought up and put to good use, and how quickly the lightly armed *stosstruppen* moved around the flanks. Parties of the units from 164 and 165 Brigades began to withdraw down the communication trenches, taking up positions at the next line of posts.

The attack made against 165 Brigade by two battalions of the 360th Infantry Regiment to the south of Givenchy was faced by the men of 1/4 Royal Lancaster Regiment on the (German) left and the 1/4 Loyal North Lancashire Regiment next to them. Despite suffering casualties on the British wire and in the fire from the first trenches, the attackers fought through and captured Orchard Keep and pressed on as planned. In the warren of trenches and posts, the German advance fragmented into many localised actions as British detachments attempted to beat them off. Second Lieutenant Joseph Collin of 1/4 Royal Lancaster Regiment fell in this fighting. He gave his life in the fight for Orchard Keep, and was later recommended for a posthumous Victoria Cross, the citation of which gives some idea of the close and hard-fought nature of these encounters:

> After offering a long and gallant resistance against heavy odds in the Keep held by his platoon, this officer, with only five of his men remaining, slowly withdrew in the face of superior numbers, contesting every inch of the ground. The enemy were pressing him hard with bombs and machine-gun fire from close range. Single-handed, 2nd Lt. Collin attacked the machine gun and team. After firing his revolver into the enemy, he seized a Mills grenade and threw it into the hostile team, putting the gun out of action, killing four of the team and wounding two others. Observing a second hostile machine gun firing, he took a Lewis gun, and selecting a high point of vantage on the parapet whence he could engage the gun, he, unaided, kept the enemy at bay until he fell mortally wounded. The heroic self-sacrifice of 2nd Lt. Collin was a magnificent example to all.[50]

Behind the Germans' left shoulder, the British garrisons of Spoil Bank Keep and Death or Glory Sap, both on the canal bank, were cut off; despite their predicament, they not only continued to fight but caused numerous casualties among the Germans attempting to advance westward. Elsewhere, Rupert Newman, the chaplain attached to 2/5 Lancashire Fusiliers, managed to escape from the Germans who had taken him prisoner and at 10.00am reported to Battalion HQ, now at Pont Fixe, that the enemy were at Windy Corner.[51] D Company was ordered to eject them. The attackers had also occupied the ruins of Givenchy church and were menacing the headquarters of the 1/4 Loyal North Lancashire Regiment. Some got across the Givenchy–Cuinchy road and as far as Gunner Siding trench, where a single 18-pounder gun fired 150 rounds at the attackers at no more than 200 yards' range, despite being so badly damaged that the breech had to be opened with a pickaxe. But the rear posts and counter-attack platoons held on, striking back as instructed and gradually pushing the enemy back. The artillery of 55 Division, assisted by fire coming across the canal from 1 Division, fired on the German support lines and reserve trenches, cutting off any possibility of reinforcement; according to later reports from British prisoners, this fire caused severe casualties among the reserve units moving up.

By early afternoon the men of 164 Brigade had driven the enemy out of Givenchy and reconnected with the garrisons of Spoil Bank Keep and Death or Glory Sap. Many German detachments, reputedly including a brass band ready to march in triumph through Béthune, were captured as the flank counter-attacks closed their escape routes. Enemy soldiers found with supplies looted from the temporarily lost divisional canteen near Gorre were soon relieved of their booty. As darkness fell even the original forward posts and saps were retaken; it was a serious defeat for 4 Ersatz Division.

It was in the hard-fought actions which drove the enemy out of Givenchy that John Schofield of 2/5 Lancashire Fusiliers earned his posthumous Victoria Cross:

> Second Lieutenant Schofield led a party of nine men against a strong-point and was attacked by about 100 of the enemy, but his skilful use of men and weapons resulted in the taking of 20 prisoners. This officer, having made his party up to ten, then proceeded towards the front line, where he met large numbers of the enemy, on whom his party opened fire. He climbed on the parapet under point-blank machine-gun fire and by his fearless demeanour forced the enemy to surrender. As a result 123 of them, including several officers, were captured. He himself was killed a few minutes later.[52]

Jeudwine's real headache now was his northern flank and the exposed position of 165 Brigade. By 9.30am, although some detachments were still fighting, the enemy had swept around them and was pressing on the Village Line. On the brigade's right, and the junction with 164 Brigade, enemy infantry advanced to the ruins of houses at Windy Corner and as planned turned north to roll up the line. Le Plantin South Post fell to the enemy after a heavy trench-mortar bombardment, although it was soon recaptured by counter-attack. On the brigade left front the situation was broken and obscure. A flank defence had been taken up between the Cailloux Keeps and thrown back to Loisne Central, but in the middle of this line the enemy captured Route A Keep at about 11.30am. It was vital that the flank should be held and extended as far west as practicable. The enemy was throwing men forwards and there seemed no end to the German attack, but no major breakthrough could be forced even against scattered positions that were still enduring exceptionally heavy and nerve-wracking shell-fire. Lieutenant-Colonel Albert Buckley of the 1/5 Liverpools recalled:

> At about 12.30pm the Germans launched a whole battalion on our left rear, between Route A Keep and Cailloux. They came across the open in drill order, advancing in rushes by platoons. I ordered all details out of HQ against them (about forty in all) and as this [German] party advanced across the open they took fright and retired. They were also, of course, enfiladed by Lewis Gun and rifle fire from my defensive left flank (very weak) but a little determination on the enemy's part and nothing could have saved us.[53]

James Briggs and his comrades of the Liverpool Scottish arrived to plug some of the gaps, only to find the Tuning Fork line an inferno of shell-fire. As the German attack continued, Jeudwine ordered every unit possible on to the left flank. Appeals to XI Corps were of no avail: 51 (Highland) Division was on its way up but there were no other troops in the immediate area. Gradually help came with the continued arrival of groups of men from 166 Brigade into the northern flank, and by early afternoon 1/5 Royal Lancaster Regiment filled the gap between Loisne Central and Le Touret. Even so, it was a thin red line indeed. At one point Loisne Central post was only held by 20 men of the Royal Field Artillery armed with rifles and a Lewis gun. The divisional pioneers (1/4 South Lancashire), Royal Engineers Field Companies and 251 Tunnelling Company arrived at Mesplaux Farm to hurriedly build defences, cover the gap to the River Lawe and act as reserves. For a while the situation looked desperate as the enemy continued to press westward, but it was at this time that the policy of having an in-depth pattern of strong posts and defended localities began to pay dividends. Boyd-Moss would later say that his brigade could not have held out in a continuous line once his left flank had turned.[54]

Jeudwine ordered Kentish to scratch together whatever troops he could find, including the many gaggles of Portuguese now in the divisional area, in order to reinforce the flank and ensure that 165 Brigade was not cut off. Finding that he was no longer in telephone communication with Boyd-Moss, Jeudwine gave his Divisional Intelligence Officer, Lieutenant Summers, the unenviable task of taking the vital message overground from Les Caudrons to Brigade HQ:

> I was then asked to try to get a message to 165 so out came my Triumph and off I went. About a mile out of Locon I got on to the

Béthune–Armentières road, only to see half a dozen barrages of enemy artillery bursting in front of me. Down went my head and up went my speed. Beyond the barrages the country – open and flat – was crawling with German infantry advancing in extended order, each man seeming to carry a machine gun or extra piece of equipment. I veered off the road as soon as practicable and headed across country to Brigade HQ, which was in a deep dug-out about 25 feet below ground. The silence when I dismounted was 'deadly' as my machine – for exhaust – carried a lesser organ pipe from Ypres Cathedral. I reached the top of the steps leading down to Brigade HQ to be greeted by a surprised Brigadier-General from below: 'Oh, it's you! I know we are cut off – I thought we were surrounded.' 'We are, sir, but here's your pass-out' – and I handed him the old man's message.[55]

The thin line held. At 2.40pm 166 Brigade reported that the Portuguese detachment had been rallied and was reorganising north-east of Le Hamel, adding to the reserves at the disposal of division. Loisne Central was taken over by the Liverpool Scottish and the line, with the exception of Route A Keep, consolidated as well as possible. Nonetheless the German advance, sweeping to the river in the area of the Portuguese Corps, continued westwards and the scratch garrison of the Mesplaux posts became engaged in a heavy firefight.

Shellfire continued to fall on the rear areas throughout the day, making resupply problematic. Many artillery batteries began to fall short of ammunition. It was also difficult to evacuate the wounded. The experience of Private M2/048544 Richard Masters, an Army Service Corps driver attached to 141 Field Ambulance, led to him becoming the third man in the area to be awarded the VC for his work on 9 April:

Owing to an enemy attack, communications were cut off and the wounded could not be evacuated. The [Gorre/Tuning Fork] road was reported impassable but Private Masters volunteered to try to get through and after great difficulty succeeded, although he had to clear the road of all sorts of debris. He made journey after journey throughout the afternoon over a road which was being shelled and swept by machine-gun fire and once he was bombed by an aeroplane. The greater number of wounded (approximately 200 men) were evacuated by him as his was the only car which got through.[56]

At 4.40pm 55 Divisional HQ completed a retirement from Les Caudrons to Hinges.

By early evening the division had achieved the establishment of a more or less continuous flank, although all units were much depleted. It had given ground in the north, with the loss of Route A Keep being a decided nuisance, but despite the scares and the losses it had been a good day for the division. Givenchy was being held by 1/4 Royal Lancaster Regiment and 1/4 Loyal North Lancashire, supported by 2/5 Lancashire Fusiliers and two companies of 1/5 South Lancashire; the line here had been restored almost to that held prior to the attack, with the exception of Warlingham Crater, which was now in enemy hands. The old Village Line was still held north of Givenchy by the 1/5, 1/6 and 1/7 Liverpool Regiment; this line included Cailloux North Keep but ended there. A second line now ran north from the canal through the Tuning Fork up to Loisne Central, Le Touret Central, round Mesplaux Farm and up towards the footbridge across the Lawe at Le Vert Lannot, where contact was made with 151 Brigade of 51 (Highland) Division. This line was held by details of several battalions, with the Liverpool Scottish south of Loisne Central and holding the Tuning Fork Switch, with 1/4 Royal Lancaster Regiment at Le Touret and 1/4 South Lancashire and 419 and 423 Field Companies RE further north. At the southern end of this line, 1 Gloucestershire Regiment of 1 Division had crossed the canal from Cuinchy and was holding positions along the embankment to protect the bridges. Behind it were a few reserves, comprising the Portuguese detachment, 422 Field Company RE and 251 Tunnelling Company RE but precious little else. The Field Company, positioned between Le Glattignies and the Lawe, was in contact with 154 Brigade, now holding Locon.

Jeudwine was able to report that he was confident he could hold against five-fold attack, should any come. The same could not be said of 40 Division, the British force on the far side of the Portuguese.

The Lys is crossed
The nine tired battalions of 40 Division were as thinly stretched as the Portuguese, holding a front of 7,500 yards from Picantin to the Shaftesbury Avenue communication trench south-east of Bois Grenier. The division had arrived in the area after a severe mauling in 'Michael' and relieved 57 (2 West Lancashire) Division on 2 April, although the artillery did not accompany the division and the guns of the West Lancashires remained to cover it. On arrival the division was placed under the command of du Cane's XV Corps. Major-General John Ponsonby set up Divisional HQ at Croix du Bac and placed two brigades into the front line. By 9 April 119 Brigade under Frank Crozier was occupying the right (Fleurbaix) sector and Campbell's 121 Brigade the left in front of Bois Grenier. 120 Brigade was in reserve positions north of the Lys although under orders to move across the river in the event of an enemy attack; their Brigadier-General Clarence Hobkirk had only been in command since 23 March.

The front was not dissimilar to that held by 2 Portuguese Division, being uniformly flat with the familiar pattern of villages, farms, trees and ditches. The forward system consisted of a continuous breastwork with small posts running behind it, from Le Trou near Picantin, past Cordonnerie Farm and La Boutillerie, gradually turning north-eastwards past Grand Flamengrie Farm to the Armentières–Lens railway line south of Chapelle d'Armentières, from where it was taken on by 34 Division. The front line had barely altered in position since 1914, but those men who had been here before thought that the defences had deteriorated. It was not an appealing prospect for a division that had recently suffered the loss of 2,800 men in similar circumstances. Clarence Hobkirk was not alone in believing that the front line was simply indefensible:

> The method of holding the line on [this] front was by a chain of small posts at wide intervals in the continuous line of a strong and well built parapet, whereas in 1916 when I was commanding the 14 Australian Brigade in the Fleurbaix defences the whole line was strongly held in front and support lines ... I was visited on 3 April, just before the relief by 119 Brigade, by Sir John du Cane who asked me how I proposed to hold the line in case of attack. I answered that in the event of a really big attack the front line posts would be wiped out and the barrage and lack of numbers would prevent an adequate force being sent forwards and that my main defence would be in the support [that is, B] line.[57]

Unfortunately for the division the B Line was only continuous in front of Fleurbaix. In the northern sector the next defensible line comprised a number of posts a mile behind the front, in the middle of the designated Forward Zone. These were at Elbow Farm, Chapel Farm, Command Post and the defences of Bois Grenier. Another chain of posts protected Fleurbaix at the front edge of the Battle Zone: from south to north the principal ones were Charred Post, Windy Post, Croix Blanche and Rue Maréchal. From the south of Fleurbaix there was a wide gap northwards to Canteen Farm. The Laies brook, famous from 1915, also ran through this area. Behind these, the Village Line and Corps Line became almost indistinguishable as the River Lys behind closed the depth from no-man's-land to the river bank to as little as 3 miles. The so-called Rear Zone was a compressed bridgehead area south of the river and just a few hundred yards deep in front of the Lys crossings at Nouveau Monde, Sailly sur la Lys, Bac St Maur and Fort Rompu, with few obviously defensible zones. Little wonder that Hobkirk was less optimistic than his opposite numbers at 4 (do Minho) Brigade, whom he was amazed to find on 6 April expected nothing more serious than some raids and appeared cheerful and confident.[58]

Facing 40 Division was the German 32 Division and one regiment of 38 Division, with 11 Reserve Division behind them, all of which came under the orders of General of Cavalry Otto von Stetten's II Bavarian Corps. All had recently moved from the Ypres area and were experienced Western Front formations. As Frank Crozier would say, from the moment the German bombardment opened at 4.15am, for 40 Division it was all 'mystery and gas'.[59]

As the front-line troops sheltered behind the breastworks and in the forward posts, the batteries, crossroads, bridges and rear strong-points were plastered by the enemy guns, although some suggest that the bombardment was not as heavy in this sector as it was on the Portuguese. At 4.45am, despite their fears that it might just presage a heavy raid, XV Corps called an order through for 120 Brigade to prepare for the pre-planned move across the river to take up a defensive line between Cockshy House and Charred Post, and to leave 120 men to supervise traffic across the Lys bridges. The divisional Royal Engineers also moved to the river. After the Somme losses they were so few that they were virtually all on this duty and inevitably scattered, but the Sappers swung the many temporary bridges into position. The 10/11 and 14 Highland Light Infantry, together with the newly arrived 2 Royal Scots Fusiliers, duly left Estaires for their assembly positions at Sailly and at 7.50am went forwards to the Battle Zone. Although there were reports from the right-hand company of 18 Welsh Regiment as early as 5.55am that the enemy was crossing the Portuguese front in large numbers, an officer of the adjacent 8 Battalion notified the 18 Welsh that they were not yet being attacked. The message went up the chain to Divisional HQ, whereupon Ponsonby made contact with Costa. He got a grateful reply for the news, being told that the Portuguese HQ had lost all contact with its units. It was the last meaningful dialogue between the two formations.

With the German shells continuing to slash down, further reports of an enemy advance on the right continued to come in. The garrison of Charred Post reported Portuguese troops on the right retiring and enemy infantry advancing into the area held by 4 (do Minho) Brigade at about 7.30am, and that they had opened fire. For those manning the machine guns, there was a good deal of uncertainty. Many men later confessed that in the thick fog and smoke it was very difficult to know whether the figures that could be seen were German or not; most men of 40 Division had not yet seen a Portuguese helmet or uniform. After the battle some were convinced that they had shot down their retreating Allies in error.[60]

Although the records give conflicting evidence, it appears that the problems for 18 Welsh really began at about 8.00am, when the Germans attacked the *left* of the battalion front, capturing C and D Posts. Within minutes the battalion also began to be enveloped from the right, and it soon became all too evident that large forces were behind them and turning the flank of 40 Division. The front-line posts quickly fell and those garrisons which could do so withdrew to the support line. Here the battalion resisted as far as possible, although a large proportion of the men were newly arrived 18-year-olds who were in the front line for the first time. Reports of enemy casualties were heavy. But inevitably the battalion was all but wiped out as the Germans overwhelmed the defence. Only 2 officers and 20 men escaped rearwards, the remainder being killed or captured.

With the Welsh destroyed and the front of 4 (do Minho) Brigade broken, by 9.00am enemy infantry were moving in large numbers down VC Avenue and Impertinence Trench towards Picantin and onwards to the line of posts half a mile distant. Crozier had ordered his reserve 21 Middlesex up but about half could not advance much beyond Fleurbaix owing to the heavy shell-fire; some appear to have reached Two Tree Farm near Petillon, where they came into action; another detachment garrisoned Winters Night Post, where they were joined by a remnant of 18 Welsh. There they were wiped out by shells and machine-gun fire. Others fell back with some survivors of 18 Welsh towards Sailly. By now 119 Brigade could form no coherent defence. German attention moved on to 13 East Surreys. Attacked from front, side and rear, they were surrounded on three sides by 9.00am and the battalion was destroyed much as 18 Welsh had been, although isolated posts fought on into the early afternoon as the enemy attack swept past. The battalion lost 20 officers and 524 men; the remnants made their way to Bac St Maur. By 3.30pm what was left of 119 Brigade had been reorganised and was holding an exposed 4,000 yards of the north bank of the Lys from opposite Sailly to Fort Rompu.

The next regiment in the line, 20 Middlesex of 121 Brigade, having lost many men in the bombardment and somewhat disrupted by the abortive dawn raid, also soon found itself almost surrounded. It did not give up without a fight. Alfred Hulls, having got back from no-man's-land, organised his company in Tin Barn Avenue:

> About 11.00am he made an attack from front and rear; at the same time parties commenced to bomb down both ends of my trench. We beat off this attack but I ascertained afterwards, however, that we had practically no ammunition left – about 15 rounds per man. I managed to scrounge another 5 rounds per man from the MGC. About 12.30 the enemy made another attack which was beaten off – had about 4 casualties. Poor old Teddy Groves caught it through the head. He asked for me. However, when I reached him he was unconscious and blood was simply gushing from his nose and mouth. If ever fate dealt hardly with a man it did with Teddy Groves. I was

very fed up. About 1.00pm he was about to attack again when Captain Samuel ... said it was no use ... so we smashed all Lewis and Vickers Guns and surrendered. Personally I never expected to be taken alive, as we must have inflicted tremendous casualties on the enemy.[61]

The few remaining elements of the battalion fell eastwards towards 13 Yorkshires and formed a flank defence with them along the Shaftesbury Avenue communication trench. Campbell's last unit, 12 Suffolks, ordered to the Fleurbaix defences and in position by 7.00am, came under tremendous pressure in the Croix Blanche and Croix Marechal areas from mid-morning. Under heavy machine-gun fire, the battalion held on grimly and inflicted severe casualties on the enemy, but the men were inevitably outflanked on their right and forced to withdraw towards the river during the afternoon.

Around 11.00am German forces reached the posts on the forward edge of the Battle Zone, the position meant to be occupied by 120 Brigade.[62] Arriving after an exhausting march through fog and shell-fire, amid the considerable confusion caused by the hordes of Portuguese who blocked the roads and fields of fire, the brigade was instead forced to take up a line behind Laventie, stretching back to Nouveau Monde and across past Laventie towards Fleurbaix. There were no British troops on either side, except for groups of men making their way from the front towards the river and the gunners of the Royal Field Artillery, many of whom continued to fire until the last possible moment before enemy infantry engulfed them. Lieutenant Cecil Lyne's battery of 64 Brigade found itself particularly exposed, as it had been ordered forwards to Barlette Farm in order to support Alfred Hull's trench raid. Lyne received an urgent wire to send up gun teams and limbers to a position of readiness near the battery, calling at Brigade HQ for orders on the way:

Brigade HQ was in a house near the bridge at Bac St Maur just where the road was marked 'dangerous corner'. It has never been so dangerous as it was that day. When I got there, all was confusion; they had had a direct hit on the mess. There was blood everywhere; the Adjutant had been badly hit; the Colonel had only just taken over command of the brigade and was also wounded for the fourth time. When I got up to HQ the Colonel was waiting for me on the bridge. He said, 'I've had no communication with the front line for the last 20 minutes and for all I know they have already been over-run by the German attack, so I can't give you any orders about trying to go up and collect the guns. However, if you feel like going, I won't try to stop you but must leave it entirely to you.'[63]

Much daunted, Lyne asked for volunteers and set off, little thinking he would see the wagon lines again:

> Fortunately most of the shelling was directed against the main road which we had avoided and our cross-country journey was reasonably free. There was a good deal of rifle fire in front but I came across no retreating infantry who could give me an idea how far the advancing Germans had actually come and it was a great relief when I pulled into the field where the gun position was, to find my gunners still clustered round the guns and cheering our arrival. Actually, they were on the point of destroying the guns as they had given up any hope of being able to get them away, since the Germans were already firing at them from hedges a few hundred yards away.

Lyne was amazed to find a complete absence of any of his own infantry, who seemed to have completely vanished. Despite having only five limbers, he somehow managed to hitch up all six guns and get the teams back across Bac St Maur bridge with few casualties.

With the infantry of 40 Division scattered and to a large extent destroyed, it is hardly surprising that Lyne saw none. His experience was not unique: as German infantry closed in on the river bridgehead, British gunners near Sailly station saw enemy troops just 600 yards away, coming up unopposed from Rouge de Bout. With the river bridges under heavy fire, there were few opportunities to withdraw guns as Lyne had managed to do. The heavy artillery brigades of XI Corps were almost wiped off the map as the enemy closed on the battery positions: 42 Brigade, Royal Garrison Artillery lost all but four of its guns, 49 Brigade all but one and 70 Brigade every gun. Losses among the heavy gunners were severe, amounting to 24 officers and 282 men. By 12.10pm the enemy had also reached Canteen Farm, north-west of Bois Grenier, and the gunners from batteries in that area were forced to make for the river at Fort Rompu and Erquinghem.

British reserves come in
The few days of preparation enjoyed by XI Corps since its arrival in the area were not wasted. XV Corps had no such luxury and hardly barely begun to unpack after its journey from the Somme when the Germans struck. Each corps had as a reserve one division, terribly depleted and exhausted after 'Michael', and both were already in the process of reorganising after receiving large drafts of young conscripts. Major-General Henry Jackson's 50 (Northumbrian) Division had arrived and been assigned to XI Corps as recently as 5 April, but had had some opportunities to carry out reconnaissance, as had two Corps Troops units, the XI Cyclist Battalion and 1 King Edward's Horse.

Their work provided the basis of a plan for an early deployment of reserves in the event of an emergency. All were quite relieved and happy to be in a quiet and not unpleasant area, with Estaires and Merville, still occupied by civilians, among its attractions. Just before the battle 50 Division was shuffled across to XV Corps, being replaced in XI Corps by 51 (Highland) Division. The men of the latter, looking forward to a period of rest in the backwater of Busnes, were completely unfamiliar with the ground they were about to defend. The divisional commander Major-General George Carter-Campbell would have known the area a little but probably had mixed feelings: he had been wounded at Neuve Chapelle in 1915. In the event of a German attack, the plan was that 51 and 50 Divisions would cross the Lawe and Lys respectively and take up positions behind the Portuguese and 40 Divisions to guard the river approaches.[64]

Both corps put their reserves on alert soon after the German shell-fire began, having received calls from Guy Glover at Portuguese headquarters at 4.50am. John du Cane straightaway warned 50 Division to have 151 Brigade ready to move across the Lys from Estaires. For the brigade's 6 Durham Light Infantry (DLI), the day began disastrously. Having just reorganised to absorb a draft of 400 men, the battalion had been glad to move into billets in the town. By mischance, all the battalion officers had moved into the town's convent, with the exception of the commanding officer, the adjutant, the transport officer and one of the company commanders, Captain George Cardew. One of the first heavy German shells burst in the building, leaving only two of its occupants unwounded. The men emerged from other billets, organised by NCOs for the move across the river.[65]

At 5.45am the units of 151 Brigade received orders to move from Estaires to a position in the Portuguese Battle Zone between Cockshy House and Bout Deville. Platoons would also garrison the key Carter's, Riez Bailleul and Clifton Posts. Despite their way being blocked by the retiring Portuguese, and hampered by enemy shell-fire, the depleted 6 DLI reached the position by 9.30am. Both 8 and 5 DLI remained behind them to hold the river crossings from Lestrem to Nouveau Monde, with detachments of the former moving to the Marais posts through heavy shell-fire falling on La Gorgue. Meanwhile 149 and 150 Brigades moved into Estaires, ready to support 151 Brigade if needed.

In XI Corps Haking also ordered his two mobile units forwards, as previously envisaged. The Cyclist Battalion was to man the La Couture defences, while King Edward's Horse would advance to stretch over a mile-long front about Huit Maisons with their left on Bout Deville. These two units were hardly likely to worry the German planners. The Cyclists, usually used for reconnaissance and observation purposes, rode up to Vieille Chapelle and there dismounted, going forwards on foot to La Couture.[66] King Edward's Horse also moved up on foot, after leaving a proportion of the men behind to look after the horses. Both units passed through a heavy gas barrage at Vieille Chapelle on the way and spent much of the day in masks. Lieutenant-Colonel Lionel James ordered the Horse into position, splitting his men into three groups. On the left A Squadron under Major Ralph Furse held a 1,500-yard line stretching from Wellington Post through the Huit Maisons defences and up to a half-completed pill-box 350 yards short of Bout Deville. Major John MacDonald's B Squadron made a continuous but desperately thin line from Wellington Post down some 1,500 yards to a position north-east of La Couture. C Squadron and the headquarters details formed a reserve, centred on the bridgehead defences at Fosse just half a mile from the Lawe. James was worried about the Cyclists manning the defences to his immediate right. La Couture had been a defended locality for so long that the enemy artillery doubtless knew every trench and stretch of barbed wire, and had its range to a tee. The primary defences there comprised a network of trenches close in around the village church and the streets around it; the Cyclists would surely be too few in number to hold them against heavy and sustained shell-fire.

As the two units moved up to their positions, 51 Division was ordered to send a brigade forwards to relieve them; 152 Brigade was selected. For these men, already fortunate to survive 'Michael', the sound and smell of the bombardment produced the horrible feeling that they were about to go through it all again. The older hands tried to offer some comfort to the bewildered 18-year-olds, who had only recently arrived and simply could not understand what was happening. NCOs worried about the all-too-obvious manpower and equipment deficiencies, and there is evidence that on the move up some men were forced to relieve Portuguese troops of their gas respirators.[67]

The corps had arranged for a fleet of lorries to rush the brigade forwards, but they were late in arriving and it was all down to hurried staff work. The drivers had initially been ordered to park at Busnes on the basis that 153 Brigade, being nearest to the front, would go. With 152 Brigade being sent instead, the fleet had to be redirected to Ham en Artois to pick up the battalions. Ham was an extra 3 miles in the wrong direction. With no time to lose and having received only the vaguest of orders, Brigadier-General James Dick-Cunyngham went by car to the forward rendezvous point at Zelobes in the hope of determining how best to deploy his troops once the lorries arrived. Having met no retiring Portuguese en route (he would later believe 'they had all packed up their kits and walked over to the German lines') he met a corps staff officer, who could offer him no idea of where the enemy was or in what strength. The state of the Portuguese defence was similarly a mystery. With no prior knowledge of the ground, the men of 152 Brigade arrived at Zelobes by 11.40am and prepared to advance into the still-thick fog, by that time knowing only that the Portuguese had been broken and that the Cyclists and King Edward's Horse were on their own.[68]

As the lorries arrived at Zelobes, the 6 Gordon Highlanders were told to remain where they were while the 5 Seaforths would go to relieve King Edward's Horse at Huit Maisons. The 6 Seaforths would go to La Couture to take over from the Cyclist Battalion. There was further delay as it was felt necessary to request guides to be sent back from those units in order to lead the battalions into place. It was not until 12.45pm that the move began, by which time the situation had considerably deteriorated.[69]

The Cyclists and King Edward's Horse had reached their allotted positions around 7.30am but could make no contact with any British forces on either side and were unsure of what was happening ahead of them. About 9.00am they were reinforced by units of 3 Portuguese Brigade arriving from reserve at Estaires. Among them came Soldier Aníbal Augusto Milhais of 15 Battalion, a Lewis gunner who stood just 5 feet 1 inch tall. His action on this and subsequent days would earn him great fame, as he manned his gun and kept the enemy at bay for long hours while others withdrew.[70]

Between 10.00am and noon the men of 6 and 8 DLI, King Edward's Horse and the XI Corps Cyclist Battalion found themselves witnessing a rout as the Portuguese streamed back from the forward area. A patrol sent out by the XV Corps Cyclists reported that they seemed to be retiring in groups of twelve men. Most of the newly arrived 3 Portuguese Brigade vanished rearwards into the fog with them. A party of about 30 men, probably from 2 Company, 15 (Tomar) Battalion, remained with the Cyclists, as did 4 Company, 13 Battalion with their officer Captain Bento Roma, this unit having stayed at La Couture when the rest of the battalion had advanced to its doom earlier in the morning. James reported that about ten Portuguese also remained to fight at Huit Maisons and later a Lieutenant James of 8 DLI reported that he had rallied some Portuguese to help man the Lewis guns at Le Marais South. Hard on the heels of the Portuguese front-line troops came the first German units of 8 Bavarian Reserve and 35 Divisions which, according to reports, had their light machine guns at the front and were spraying the area with fire as they advanced. By noon the defenders were hotly engaged and came under increasing pressure as the hours ticked by. At La Couture, Huit Maisons and in the posts, men blazed away with Lewis guns, rifles and hand grenades, keeping the enemy at bay and killing hundreds as they advanced in dense waves. The Germans approached to within 10 yards at one point, only to be beaten off by Private Albert Hartle firing a Lewis gun that he had salvaged from a fleeing Portuguese soldier, and there were other instances of hand-to-hand fighting.[71]

In the mayhem, communication between the British units was tenuous to say the least. It took 2 hours to get a message by runner from the Cyclists at

La Couture to King Edward's Horse, which inevitably meant that each unit fought its own battle. At times, enemy troops could easily be seen massing for an attack, and would have made splendid targets had there been any means of bringing artillery fire on to them. In the absence of information, patrols made two disturbing discoveries. The Durhams found no British troops on their left beyond Cockshy House, and the King Edward's Horse identified that Germans were now probing the gap around Bout Deville between them and the Durhams. Slightly more comforting, some touch was made between the troops in the Fosse bridgehead and the men of 6 DLI now holding the Le Marais posts 1,000 yards to the north, and news came of the imminent arrival of reserves.

Around 12.45pm the two units ordered by Dick-Cunyngham to reinforce the front began their advance. The leading company of 6 Seaforths came under fire while crossing the Lawe at Boundary Bridge, 1.3 miles west of La Couture. The fire came from La Couture itself and Le Touret North Post, the enemy having worked their way around the Cyclists' right. Three platoons crossed the river but were withdrawn an hour later. They took up the river line from 200 yards south of the bridge up to the Vieille Chapelle road; there they experienced much firing but no close infantry action until evening. The 5 Seaforths had a less eventful journey and established battalion headquarters in Fosse Post, while two companies joined the hard-pressed King Edward's Horse at Huit Maisons around 1.45pm, although one was delayed due to its guide having been killed on the way.

Through the afternoon the battle north of Givenchy developed as a two-pronged attack against the two rivers in the areas Vieille Chapelle–Lestrem and Estaires–Nouveau Monde–Sailly sur la Lys. The bridges across the Lys were jammed with traffic: headquarters details, artillery, support units, lost individuals and civilian refugees all rushing to get away from the enemy's guns. Behind them, the posts in the Village and Corps Lines were systematically destroyed by the German attack and for the most part the garrisons were killed or captured. Reports from corps, divisions, brigades and battalions vary greatly in the stated times at which the various posts were lost. It seems that Cockshy House was reduced by shell-fire and fell to infantry attack from Laventie by 1.00pm; Marais East fell at the same time. Within minutes Marais West also fell to German units advancing through Bout Deville and directed on Lestrem. Guy Glover later recalled that at about this time a German attack on the Lawe bridge at Pont Riqueul was repulsed by Lewis gun fire; it was a weak attempt and Glover commented that with more determined leadership 'they could easily have crossed and taken Lestrem by 2.00pm and advanced without opposition'.[72] In mid-afternoon the defences at Riez Bailleul and Clifton Post finally fell. By 4.40pm 8 DLI had been cleared out of the last of the Marais posts.

Behind the posts many gun positions were abandoned, in many cases their teams having been completely unaware of how close the enemy had come until the last moment. Forwards of Sailly and near Fleurbaix, 1 and 45 Brigades of the Royal Garrison Artillery had no chance of moving their huge guns out of harm's way in time. Major Lindsay Mackersy was later awarded the Military Cross despite losing his section of two 9.2-inch howitzers. His experience with 12 Siege Battery typifies the experience of the day for many gunners: '[He] fought his section to the last under continuously heavy barrage; and when the enemy entered the position, retired fighting on the infantry in rear with the remainder of his men.'[73] Hundreds of guns and tons of ammunition and supplies were thus relinquished to the enemy, much of this booty undamaged. Reserve units moving up were surprised to see intact but completely abandoned quartermaster's stores as far as 3.5 miles from the front.[74]

It was now a question of whether and for how long the fragile bridgeheads could hold, and to what extent their garrisons could escape destruction. To some extent their salvation was assisted by the lifting of the fog. Finally, from about 2.00pm, RAF squadrons were able to take off and contact patrols were sent out first, spotting the forward German positions and sending back valuable information for the artillery. They were, for the most part, unhindered in their work.[75]

The men of 6 DLI, now outflanked, were ordered to withdraw to the junction of the Lawe and Lys near La Gorgue and take up a position between 8 and 5 DLI. By 1.45pm Le Drumez and Carter's posts had both gone and the way was open for a German advance on the Lys. Shortly before this, the men of the 4 Yorkshires and the 4 East Yorkshires of 150 Brigade moved down under shell-fire from Trou Bayard and arrived on the north bank of the river east of Estaires. They found remnants from 119 and 120 Brigades already there and made contact on the left with the 21 Middlesex, still holding out across the river at Sailly. Within minutes enemy troops of 35 Division appeared on the south bank at Nouveau Monde and put the two battalions under machine-gun fire, taking advantage of being able to occupy the upper storeys of houses that enjoyed an unbroken view across towards Trou Bayard. Jackson sent 5 and 6 Northumberland Fusiliers of 149 Brigade to assist, with orders to counter-attack any part of the line that might be broken.

A mile to the north the battalions of 120 Brigade extended the line up to Sailly. So rapidly had the military situation developed that some of the normal elements of life were still going on: the brigade received a draft of 150 new men during the battle. One can only wonder at the shock experienced by the draft, most of whom were 18-year-olds arriving straight from England. They proved to be 'extraordinarily brave, though much of it was the bravery of ignorance'.[76] The 2 Royal Scots Fusiliers (RSF) under Lieutenant-Colonel John Utterson-

Kelso, together with the remnants of 14 HLI and 10/11 HLI, had retired from the chaos of the planned advance towards Laventie East and Charred Post having lost large parts of each battalion. Outflanked on their right as the German 42 Division rounded Laventie, the brigade fought a courageous holding action until it was in serious danger of being cut off. Repeated enemy attacks were halted, particularly by fire from 2 RSF. With the enemy closing in on the river line, the Royal Engineers began to destroy the Lys bridges. Bac St Maur went at 2.15pm, blown up by Lieutenant Carr despite it being necessary to repair firing cables broken by shell fragments; Nouveau Monde at 3.40pm. Efforts to destroy the bridges at Pont Levis and Sailly did damage but were not completely successful. Rearguard detachments kept enemy infantry at bay while the brigade took its last opportunity to cross, using pontoon bridges at Nouveau Monde brewery and Rouge Maison. The Scots Fusiliers and 21 Middlesex were last to go, crossing at Sailly bridge between 4.00pm and 4.30pm. Already under fire as the enemy advanced into the vacuum, the brigade lined the river bank and gritted their teeth for the next assault. Their situation was not helped by the fact that the German 370 Regiment of 10 Ersatz Division was crossing at about the same time, a mile and a half downstream at Bac St Maur, using an intact pontoon bridge. The few remaining defenders of 119 Brigade, who had put up strong resistance by firing from the upper windows of buildings near the bridge, before escaping across the Lys and taking up a position on the far bank, were forced away from the river by devastating machine-gun fire from the same buildings and from field guns that the Germans had rushed to the area.

It was perhaps fortunate that the enemy force now crossing at Bac St Maur was not larger and that it was already beginning to encounter transport and supply difficulties, having reached as far as the river from the morning's start line. Although the Germans pressed on towards Croix du Bac, sweeping away the remaining elements of 40 Division and two companies of the Royal Scots, just enough British reserves were assembled to halt the German advance before nightfall. The 4 Yorkshires of 150 Brigade extended from Sailly to form a flank that would ensure the enemy could not approach Estaires from the Bac St Maur direction; 101 Brigade, 34 Division was now in place near Fort Rompu with a flank formed to stop any advance towards Erquinghem; and help arrived in the shape of 74 Brigade, officially part of 25 Division but placed temporarily under the command of 34 Division.

The three battalions of Brigadier-General Hugh Craigie-Halkett's 74 Brigade (comprising 9 Loyal North Lancashire, 11 Lancashire Fusilier and 3 Worcestershire Regiments, together with a company from 25 Machine Gun Battalion) were some 6 miles north of the battle front near Bailleul when the day began. Roused from rest, for they too had recently arrived from the

Somme, the brigade arrived at Steenwerck in mid-afternoon and received orders to clear Croix du Bac. Information was scanty to say the least:

> We could get no definite information as to the exact whereabouts of the enemy. The retiring brigade [119] had apparently melted away, and it was only later that I met its Brigadier [Frank Crozier] in a car when he had just got clear of Croix du Bac and was looking for his men. Maps issued to us were deceptive. Strong-points were shown along the left [northern] bank of the Lys, and I issued orders later to every man to seize and hold them. As a prisoner next day I saw these were only scratchings in the soil and my men, having vainly tried to take cover there, died in them.[77]

They were joined by fewer than a hundred Royal Engineers of 119 Brigade, hastily organised as infantry by Frank Crozier and led by Major Frederick Clark of 229 Field Company. Advancing with 11 Lancashire Fusiliers in the centre, with their right on the Le Séquenteau–Croix road, the North Lancashires on the right and the Worcesters on the left, going through Hallobeau to the river, the brigade brought the enemy attack to a temporary standstill. The 3 Worcesters were on the river and in touch with 34 Division on their left. Two brigade counter-attacks during the night pushed the enemy – by now suffering from ammunition shortages – back out of Croix du Bac, but suffered heavy casualties in doing so, leaving insufficient strength to throw the Germans back across the Lys.[78]

The Cyclists and the Portuguese detachment at La Couture had been reduced by constant attack since mid-morning and fought a magnificent defence in spite of overwhelming odds. Inevitably, sheer numbers and the German penetration beyond the south side of the village had their effect. By 3.00pm the enemy had broken through the defences and were mopping up the trenches and dug-outs among the ruins. Those of the Cyclists that could do so slipped away towards the river, leaving half of their number dead, wounded or captured there. The 6 Seaforths, moving up to relieve the garrison, reported at 3.40pm that it could not reach La Couture and that the enemy seemed to have broken through between there and Le Touret (this was at the time when German infantry were moving in against 55 Division at Mesplaux Farm). Meanwhile the King Edward's Horse was also being outflanked to the north, for the Germans cleared the remaining Marais posts between 3.00pm and 4.40pm. Furse's A Squadron was almost surrounded and faced the prospect of being cut off; he withdrew what little remained of his force into Fosse. Despite the enemy's advance enabling them to put enfilade machine-gun fire into Fosse, the KEH men, together with the 5 Seaforths that had got through, held on. By 5.00pm the enemy had reached the Lawe at the Rault Lock. Half an hour later James also ordered the retirement of his force to Fosse, which it reached by 8.00pm. As it did so, the enemy filtered across the lock and stood for the first time on the western bank of the Lawe.

The movement of 153 Brigade from Busnes to the Lawe had been much delayed due to crowds of civilian refugees and Portuguese troops on the roads. Not until 5.45pm did the leading unit, the 7 Gordon Highlanders, arrive. Their intended line was from north of Fosse Bridge to Marais West Post, but on reaching the railway south of Lestrem at 6.35pm the battalion learned from 8 DLI that the enemy had crossed the Rault Lock. Arrangements were made for the Gordons to wait in support while three platoons of the Durhams launched a counter-attack. Although this was not entirely successful, being broken up by intense machine-gun fire from across the river, it had the desired effect. The Germans, if there were any left on the west bank, evidently withdrew from their fragile bridgehead and by nightfall neither side held the Lock. The 6 Black Watch also arrived and extended the line to Lestrem and the large bend in the Lawe. A company of 6 Gordon Highlanders under Captain James Christie was ordered to Vieille Chapelle Post to assist a detachment of King Edward's Horse.[79] The various battalions also placed sixteen machine guns along the river between Boundary Bridge and Fosse.

Around 7.00pm Jackson ordered all that remained of 151 Brigade to withdraw across to the western bank, leaving 8 DLI in the river loop a few hundred yards on either side of Rault Lock. A small detachment of Royal Engineers, holding the Lawe foot-bridges south of Lestrem, was relieved by the 7 Gordons at 11.00pm.

There were strenuous but localised German efforts to cross the Lawe during the night. The 8 DLI came under great pressure around 1.30am when much of its garrison was destroyed by close-range artillery. All remnants in the Pont Riqueul area withdrew to the western bank, among them barely a hundred men of 6 DLI, which had been engaged throughout the day. The 6 Seaforths also came under heavy attack near Boundary Bridge, where the enemy could get very close in the darkness by taking advantage of the cover of trees and undergrowth. However, the German efforts failed, cut down by fire from the DLI and Scots units holding the Lawe, as well as the 51 Divisional artillery which had now come into position. With 55 Division having held its ground to the south, the river line formed the fighting front through a tense night. To the east of Bac St Maur, 40 and 34 Divisions had contrived to make a more or less continuous flank.

On the extreme right of the Germans' selected assault front lay Armentières, a town of light industries long since evacuated of civilians and partly lying in ruins barely 2 miles from the trenches. Erquinghem-Lys, a pleasant village just 1.5 miles west along the river, was still occupied by civilians despite having been within a short distance of the firing line since 1914. The British front dropped down from Ypres along the east of the Messines Ridge, curved gently around the town to the south and into the flat country at Bois Grenier. Occupying this sector was 34 Division, another tired and depleted formation recently arrived from fighting near Arras. Holding 8,000 yards of front with just two brigades, the division was fortunate to escape the worst of the fighting on 9 April. It was a difficult sector to defend, with Armentières and the Lys being close behind the front and giving no opportunity for laying out a deep zonal system. As elsewhere, the front-line system appeared to the division to have been neglected and much labour was expended over the days before the battle in a last-minute attempt to strengthen the wire defences, dug-outs and posts. Major-General Cecil Nicholson, commanding, placed 102 Brigade on the left, holding from the Lys to the Armentières–Lille railway line, with 103 Brigade taking the line on and connecting with 40 Division at Shaftesbury Avenue. At this time 103 Brigade had the 9 Northumberland Fusiliers on the extreme right, with the 13 Yorkshires holding the line up to the railway. For the most part their front consisted of a front-line trench with a support line just behind it, and the position was interspersed with smaller machine-gun nests and posts. An intermediate trench ran parallel to the Armentières–Bois Grenier road and behind it the Village Line continued in the form of a chain of posts, with Canteen Farm, Red House Post, Streaky Bacon Farm, Gunner Post, La Vesée Post and Rue Fleurie being the primary defences. The division's other infantry element, 101 Brigade, was for the moment acting as XV Corps reserve. It did not amount to much: the 15 and 16 Royal Scots at Erquinghem, and the 11 Suffolks at La Rolanderie Farm, equidistant between Erquinghem and Streaky Bacon Farm, a mile ahead.

The division's artillery was in a state of flux. Having arrived from Arras on 7 April, just days before, it began replacing the outgoing 38 (Welsh) Artillery the next day, a section at a time. This was still in progress when the German attack began. In order to maintain some command coherence, the Welsh gunners returned and took over 34 Division's guns. Other elements of 34 Division's own artillery moved into position and came into action during the afternoon.

Armentières and the area towards Nouvel Houplines came under a terrific gas bombardment from 8.30pm on 7 April until 7.00am next day.[80] Tens of thousands of 'yellow cross' mustard gas shells fell, opening with their characteristic 'plop' and drenching the town. Impossible to clear from the streets and buildings, the gas drifted on a toxic westward breeze to the front lines. The division suffered some 900 gas casualties, many of them from the newly arrived drafts. Half of the 25 Northumberland Fusiliers of 102 Brigade were incapacitated, and as they were holding the front line they had to be replaced by two companies from the 15 Royal Scots. The sappers of 207 Field Company also suffered heavily, and all the officers and a hundred men of the divisional pioneers, 18 Northumberland Fusiliers, were lost.

Facing 34 Division was a regiment from the same 38 Division, II Bavarian Corps, which had assaulted 40 Division. It launched no meaningful attack on the front of 34 Division on 9 April, but the rapid breakthrough of the area to the west soon brought the reserve 101 Brigade into action. The initial German bombardment did not play on the front line around Armentières but the rear areas, town and roads from the north were heavily shelled in the fog. Soon after 5.00am SOS rockets were observed going up in 40 Division's front and the engineers were ordered to swing the many emergency bridges into place across the Lys behind the town. XV Corps put the units of 101 Brigade on alert but it was not until 10.00am that the decision was made to order them from Erquinghem to provide support for the embattled and scattered units of 40 Division south of Bac St Maur. It was all too late. With cable signals having been destroyed by shell-fire, it took until 11.20am for the order to reach the battalion and a half of Royal Scots, and by the time they reached the area the enemy was already in possession of the ground they had hoped to reach. The battalions took up a flank position at Fort Rompu and Du Cane ordered them to link up with 103 Brigade. Despite coming under terrific pressure, the units of 101 Brigade nonetheless managed to create a continuous defence which also incorporated the 12 Suffolks of 121 Brigade, retiring from their extended defence of Fleurbaix by making a fighting withdrawal to the south-west of Fort Rompu, and 103 Trench Mortar Battery. The problem with the south-western orientation of the line now being taken up was that it cut across the main trenches at 90 degrees; the only prepared positions were the communication trenches, and they existed only at the southern end of the flank.[81]

On the extreme right of 103 Brigade, at about 4.00pm the 13 Yorkshires – by now isolated from the rest of their division – informed the 9 Northumberland Fusiliers that they were forming a defensive flank, which by nightfall ran in a thin line from Grande Flamengrie Farm along Shaftesbury Avenue to La Vesée and across the Laies brook. Lieutenant-Colonel Walter Vignoles ensured his battalion would link up with the Yorkshires and up towards 101 Brigade. The fragmented and frail nature of the line formed can be judged from his later report. It was becoming a subaltern's and sergeant's battle, with company, battalion and brigade commanders barely able to keep in contact with the small and separated elements making up their command:

> We accordingly formed a defensive line facing south-west as follows: two Platoons A Company in Park Row; two C Company around Ration Farm; B Company holding a line facing south-west through

La Vesée; B Company of 10 Lincolns continuing the line through
Gunner Post; D Company from Gunner Post to Streaky Bacon
Farm, with orders to get in touch with troops on the right.[82]

By day's end the division found itself holding a much sharper salient round
Armentières with the enemy already across the river at Bac St Maur. Should
the Germans continue the attack next day from that direction, it faced the
prospect of being cut off and destroyed in detail.

Behind the lines

Little news of the enemy attack reached GHQ during the morning and with
the Royal Air Force unable to fly Haig had only the scantiest idea of what was
happening. It became clear by mid-day that the Portuguese line had broken but
the near-destruction of 40 Division and the desperate fighting at Givenchy had
barely begun. Situation reports from the other armies through the day were
mercifully quiet, although First Army came under heavy shell-fire and gas
bombardment south of the La Bassée Canal. During the afternoon, as the
ground mist cleared, contact (spotting) flights began to be made, bringing in
accurate news of the enemy's advance. Camels and SE5As of 4 (Australian),
40 and 210 Squadrons also began the dangerous job of ground strafing and
bombing from low level, aiming principally at the few useful roads that
stretched across from the German start line towards the river bridges. At least
one German regiment moving up towards Festubert was held up by these air
attacks and suffered losses.

At 12.45pm Haig met with Foch, Weygand and Wilson at Beaurepaire.
Believing this attack to be the second stage of a German offensive now clearly
pointing at the intended destruction of the British Army, Haig pressed for
assistance. He needed the line to be shortened and suggested – not for the first
time – that this could be done on the Somme; at the same time he needed the
French to relieve six divisions on the Ypres front or four French divisions to be
assembled as a reserve behind Arras in the area Frevent–Doullens. Foch
declined, but agreed to put four divisions with their heads on the River Somme
between Amiens and Picquigny, ready to move in a north-easterly direction if
and when required, his intention being to maintain French reserves intact
to meet emergencies. Both commanders remained fixated on the danger of
a German attack against Arras, and when Haig went to see the Third Army
commander Lieutenant-General Byng later that afternoon, he got the message
that he too believed he was about to be attacked again in that area.

With no Frenchmen likely to be sent to the Lys, and with more than an eye
on events further south, Haig had no choice but to strip Second Army of anything it could spare around Ypres. Lieutenant-General Herbert Plumer did his

best, releasing his 29 and 49 (West Riding) Divisions. At 4.55pm XV Corps was advised that the first brigade of 29 Division would arrive at Steenwerck, and 147 Brigade, a Machine Gun Company and a Field Company of 49 Division at Le Crèche, later that night. Plumer also released the 9 Cheshires from the reserve of 19 Division at Wulverghem with orders to move to join 34 Division at Nieppe.

The fighting front having been pushed quickly backwards, the whole panoply of the army behind it had to be moved lest it too fall into enemy hands. Estaires, Merville, Armentières and many of the villages were devastated by the ceaseless shelling and burned through the day and night. Unable to go safely through these places, many people crossed fields and followed farm tracks or railway lines in order to get away. La Gorgue aerodrome, home to 208 Squadron, came under fire during the morning; when reports came in of enemy infantry closing in, it was still too foggy for aircraft to take off, so the decision was taken to destroy the squadron's fleet of Camels where they stood. Other, more distant, units moved out later in the day, with 4 and 42 Squadrons evacuating Chocques. Below them the roads of Flanders were crammed solid with headquarters, signals units, field ambulances, casualty clearing stations complete with wounded, labour and railway units, transports of the Army Service Corps and sad, frightened and pathetic clusters of civilians, all fleeing west and north. Ambulance trains, barges and motor ambulance convoys were also heading in the same directions, evacuating 3,538 men from the casualty clearing stations. During the day 212 officers and 3,469 wounded were admitted from the battlefield to the medical units of First Army. As yet, the numbers of dead and captured could not be calculated.[83]

Chapter 4

The German Attack Develops

The fight for Messines Ridge

North of Armentières the British front had remained unmolested on 9 April but as the fog came down again in the early hours of the next morning, eight fresh German divisions made final preparations and lined the front there ready to extend the offensive. The ground in this area differs from that already attacked, in that it is not flat but rolling and better suited for infiltration. In the gentle folds of the landscape and in thick fog the defending units were easily separated, enfiladed and obliterated. The front line followed the high water mark of the British success of June 1917, broadly parallel to and on the gentle forward slope of a line of high ground along which the Armentières–Ypres road ran: the British called it the Messines Ridge. The forward defence comprised widely distributed small posts although some of them were concrete constructions. Others, big enough to house an entire platoon, were very thickly wired all round and had overhead netting meant to camouflage them from the air, but as they were on a forward slope they could be seen from the German trenches. Behind them the support line was more effectively concealed and had a better field of fire. At least one brigadier-general asked before the battle to evacuate the posts and take up a better position in the support trenches; his divisional commander supported the idea but Corps and Army authorities refused. As the attack began, these posts were accurately engaged by shell and mortar fire, and when the German infantry advanced behind the barrage, men were slaughtered in them like rats in a barrel.[84]

Behind much of the forward system lay up to 5,000 yards of devastated and waterlogged ground, churned and cratered by the immense bombardment of June 1917, and across which movement was confined to duckboard walkways. It represented a serious obstacle to any rapid German advance. At the northern end of this wilderness stood the shattered remains of Ravine, Denys and Oosttaverne Woods, with the ruins of Wytschaete and Messines along the top of the ridge and the dense mass of Ploegsteert Wood to the south. The entire area was riddled with trenches and dug-outs. A mile and half or so west of the front-line system and still in the devastated area lay the Corps Line, which ran up from the Douve Valley past Bethleem Farm, then east of Messines up to Lumm Farm, on to Onraet Wood and then bending eastwards

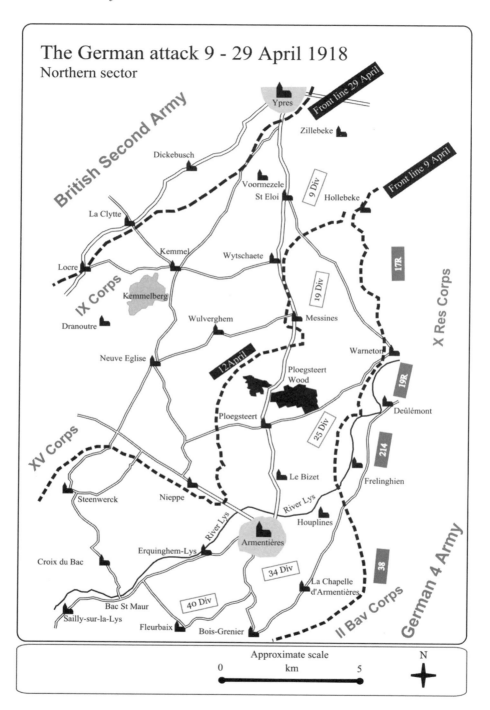

The German attack 9 - 29 April 1918
Northern sector

Front line 29 April

Ypres

Zillebeke

British Second Army

Dickebusch

Voormezele
St Eloi

9 Div

Hollebeke

Front line 9 April

La Clytte

Kemmel

Wytschaete

17R

X Res Corps

Locre

IX Corps

Kemmelberg

19 Div

Dranoutre

Wulverghem

Messines

Neuve Eglise

12 April

Warneton

19R

Ploegsteert
Wood

Deûlémont

Ploegsteert

25 Div

214

XV Corps

Le Bizet

Frelinghien

Steenwerck

Nieppe

River Lys

River Lys

Houplines

38

Croix du Bac

Armentières

German 4 Army

Erquinghem-Lys

River Lys

34 Div

La Chapelle
d'Armentières

II Bav Corps

Bac St Maur

40 Div

Sailly-sur-la-Lys

Fleurbaix

Bois-Grenier

Approximate scale

0   km   5   N

in front of Denys Wood. Its defensive potential was variable and in the Ploegsteert area the line barely existed. Westwards and on the reverse slope of the ridge a defence of sorts could be made in the trenches and craters of the old British front of 1917.

The 96 guns of the British heavy artillery batteries were arranged on the general line Ploegsteert Wood–Hill 63–Steenbeek Valley–Wytschaete–St Eloi. Arrangements were made on the afternoon of 9 April to retire some batteries and form two brigades, one each to provide fire support for 19 and 25 Divisions. Some guns were turned to fire a gas barrage on Bac St Maur during the night. Although orders were given early on 10 April for the heavies to retire, and most did so successfully, the speed and depth of the enemy attack captured 19 guns, including an enormous 15-inch howitzer near Peckham Crater, operated by the Royal Marine Artillery. The fact that artillery lorries had been loaned to bring up reinforcement infantry meant many stores and ammunition could not be removed in time and also fell into German hands.

Of incalculable advantage to the defence was an extensive signal cable network, buried 7 feet deep in a chessboard pattern connecting the front-line posts with commands as far back as Neuve Eglise. Even when the heaviest German bombardment pierced parts of the network and the frontal areas were overrun, the ability of operators to switch to alternative signal routes remained intact and enabled a continuous flow of messages across much of the front, although things became complex as formations were moved and chopped and changed. 7 Brigade, for example, was able to stay in touch with parts of its three battalions up to within minutes of the enemy closing in. As the forward area fell into enemy hands, Romarin, Neuve Eglise and Dranoutre became important signals centres, at the heart of arteries of multiple field (above-ground) cable lines. Broken lines were repaired under fire during the battle and worked well, as did the tireless despatch riders, wireless and pigeon service. They would all play a key part in slowing the enemy attack.

It was the job of the German Fourth Army under General Friedrich Sixt von Arnim and his able Chief of Staff *Generalmajor* Friedrich von Lossberg to plan and execute the attack, with the intention of helping the Sixth Army's efforts to cross the Lys and move generally in the direction of Nieppe and Steenwerck. Fourth Army's front began just north of Frélinghien. Two corps would make the assault: on the left, X Reserve Corps with 7 and 17 Reserve Divisions, and XVIII Reserve Corps to their right with 31 and 214 Divisions. Behind them were 49 and 36 Reserve Divisions in close reserve (in the event they were released to corps command at 8.10am) and 11 Bavarian and 22 Reserve Divisions not far away in OHL reserve. All were Western Front experienced and rested, either having enjoyed a period out of the line or having recently come from quiet sectors. Facing them, Lieutenant-General Sir

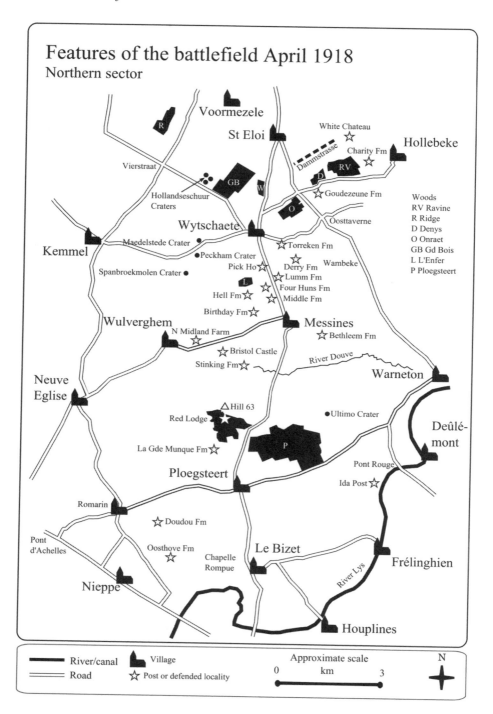

Features of the battlefield April 1918
Northern sector

Voormezele

St Eloi

White Chateau

Hollebeke

Charity Fm

Dammstrasse

Vierstraat

R

RV

D

GB

W

Hollandseschuur
Craters

Goudezeune Fm

O

Oosttaverne

Wytschaete

Woods
RV Ravine
R Ridge
D Denys
O Onraet
GB Gd Bois
L L'Enfer
P Ploegsteert

Maedelstede Crater

Torreken Fm

Kemmel

Peckham Crater

Pick Ho

Derry Fm

Wambeke

Spanbroekmolen Crater

Lumm Fm

L

Four Huns Fm

Hell Fm

Middle Fm

Birthday Fm

Wulverghem

Messines

N Midland Farm

Bethleem Fm

Bristol Castle

Stinking Fm

River Douve

Warneton

Neuve
Eglise

Hill 63

Red Lodge

Ultimo Crater

Deûlé-
mont

La Gde Munque Fm

P

Pont Rouge

Ploegsteert

Ida Post

Romarin

Doudou Fm

Pont
d'Achelles

Oosthove Fm

Le Bizet

Chapelle
Rompue

Frélinghien

River Lys

Nieppe

Houplines

━━ River/canal	🏠 Village	Approximate scale
══ Road	☆ Post or defended locality	0 km 3

N

Alexander Hamilton-Gordon's IX Corps held 17,000 yards and comprised three more British formations that had been cut up in 'Michael' and were tired, below strength and still assimilating recently arrived drafts: from right to left they were 25, 19 (Western) and 9 (Scottish) Divisions.[85]

The night of 9/10 April was quiet in this area although the sound of feverish activity behind the German lines was unmistakable. There was room for concern at both ends of IX Corps' front. Lieutenant-Colonel Charles Birt's 8 Border Regiment (75 Brigade, 25 Division) held the rightmost position of the division's 7,000-yard front, adjacent to 34 Division. Patrols that he had sent out during darkness had not returned and he was worried that the German machine guns were firing to cover the sounds made by bridging the Lys (which was indeed the case). Birt knew that inexperienced men – and he had more than his fair share – could not be expected to hold such an ill-defined line as that through the marshes along the river, and with 74 Brigade having been sent yesterday to Steenwerck, there was nothing behind him but the 2 South Lancashire Regiment.[86] Conversations with Brigadier-General Cathcart Hannay (a Gallipoli veteran who had taken command only the evening before), aimed at agreeing a withdrawal to a shorter line, were not helped by the general having lost his voice after being gassed two days previously. No such change in the line took place before the enemy attacked. Patrols sent out by the neighbouring regiment, 11 Cheshires, discovered German plank bridges already in place, a foot below the river's waterline.[87]

Some 7 miles to the north 9 Division was holding its whole sector with just 27 Brigade in the front line, and during the night its men were ordered by Corps HQ to extend 500 yards into the front occupied by 19 Division. In this desolate area, in darkness and without any opportunity to reconnoitre, the relief began just as the German bombardment opened at 2.45am. 'Relief' soon proved a highly optimistic notion, for the Scots never did find any of the men of 19 Division. In the circumstances it was quite a feat to locate the positions to be held, with the move only just completed and the last outpost garrisons filtering into position by daybreak when enemy infantry attacked. Although news of the enemy's attack on the Lys had come through, a German assault near Ypres had not been anticipated. The war diary of 7 Seaforth Highlanders, which had just been relieved from the front line and arrived in billets at Seddon Camp, Vierstraat, is illuminating:

> Up to this date no convincing evidence had been secured to indicate the coming of an enemy offensive on this front and the general appreciation of the situation ran to this: that the enemy was too much engrossed in his enterprise on the Somme to be capable of launching an attack in this sector; that the nature of the country in the Ypres

salient was too difficult to encourage offensive ideas; and that, in any case, the enemy had neither the troops nor the guns to supply an attack. That view, moreover, corresponded with what the Army Commander had said on the occasion of the divisional inspection on 3 April.[88]

Whether it was down to poor intelligence, wrong assumptions or the simple desire not to damage morale, the information being fed down to the units was far from accurate. The enemy's assault certainly came as a surprise to the Seaforths and by 1.00pm they were ordered to return to the forward area.

The pattern of the first hours of shell-fire and infantry assault was similar to 'Michael' and the first day of 'Georgette'. German artillery blasted away at the British batteries and key points in the rear areas for some hours, dousing all with concentrations of gas which hung around in the fog. The infantry came on largely unseen, moving quickly around difficult spots and probing into the gaps, often coming on British posts from behind them and before they had any intimation of their approach. This anonymous quote is typical of the experience of those in the forward posts:

> The Boche started again and he gave us such a dosing as I have never had and he kept at us until half past twelve when it all died down and he attacked us on our left rear, the weak spot. I saw them coming over the open, three, four or five hundred. I can hardly tell but there were a great number and I really thought it was all over.

The 8 Border Regiment and 11 Cheshires south-east of Ploegsteert Wood and around Le Touquet were quickly enveloped by the Germans of 214 Division who had bridged the river at Frélinghien and Pont Rouge; it is not clear whether a single man of the Cheshires escaped. Charles Birt himself organised elements of the 8 Borders to form a flank west of Le Bizet, hoping in vain to make contact with the Cheshires on his left. Out of communication and with visibility so poor, he spent all day in the fighting front and on his own initiative organised a gradual withdrawal towards Chapelle Rompue and Oosthove Farm. He was to later say, 'I believe I was never in a show where one knew less of what was going on.' Birt was almost taken prisoner at one point, such was the rapid nature of the enemy advance and the close in-fighting experienced by his regiment, and sustained a wound before the day's end. No. 5069 CSM James Gent, finding that all his company officers had become casualties, organised another party of the battalion and oversaw their withdrawal towards Ploegsteert.[89] With 75 Brigade's front having been pierced, German infantry worked their way north through Ploegsteert, up to Hyde Park Corner and by 1.00pm were in the southern end of Ploegsteert Wood. There they found the wrecked guns of 2 New Zealand (Howitzer) Brigade, destroyed by the gunners as they slipped away at the last moment.

During the morning half of 2 South Lancashire Regiment was ordered up from camp near Nieppe and took up a position on slightly higher ground about Regina Farm, 1,400 yards west of Ploegsteert. About a hundred stragglers from 8 Border Regiment joined them, as did the 6 South Wales Borderers, 134 Army Troops Company, Royal Engineers and 1 Australian Army Troops Engineers, which the Lancashires' commander, Lieutenant-Colonel Jerome Allsopp, placed on his right.[90] 25 Machine Gun Battalion also arrived and took up a position on the left. Although Ploegsteert was already in enemy hands no attack was forthcoming from that direction and the units dug in and wired as best they could, under intermittent shell-fire and some sniping. Between 5.00pm and 5.40pm this scratch force mounted a counter-attack with the intention of retaking the village. Without adequate artillery cover and with communications in this area still poor, the attackers were raked by machine-gun fire and fell back. At 7.00pm the force was reorganised with the two fresh companies of the Lancashires rejoining from Le Bizet; the various elements of 8 Border Regiment also regrouped at that place and the engineers withdrew to Romarin.

German infantry of 31 Division began the attack against 7 Brigade at 3.30am. Holding the line up to the morass of the Douve Valley, with the 1 Wiltshires on the right and 4 South Staffords on their left, the brigade's front was quickly penetrated in several places. The Wiltshires lost most of A Company, which had been in the front trenches of La Basse Ville, but managed to withdraw most of the rest around Ultimo Crater and from there back into the north-east of Ploegsteert Wood. Here the battalion resisted numerous attacks during the day and caused heavy casualties to the Germans, but at considerable cost to themselves. The Staffords also lost their front posts facing Warneton, with B Company being completely destroyed except for a platoon that judiciously withdrew into the cover of Watchful Post. After mounting a tenacious defence all morning, the battalion retired through Grey Farm at about 2.00pm, making for the deep shelters of the 'catacombs'. Dug below the slopes of Hill 63, this was a complex of concrete tunnels and shelters, completed by Australian engineers in early 1917.[91]

North across the Douve, 57 Brigade had all three of its battalions in the line: 8 Gloucesters on the right, 10 Worcesters in the centre and 10 Royal Warwickshires on the left. In addition to holding the scattered forward posts, these battalions had been making efforts to join up the discontinuous third line. All had been in the trenches for eight days and were due for relief, but the orders for such a welcome change had been cancelled on 9 April. In the evening of that disappointing day, brigade received intelligence of a build-up of enemy forces in the vicinity of Deulemont and put the battalions on alert at 9.00pm.

After a relatively quiet night, other than some gas shells falling on batteries west of Messines and periods of shell-fire on the battalion headquarters and forward positions, the great bombardment opened and 17 Reserve Division advanced to the attack at about 6.00am. During the day no fewer than thirteen German battalions were identified as having engaged the brigade. Within minutes the front and support posts were lost along the whole brigade line and most of their garrisons were never heard of again. V Australian Heavy Trench Mortar Battery lost all six of its guns as the enemy closed quickly on them east of Oosttaverne. Nevertheless the gunners stayed put, fighting and organising stragglers throughout the day. By 6.30am there were clear signs that the 4 South Staffords across the Douve had also lost their front system, for the enemy was advancing north along the Warneton road towards Gapaard. General Cubitt, experiencing all the uncertainties of an obscure position in the fog, reacted quickly, ordering his only reserves – 81 Field Company and B Company of the divisional pioneers, 5 South Wales Borderers – to man the Corps Line in front of Messines. Hamilton-Gordon also saw the dangers of a deep enemy advance up on to the ridge line if Cubitt's men could not hold. He immediately released the 8 North Staffords from his reserve and two companies were ordered to reinforce the Corps Line, but by the time they reached Messines parties of Germans were already in the eastern edge of the village. The North Staffords wisely withdrew to the western edge and took up a line through the ruined hospice where they were reinforced by two platoons of 8 Gloucesters. Behind them, 84 Field Company occupied the line from Maedelstede to Stinking Farm.

Shells continued to rain down on 19 Division's area throughout the day. Kenneth Godsell's 82 Field Company, Royal Engineers started the day in reserve in an old German trench just west of Grand Bois:

> Some 100 yards in front of us was a 6-inch howitzer battery. Being very crowded, I sent four sections to dig themselves in south of the Vierstraat–Wytschaete road. I remained with HQ and 12 cyclists. Less than a quarter of an hour had elapsed after their departure when a [shell-fire] concentration began, presumably aimed at the battery. Things got really very nasty so we evacuated the trench and got into a disused German pill-box 20 yards in front. The concentration lasted nearly 40 minutes and in this time the trench we had occupied was completely demolished, all the bicycles destroyed, and all our kit much damaged. Had we stayed there doubtless we should all have long since been growing daisies.[92]

A little to the north Lieutenant-Colonel Arthur Fitzgerald of the 10 Warwickshires had his headquarters in the kitchens of Lumm Farm, a mile and a half behind the forwardmost of his 560 men holding posts between the Blauwe-poortbeek and Wambeek streams. His experience was typical of many battalion commanders on this day:

> The first intimation I had of an attack on my front was from the commander of my support company, who ran into my headquarters and said the three front companies had been surrounded and if I didn't get out now with my HQ I should never get out. I immediately manned what defences were available, only to find that the Germans were advancing on us from our right rear, making it clear that the 10 Worcesters had been pushed out of their position. Hand-to-hand fighting took place at my HQ until, with the help of the fog, most of us were able to retire.[93]

Fitzgerald led his men under heavy shell and machine-gun fire to Pick House, a cluster of concrete bunkers on the Wytschaete–Messines road. With no sign of a serious enemy attack to his north, and now in touch with the 6 Wiltshires on his left, he arranged his remaining hundred men into a line running south-west to north-east, across the road. By now 58 Brigade was acutely aware that its neighbours were being pressed back, and took steps to form a south-facing defensive flank south of Oosttaverne along Manchester Street to Torreken Corner cutting.

Just 150 yards away from Fitzgerald's line, a battery of 18 pounders was still in action – and they were not alone, for the guns of 19 Divisional Artillery were handled with great bravery and skill on this day. The two brigades, 87 and 88, had been split into two groups under Lieutenant-Colonel Edward Peel and Major Herbert Russell and placed along the reverse slope of the ridge, with a gun for anti-tank purposes on the forward slope. The batteries remained in position and came under machine-gun fire as the enemy closed. Two batteries on the right were withdrawn to beyond Wulverghem, where they later supported an attack by the South African Brigade, but such was the remaining gunners' tenacity that other than the forward gun, only one other was lost. Among many acts of great personal courage, Captain Eric Dougall of A Battery, 88 Brigade organised gunners and infantrymen alike to keep the enemy out of Messines.[94]

The remaining two companies of 8 North Staffords, together with 700 recently arrived drafts who had not yet even been assigned to battalions, dug in along a line west of Wytschaete and Messines, broadly corresponding to the old British front of before 7 June 1917 and running from Maedelstede Farm, east of Spanbroekmolen to In de Kruisstraat camp and on to Bristol Castle.

58 Brigade, having formed a defensive flank once it became clear that the 10 Warwickshires were being force to retire, came under fire from higher

ground south of Wambeke but managed to destroy several German attacks before they had fully developed. It was not until around 4.30pm that the situation changed, when the 9 Royal Welsh Fusiliers on the brigade left were ordered to evacuate the front posts.[95] The 6 Wiltshires on the right were forced to comply and retired into the relatively strong support line, where for some time their fire kept the enemy at bay. While they were doing so, to their south the South Africans were doing their level best to recapture Messines.

Shortly after noon the South African Brigade of 9 Division, resting in huts between La Clytte and the Scherpenberg, was placed under 19 Divisional command with orders to mount a counter-attack to regain the Corps Line. It was asking a lot, for after a stiff fight at Marrières Wood in March the brigade amounted to less than half a battalion. The reinforcement camp in England was swept clean and a draft of almost 1,000 men arrived at Ridge Wood in early April, but still the brigade could only muster 1,500 men with no prospect of any more. They also had a new commander in Brigadier-General William Tanner, a veteran of the brigade's baptism of fire at Delville Wood in 1916. Captain W. Graham Wallace of 9 Divisional Signals Company was sent to act as signals officer for the operation:

> We were ordered to counter-attack. I arrived to take over my command just as they were moved up to the attack. I found that to organise communications between Brigade HQ and the three battalions I had six men, two telephones and half a mile of wire. Everything else had been captured. I could do nothing but commandeer some despatch runners and trust to luck. The brigade made a forced march to Neuve Eglise and in a cold spring twilight without artillery support, without bombs or reserve ammunition, in fact, nothing but the bayonet and what the men carried, the brigade so raw that the officers hardly knew the NCOs, and their NCOs certainly could not know their men, was flung into a forlorn attack on the Messines Ridge which in the nature of things was doomed to undeserved failure. I saw them go over without faltering or wavering and then they disappeared into the mud and confusion. It was a gallant show but a futile waste of brave men.[96]

It was, perhaps, not as futile as Wallace suggests, for the South Africans' advance slowed the German attack and gave it a bloody nose. At 5.45pm the troops reached the line of the Steenebeek, behind L'Enfer Wood and Birthday Farm, and deployed ready to attack between Messines and Lumm Farm. 1 Regiment took the right position and 2 Regiment the left. 4 Regiment was in close support, and one of its companies was already with 1 Regiment. Artillery cover was weak, for no obvious reason other than a communication breakdown. As the men of 1 Regiment approached the crest of the ridge they met heavy machine-gun fire from strong-points along the ridge road at Middle Farm, Four Huns Farm and the area of Pick House, and suffered 50 per cent casualties. By 6.30pm 2 Regiment had forced its way across the road and captured both Middle and Four Huns Farms. Soon afterwards Lumm Farm also fell and some men reached as far as Derry House. Messines was cleared at bayonet point as far as its eastern edge but there men were pinned down by fire from Bethleem Farm. In this severe fighting all the officers in Messines were killed or wounded, and the remnant withdrew to a point 100 yards west of the village, taking German prisoners with them.

While the South Africans were pushing into Messines, at about 6.00pm both flanks of the 6 Wiltshires near Oosttaverne finally gave way; desperate orders for a retreat to the reserve line did not reach the two companies holding the support trenches, and few of those men returned. Among the survivors was Major H. Wilfred House, who, despite an extraordinary escape, always remained rather embarrassed to be among the few that got away. He would later tell how he received no further orders once in the support line; how he was completely out of communication and runners sent with orders did not get through; how his detachment was turned from his right rear. Despite the evidently hopeless situation, his comrade Captain Kent simply refused to retire without orders. His company was killed or captured to a man. House also recalled how in the early part of the night enemy shells were falling 1,000 yards *behind* their most advanced troops – clearly the Germans were struggling with battlefield communications just as much as the British:[97]

> As darkness began to fall I had to decide what we would do. I had become convinced that Battalion HQ couldn't reach us and therefore we were almost completely, if not completely, isolated. I had about 25 or 30 men with me and whenever we tried to move in the direction of what we thought might be our own lines we were heavily fired at and as darkness came on we could see by the Very lights that the Germans had got some way behind us. I collected our little party and told them what I thought the position was and that I saw little hope of cutting our way out and therefore it seemed to me that the only thing was to form ourselves into groups of 2 or 3 men each and try to make our way through in the dark. I could only tell them what I believed to be the direction of the British line and advise them to watch the Very lights which would confirm that they were moving in the right direction. I decided that the best thing would be for parties of 2 or 3 men who were friends to work together and I arranged that

I would move off with a young officer called Findlay and that we would set off as soon as it was really dark. We didn't know the ground very well as we had only gone into the line the day before and had never been as far forwards as that before, but I had an idea that I knew roughly that there was a stream running at right angles to what had been our original line and Findlay and I decided that we would make for the water and walk in it, as being less likely to meet parties of Germans.[98]

Fired on from all directions but moving steadily in the direction of the flares, House and Findlay followed the line of the stream and after narrowly avoiding a deep flooded gravel pit took cover when they heard foreign conversation. Their relief on finding that the voices were of native speakers from the two Welsh battalions of their brigade was palpable. The 9 Royal Welsh Fusiliers had also endured a difficult time. The bombardment had proved exceedingly heavy and accurate on their left front at Ravine Wood and up towards Charity Farm, and once the German infantry came on, all posts there were lost by 3.00pm. The battalion ordered a withdrawal from its posts at Rose Wood and about the same time lost touch with the 6 Wiltshires on the right.

At the northern extremity of the German attack 27 Brigade occupied a 4,000-yard line of posts and pill-boxes, with some men in a more or less continuous trench system a few hundred yards behind. In the area taken over from 19 Division during the night there were no serious defences behind the forward posts. 26 Brigade was in reserve near Vierstraat, over 3 miles behind the front, with half of 9 Machine Gun Battalion close by (the division's other major element was the South African Brigade).

With no German activity other than shell-fire on their front during the morning, the Scots units remained on alert and came into action between 1.00pm and 2.00pm. German infantry of 17 Reserve Division rushed the outposts held by the 11 Royal Scots but were beaten off; a second attack was very much stronger, reaching as far as the stables of the old White Chateau north of the Dammstrasse. The sight contributed to the 9 Royal Welsh Fusiliers' orders to also withdraw. Fortunately two companies of the 12 Royal Scots were able to reinforce the line and the divisional pioneers, 9 Seaforth Highlanders, were also ordered to that area. In mid-afternoon 26 Brigade, which had been held back by Corps, was returned to divisional control, and 58 Brigade temporarily switched from 19 Division. The situation around Wytschaete was obscure but we now know that positions were being held at least at Pick House and Torreken Corner; around Oosttaverne the enemy appeared to have completely occupied the former British lines by this time. 9 Division would have given much for such hard information.

About noon 8 Black Watch had moved from Vierstraat forwards to Grand Bois, north of Wytschaete. A platoon was sent out at 4.00pm under Lieutenant John Robertson with orders to patrol through Oosttaverne Wood to try to ascertain the situation and determine which British units, if any, were out in front. Stumbling across the battalion headquarters of 9 Royal Welsh Fusiliers on the eastern edge of the wood at about 5.30pm, Robertson discovered that the commanding officer, Major H. Lloyd Williams, had no information about the location or status of his forward companies. Robertson decided to go on:

> I continued through Denys Wood to the Dammstrasse and saw not more than 20 men of 58 Brigade scattered along this line (including some in Goudezeune Farm). We saw Germans about 500 yards away and from the Dammstrasse it seemed there was fierce fighting at the stables and White Chateau. As it was getting dark I commenced to return, intending to revisit the Battalion HQ of the RWF. On approaching the north side of Oosttaverne Wood I met the medical officer of the RWF who informed me that the Germans were in the wood and had captured all the officers of RWF HQ. I was never more surprised in my life.[99]

During his patrol, the enemy had broken through the 6 Wiltshires. Robertson and his men were fortunate to have moved northwards from Oosttaverne Wood, or they would have shared the fate of the many others who were killed or captured there.

By 8.00pm 26 Brigade had reinforced 27 and manned the line Stables– Delbske Farm– Ravine Wood–south of Denys Wood–Goudezeune Farm, with the Black Watch between Onraet and Oosttaverne Woods. Also joining in was 62 Brigade of 21 Division, less one of its own battalions but with one of 146 Brigade attached. First into action were the 2 Lincolns, advancing from Vierstraat towards the north of Wytschaete; the 12 and 13 Northumberland Fusiliers moved from Kemmel past Maedelstede Farm and met no troops whatever until they too were in the village. The two battalions were in contact and in touch with 26 Brigade, so the line north of Wytschaete was by night thin but continuously held; below Wytschaete the Northumberland Fusiliers were not yet in touch with the South Africans. Weak German patrols were encountered, but things quietened down considerably as night fell, with both sides having fought to exhaustion.

While not as spectacularly repulsed as at Givenchy, the right flank of Rupprecht's offensive had failed in its initial objectives. The British line had been pressed back and the crest of the Messines–Wytschaete Ridge reached – but no more. 9 Division had held its ground and only relinquished its forward posts, while to the south of Fourth Army's attack Ploegsteert Wood was still largely in British hands. The way was open for a march on Kemmel and Dickebusch, with the prospect of outflanking the British holding the Ypres salient, but it was clear from the aggressive resistance and counter-attacks that this would be no easy task. Much would depend on how Sixth Army progressed in building on its undoubted success of the first day.

Across the Lys
With the fillip of having gained a bridgehead across the Lys, and having clearly caused untold damage and disruption to the British and Portuguese, Sixth Army found new energy and sufficient transport to bring up enough artillery and ammunition to resume its offensive from 6.00am.

After its failure at Givenchy the previous day, German IV Corps made no serious effort to recapture the knoll or village there, but concentrated instead on an attempt to outflank 55 Division in the area of Loisne and Le Touret. During the night and in spells when the shell-fire slackened, the defenders – who continued to occupy positions they had held since the fighting died down on 9 April – repaired trenches, connected up shell-holes, improved their wire and parapets and gathered in guns and ammunition ready for the next attack. German artillery fired a heavy and almost continuous bombardment during the day, obliterating many posts and destroying lengths of trench; only the scattered nature of the detachments of 55 Division and the fact that some were in concrete shelters saved them from heavier casualties. When parties of Germans were seen, in most cases they were destroyed or driven off by murderous machine-gun and rifle fire, or were ejected by platoon-sized counter-attacks. The fighting was severe, and with the bombardment gradually reducing platoons to mere remnants, the men were under great strain. Minor but most welcome relief came in the form of rations and rum, brought up under heavy fire. The 1/5 Royal Lancaster Regiment at Le Touret endured and repelled an attack at around 8.20am, but the enemy regrouped and came on again at 1.00pm. In this fighting 100 of the 140 men of B Company were lost as the battalion was pressed back some 200 yards. A counter-attack at 2.20pm regained the ground, before relief arrived in the welcome shape of 1 Northumberland Fusiliers of 9 Brigade, marching up from Essars. 4 Royal Fusiliers had also arrived but remained in reserve near Gorre, and two companies of 1 Gloucesters were at Pont Fixe with Battalion HQ at Le Preol. For the second day 55 Division's line had shaken and cracked a little but it still held, and the subalterns and NCOs leading the scattered detachments had inflicted another significant defeat on a much greater attacking force.

Some 2 miles north of Le Touret the King Edward's Horse and 6 Gordon Highlanders likewise held fast in Huit Maisons and Vieille Chapelle during the night and continued to pour fire on to German moves both in front and to north and south. The same was true of the smaller bridgehead at Fosse held by the Horse and 5 Seaforth Highlanders.[100] But it was becoming increasingly evident by mid-morning that both garrisons were in serious danger of being cut off, for the enemy had advanced well past the villages and had crossed the Lawe on both flanks. During the night parties from 8 Bavarian Reserve Division had managed to quietly cross by Boundary Bridge. Supported by machine-guns and artillery pieces that had been moved right up and lined the river bank, they surprised the 6 Seaforths and brought down on them enormous volumes of fire. Movement above ground became simply impossible between the river bank and the Locon–Zelobes road. Support from 51 Divisional artillery appears to have been slight; Dick-Cunyngham reported that there was none except for a single heavy howitzer that had been passing and was commandeered. Despite the Germans' evident fire superiority, enough British fire came back at them to ensure that few men could cross the bridge to reinforce the small bridgehead force, which by now had seized two farm buildings. The 6 Gordon Highlanders made two small counter-attacks, the second of which recaptured the more northerly of the farms, but with only 15 men left of the 97 who went into action it proved impossible to take the second. At dusk this detachment linked up with the rest of its battalion, and with the 7 Argyll & Sutherland Highlanders to the south. With this river crossing effectively halted for the time being, the Vieille Chapelle defences were safe from being outflanked to the south.

At Pont Riqueul, another 2 miles to the north, the same 8 Bavarian Reserve Division made a very much more serious incursion across the Lawe. At 8.00am a party from 23 Bavarian Reserve Infantry effected a crossing, under cover of a field gun brought up to close range under *Oberleutnant* Paul Hermberg and an intense machine-gun barrage.[101] At the same time infantry also moved across the disputed Lock de la Rault. Inevitably the thin garrison holding the river loop (comprising elements of 6 Black Watch and 7 Gordon Highlanders) was compromised and pushed back on to the Lestrem–Fosse road across the 'chord' of the loop. There they joined about a hundred men of 8 DLI, who were manning Lestrem Post. Around 10.30am German troops also crossed the river by Lestrem bridge. The eastern outskirts of the village were cleared and Lestrem Post captured. This was temporarily restored by a strong counter-attack made by 8 DLI at 11.30am, but again artillery support was weak and with enemy forces growing in the loop bridgehead it was only a matter of time before a fresh blow fell.[102]

It took the Germans a while to bring up enough artillery and ammunition across the cratered and muddy area formerly held by the Portuguese, and it was not until 6.00pm that the attack was renewed. The original force had now also been strengthened by the arrival of 16 Division. The delay had given the men of 51 Division some time to reorganise, but they were now holding an area with fewer defence works and little by way of natural cover. There was a deep wire belt in front of Locon and more around Zelobes Post, but precious little else. The whole area came under heavy bombardment from 6.00pm and an hour later the German infantry advanced under its cover. Attacked from the direction of the Rault Lock, the Fosse Post defences finally gave way. Those men of the 5 Seaforths and 7 Gordons that were able to do so escaped under heavy fire across the river bridge, which was destroyed in their wake. Lestrem Post once again fell into enemy hands; German parties spread out to north and south, reaching the northern edge of Lestrem and edging past the western approaches to Fosse bridge towards Zelobes.

As the enemy streamed past to the north of Vieille Chapelle, their attentions turned increasingly to wiping out the defences there. The situation in the village grew desperate as the volume of fire increased. Lieutenant Robert Morpeth, an officer of 51 Machine Gun Battalion, was among the garrison:

> In the early morning our farmhouse was severely shelled and both the Seaforth Captain and I had to evacuate it. . . . They seemed to be firing at point-blank range. Two of our machine guns were shelled out of position sustaining several casualties. . . . We managed to keep touch with infantry on our left and right flanks all day, and also with Brigade HQ who ordered us to hold on at all costs. I myself sent back several messages reporting that the position was very bad and asking to be allowed to retire to a position where my guns could be used to better effect. I never knew whether my messages reached Company HQ as no messages were received by me.[103]

The defences of Huit Maisons–Vieille Chapelle by now formed a pronounced salient, with the continuous but disorganised and thin British line pressed well back on either side. Nonetheless the garrison continued to hold. By night the line to its north folded back through Zelobes and Croix Marmuse, followed the road to L'Epinette and thence to the west of Lestrem.

On the Lys front held by 50 and 40 Divisions, Estaires was shelled heavily through the night and the proud old town gradually turned to dusty rubble. Some reorganisation of its brigades and units was carried out by 50 Division during the hours of darkness; we have already seen how 151 Brigade fared in the Pont Riqueul area. On the division's left a strong attack was mounted early in the morning fog by the German XIX Corps against 149 Brigade. By 7.45am elements of 35 Division had crossed at Pont Levis in the face of strong British machine-gun fire coming from the area of Trou Bayard, forcing back on Estaires the small detachment of 5 Northumberland Fusiliers holding the bridge. Last-minute efforts to blow up the bridge failed; the sappers believed it was due to their electric leads being continually cut by shrapnel. Fanning out from Pont Levis, German units soon took Ferme de Quennelle and also moved on through the town. An urgent counter-attack was organised, in which 6 Northumberland Fusiliers pressed back through the ruins of the streets of Estaires, clearing out the Germans as far as the approaches to Pont Levis and gaining touch with 5 DLI, which was still holding the Pont de la Meuse.[104] Machine guns were set up in the highest buildings around the latter bridge and poured fire on to enemy troops seen approaching from the south or through the town from Pont Levis. Pressure began to build again during the afternoon as the German bridgehead was reinforced. By 3.30pm progress was being made in pushing the battalions of 149 Brigade westwards; XV Corps blithely issued orders to retake the town but with dwindling strength and little by way of artillery support or reserves within the vicinity, it was all that the North-umberland Fusiliers and Durhams could do to hold on as best they could. Around 4.30pm salvoes of shells destroyed the buildings at Pont de la Meuse and large numbers of German infantry took advantage of the reduction in fire to push the defenders back to a position near the water tower on the north–west edge of town.[105]

The task of 40 Division and its attached 74 Brigade, bucked by the news that 29 Division was on its way as reinforcement, was to ensure that the enemy did not capitalise on its bridgehead at Bac St Maur, and if possible to push the Germans back across the Lys. The division had been badly damaged by the previous day's assault, with 119 and 120 Brigades suffering such severe losses that each could only muster little more than a composite company. Other elements of the division were on the other side of the river under the wing of 34 Division. At 4.00am du Cane ordered the division to hold the Steenwerck Switch (a lengthy communication trench with few wire defences or strong-points, west of and parallel to the Grande Becque stream from Steenwerck down to its confluence with the Lys south of Pont de la Boudrelle) with 119 Brigade. The remnants of the 21 Middlesex Regiment would line up to the brigade's right and the pioneers of the 12 Yorkshires rather uncomfortably on the left, out of touch with any British troops on their flank. South of the Middlesex men were the 2 Royal Scots Fusiliers, still holding at Sailly bridge and, not for the first time in this battle, doing so alone. Behind this force 120 Brigade took up a position near Petit Mortier. Further Corps orders, which at this distance in time look extraordinarily optimistic, came at 8.00am, speci-fying that the force, together with 74 Brigade, would counter-attack. Craigie Halkett could not wait. Despite having taken heavy losses in the previous evening's attempt, he was conscious of increasingly heavy enemy shell-fire and the inevitability of a German build-up at Bac St Maur, and he ordered 74 Brigade to advance from Croix du Bac. Neither 119 nor 120 Brigade had the faintest intimation of his intentions, for there had been a complete breakdown in lateral communications resulting from breaks in signals routes, the confusion arising from the fragmentation of units and the unfamiliarity and inexperience of many of the remaining officers. The first 120 Brigade knew of it was when men from 74 Brigade began streaming back into their positions, for the Germans had met the counter-attack head on and destroyed it with volumes of machine-gun fire. The scattered companies of 74 Brigade became engaged in a severe fire-fight that lasted for some hours, but they were inexorably pushed backwards. There are reports that in the confusion some men fired on 120 Brigade in the Switch line. With so much movement, and with units so broken and scattered, it is little wonder that the battalion system of supply broke down. One battalion of 50 Division reported that the arrival of a single limber with seventeen boxes of small arms ammunition saved the day for them around 4.00pm; there are other instances of units reporting shortages. By 3.30pm the German 10 Ersatz Division was at Steenwerck, where hand-to-hand combat took place; in this fighting Lieutenant-Colonel Edward Martin, commanding the 11 Lancashire Fusiliers, was wounded and taken prisoner. There were moments of great anxiety as gaps were forced and the way apparently left open to La Crèche and Bailleul. Somehow parties of stragglers, Royal Engineers and details were found and deployed piecemeal to stop the gaps. For the few officer veterans of 1914, it felt very much like the First Battle of Ypres. To stop a yawning gap opening up between 119 and 74 Brigades, the former arranged a counter-attack at 4.00pm, which succeeded temporarily in advancing half a mile at bayonet point. Around the same time – by coincidence, for any thought of coordination had long since gone – a mixed force of 14 HLI, 2 Royal Scots Fusiliers and 21 Middlesex also made an attack, advancing their line some 600 yards. In this continuous see-sawing and fragmented fighting the gallant 2 Royal Scots Fusiliers had been forced to give up Sailly bridge and by evening the Fusiliers were some 1,200 yards to the north of the river. Above them the ragged and exhausted line curved round to the north-west of Steenwerck and to Pont de Pierre, a mile west of La Crèche. But there was good news, to the extent that the war diarist of 119 Brigade would note at midnight that 'things looked brighter', for fresh troops in the form of 29 and 31 Divisions had arrived.

Rushed from the trenches of Passchendaele (a carefully weighed decision by Plumer, who could ill afford to weaken the Ypres front), 86 and 87 Brigades of 29 Division arrived at Vieux and Neuf Berquin by bus from the Poperinghe area between 6.00 and 8.00am. However, 88 Brigade and the divisional artillery did not accompany them. Among the first to arrive, 1 Border Regiment was ordered to move towards Estaires and occupy a wired and entrenched support line running from the Lys across the north-west face of Estaires. Unmolested by shell-fire, it remained in this position as a backstop to 50 Division until 5.00pm, when it was relieved by 2 Royal Fusiliers. The final element of 29 Division, 88 Brigade, under the remarkable Brigadier-General Bernard Freyberg, arrived at Bailleul at about 4.00pm and took up a position half a mile north of Steenwerck, plugging a gap on the left of 40 Division. Meanwhile, 31 Division began to arrive at Neuf Berquin during the evening, having encountered roads blocked by men, transport and refugees all fleeing the area. On arrival it was deployed in a reserve position covering the eastern approaches to Strazeele and Hazebrouck. 93 Brigade moved to Outtersteene and Merris, while 92 Brigade took up a line in front of Lynde Farm, east of Vieux Berquin, where Divisional HQ was established. The men of 4 (Guards) Brigade were supposed to begin their journey at 11.00pm but no buses turned up and the troops spent the night sleeping in the open along the Arras–St Pol road. During the day 61 (2 South Midland) Division had travelled with orders to detrain at Calonne and Merville, but due to shell-fire was forced to Steenbecque and Berquette. It would form a reserve behind the Lawe front.

The German push north of the Lys and the Messines attack posed grave dangers for 34 Division holding the salient around Armentières. By mid-afternoon the converging distance between German forces near Ploegsteert and those pressing at Steenwerck was only 5 miles. The furthest troops of 34 Division, south-east of Armentières, were 3 miles from Nieppe in the very neck of the bottle, and at least 4 or 5 miles from safety. The German II Bavarian Corps renewed its attack against the battalions of 101 Brigade (plus the 11 Suffolks of 121 Brigade) holding the Fort Rompu–Erquinghem-Lys–Bois Grenier line from 7.00am, and the fighting was fierce and continuous all morning. As elsewhere, enemy soldiers from 32 Division at times broke through the British defences and things looked very bleak, but then enough troops were scratched together to make a counter-attack that drove them out again. Among the various details and units that arrived to reinforce the line were 1/4 Duke of Wellingtons of 147 Brigade, 49 (West Riding) Division, 3 Australian Tunnelling Company and F Special (Gas) Company of the Royal Engineers. Weight of numbers and the difficult tactical position inevitably told, and by early afternoon German troops were on the western edge of Erquinghem-Lys. It was only the tenacious defence of these units that enabled them, and their comrades in the rest of the division, to escape destruction. It became obvious to XV Corps that the evacuation of Armentières was imperative and orders were duly issued at 10.50am, but with communications having been cut and units caught up in the extreme tension of battle, it was not until afternoon that the instructions reached the brigades and men in the line. All experienced a fighting withdrawal, with clashes taking place in the streets of Armentières itself, as fewer and fewer bridges remained. 102 Brigade, having received the orders first, managed to get its entire force across to the north side of the Lys by 6.20pm, whereupon it took up a position from the railway line towards Nieppe. 101 Brigade, despite being most heavily engaged, slipped across but lost a number of men from the 18 Northumberland Fusiliers and 1/4 Duke's who found themselves on the wrong side of the river and surrounded with no bridges left to cross. There were many acts of great personal courage during this withdrawal, such as the evacuation of all the wounded who had been at the jute factory, but none was more outstanding than that of no. 24066 Private Arthur Poulter of the Duke's. His Victoria Cross was gazetted a few weeks later:

> When acting as a stretcher-bearer during the Battle of Lys, [he] carried badly wounded men on his back through heavy machine-gun and artillery fire on ten separate occasions. During the withdrawal over the River Lys, he ran back under fire and brought in a wounded man who had been left behind. He then bandaged forty men under the same heavy fire and was dangerously wounded when attempting another rescue.[106]

The men of 103 Brigade were the last to go, beginning their escape at 4.30pm as the enemy closed in on all sides. Many crossed the Pont de Nieppe, blown at the last possible minute at 6.45pm by 208 Field Company. With them was no. 85196 Sapper Thomas Dewing (always known to his pals as 'Plugg') of 34 Divisional Signals. He recalled that 'the withdrawal was not chaotic but pretty well organised. The Germans were round us but a long way off . . . we could see Very lights going off all around.'[107]

There was no doubt that evacuation was the correct decision, and it saved many lives, but it was a severe blow. Armentières, proudly held by British troops since 1914, was now in German hands. By day's end the attacking forces had advanced over 7 miles and were now through the primary defences and across the Lys. The effect of German shellfire and the depth of the advance can be judged by the losses of XI Corps heavy artillery. The day began with 42 (which lost all but four guns), 49 (all but one) and 70 Brigades, Royal Garrison Artillery, which between them lost all 24 officers and 282 men; during the day itself these units were reinforced by 10 and 28 Brigades and two railway-mounted siege guns. The Corps Artillery HQ at Robecq was so badly damaged by enemy artillery that it could not function and the heavy guns effectively came into divisional commands. But the results to date were disappointing for Ludendorff and Rupprecht. The advance was far behind the original targets and the northern attack had not yet managed to cut the Armentières–Bailleul road. There were signs that some attacks had not been pressed home as far as they might in the face of British machine guns. Transport, material and supply were also becoming problematic. Even so, German forces were now only 10 miles from Hazebrouck, with virtually nothing by way of defences in between. Certainly 10 April had been a day of mixed fortunes for the German offensive, but the relatively small bridgehead at Bac St Maur had now become a platform for a much greater thrust towards Hazebrouck – with terrible consequences for the British armies in Flanders.

The lights burned well into the night at GHQ. In the morning Haig took the risk of stripping the Somme of his last reserves in the shape of 5 and 33 Divisions. Once again he implored Foch for assistance but the dialogue through the day ran again into the dictums 'Never withdraw', 'Never relieve tired troops while the battle lasts' and 'One does what one can'. Foch, believing that the British had sufficient resources to hold the attack and still convinced that an enemy attack on the Arras front was far more to worry about, ordered Petain to move two groups of divisions under Maistre (four infantry and three cavalry divisions) and Micheler towards Doullens. In addition 133 French Division would move up by rail to Bergues near Calais. Meeting Haig at Montreuil at 10.00pm, and reading reports of the day, Foch concluded that perhaps the German offensive was indeed designed to destroy the British army but he still thought that the main blow could yet be expected to fall between the Somme and Arras. Haig authorised his chief of staff Major-General John Davidson to communicate to the armies that they should hold fast, and that French troops were moving north to their assistance. As an extra and last insurance policy, he ordered Fourth Army to release 1 Australian Division. The Aussies would move up from the Somme by rail on 11 April, and cover Hazebrouck as a last line of defence.

Forced back

Once again dawn on 11 April found the Lys Valley shrouded in mist, thicker than the previous day's and longer lasting. At 6.30am XI Corps was informed that ground visibility was too poor for air operations. Perhaps this was just as well, for the beleaguered commands of the three British corps on the front attacked to date might have reacted badly had they known that their ten divisions were about to be assaulted once again, but this time by an expanded German force three times their number.

Both German armies gave orders to renew the attack. Sixth, having effected a broad bridgehead across the Lys, instructed II Bavarian and XIX Corps to thrust northwards from the Neuf Berquin–Doulieu front with the objective of reaching the ridge of high ground running east from near Hazebrouck and going through Strazeele, Méteren and Bailleul. On the right II Bavarian Corps would link up around Nieppe with elements of Fourth Army, which would advance from Ploegsteert. On the left flank LV and IV Corps would complete the crossing of the Lawe and move on the La Bassée Canal and the little River Clarence, which flows up from Robecq past Calonne and into the Vieille Lys. Meanwhile 16 Division, in reserve to LV Corps, was ordered to deploy between the tiring 1 and 8 Bavarian Reserve Divisions. Each objective was about 5 miles distant from the start point. Fourth Army set rather less optimistic targets, ordering *General der Infanterie* Magnus von Eberhardt's X Reserve and *Generalleutnant* Ludwig Sieger's XVIII Reserve Corps to secure the Messines Ridge by the capture of Wytschaete and Wulverghem. For these operations seven fresh divisions which had been in corps or army reserve had been brought up into close support. Three further divisions and the Alpine Corps were in deeper reserve.

After two days of almost unrelenting strain, the same British divisions that had faced the opening assault (less the scattered remains of 2 Portuguese Division, still being rounded up on the roads of Flanders) remained in the front line.[108] The brigades of 55, 50, 51 and 40 Divisions could, in most cases, each barely muster a battalion's worth of strength and were fighting in penny packet detachments. During the fighting of 11 April, when stands were made, soldiers could be as much as 20 yards apart. But the defence of the Lys was proving to be not just a question of manpower but a war of firepower and *materiel*. As long as sufficient artillery and machine guns could be concentrated where the enemy tried to attack, and as long as ammunition could be supplied, attacks could be held off by relatively few men. But 29 and 31 Divisions had already arrived and begun to deploy; 36 and 49 Divisions had sent detachments and 61 Division was not far away; there was also a promise of further help in the shape of 3, 5 and 1 Australian Divisions to come. It was vital that these forces should arrive soon, not just to balance up the manpower equation but to help provide an antidote to the almost total lack of prepared defences now behind the British front. There were few wired defences to be held, and hardly any concrete shelters. The fighting would be done in the fields, woods and ruins of the farms, villages and towns of Flanders. Frank Parker of the 5 Yorkshires tried to explain it in a letter home:

> Estaires was absolutely different [to the Somme] and was a rotten show, as it was a very flat, close country full of farms and drains and you could only see a few hundred yards and hadn't the faintest idea what was going on around you. The worst was that you could never get any cover from his machine guns owing to the flat and the way they were brought forwards and used generally was marvellous.[109]

Perhaps surprisingly, given the circumstances, morale was rising. It was becoming clearer that masses of Germans could be held, if only temporarily, by determined resistance, and with the news that reserves were on the way, things were, for some units at least, feeling brighter.

Behind the fighting front all was chaos, for the army found itself having at once to advance through and do what they could for the tens of thousands of civilian refugees reluctantly leaving their homes and tramping to wherever they thought safety lay. It was a bleak and heartbreaking sight, remarked upon by many soldiers in their letters, diaries and memoirs. Lieutenant–Colonel Walter Vignoles commanded 9 Northumberland Fusiliers, now north of Armentières:

> The village of Nieppe seemed to be full of old people who had not been able to get away, and who did not know in what direction to go; many were stranded without means of transport, too old and weak to walk. It was pitiful to see them, dressed in their best clothes, the only belongings some of them were able to save. An old man of 85 was wheeling his wife of over 80 in a wheelbarrow, with a few precious chattels, down the Bailleul road; we hoped that further back he and his burden would be picked up by one of our limbers that were still moving on the road.[110]

Farmhouses and villages were abandoned, the animals left in their fields. Above their heads flew the heavy shells, killing soldiers and civilians alike and destroying at great distances from the firing line. Lieutenant Frank Glover was with the 1 East Surreys, hurrying north to the Lys as part of 5 Division. They entrained at Mondicourt at noon, and later the battalion's train passed through Chocques, where

> a train had been shelled that morning and many corpses were strewn along the permanent way. Lillers we passed through, the station having been partially wrecked by the explosion of an ammunition train the previous week. We detrained at Thiennes about 8.00pm and I had to billet the battalion in Boëseghem about a mile away. [We] found the houses packed with refugees.[111]

The chaos and long-range shell-fire on railways and road junctions would, for some of the reserve divisions, cause terrible delays to their arrival and disorganise their usually well-ordered movement, making for a haphazard and piecemeal deployment. For the 4 King's Liverpool, moving up with 33 Division, the day included disaster when 40 men died in the shelling of their train at Doullens. The transport, quartermaster's and provost staffs had never worked so hard, and many a burial party thought the same thing.

The day was characterised by continuous attacks and counter-attacks in which the British line gradually retired. By day's end Estaires, Merville and the entire line of the Lawe and Lys had been lost and the enemy had occupied

Neuf Berquin. To the north Messines had finally fallen, as had Ploegsteert and the wood and the key Hill 63 behind it, but Wytschaete remained in British hands and the enemy had made no significant inroads north of the village. While it was a day of loss of ground for the British forces and of bitter fighting, neither of the German armies had succeeded in achieving its objectives and the results came as a great disappointment to Ludendorff, Rupprecht and the army commanders.

On the British left flank 9 Division came under attack in the area of the Dammstrasse from around 8.00am, but all German attempts to advance were soon brought to a halt by machine-gun and rifle fire and a counter-attack by the 7 Seaforth Highlanders. In fact, 64 Brigade of 21 Division was offered to area commander Major-General Henry Tudor, who was contemplating a larger counter-attack to grab the higher ground near Oosttaverne, but the local situation was now secure enough that the operation was not required.

Next down the line, 19 Division was reinforced at 1.20am by the arrival of 108 Brigade of 36 (Ulster) Division, returning to the ground on which they had fought so famously on 7 June 1917. The Irishmen were sent to support 57 Brigade, and 1 Royal Irish Fusiliers manned the road from 500 yards north of Wytschaete down to near Pick House. They came into action with 2 South African Infantry on their right when a heavy attack was made on and north of Messines around 3.00pm. Just prior to this, as news of enemy successes at Ploegsteert came through, Divisional HQ issued orders for a defensive flank to be formed along the Wulverghem–Messines road, to prevent any enemy attempt to turn north and roll up the division's position. The guns of 6 Motor Machine Gun Battery and four of 19 Machine Gun Battalion were placed on high points to cover the road, and the 9 Royal Irish Fusiliers also took up positions along the road. A heavy attack developed between 3.00pm and 3.30pm in the area of Middle Farm, during which the South Africans were pushed back some 600 yards and contact with the southern end of the 1 Royal Irish Fusiliers line was lost. A joint counter-attack soon restored the situation, although enemy soldiers worked their way through the gap, forcing the South Africans' left to bend back towards Hell Farm. Further heavy attacks through the afternoon were beaten off. About 4.00pm orders came through to all units to put into effect the move to the flanking line. The South Africans, now down to pitifully few men, and 108 Brigade would hold from North Midland Farm to Maedelstede Farm, with 57 Brigade withdrawing to a reserve position along the Neuve Eglise–Kemmel road. Two companies of the 12 Royal Irish Rifles came up to reinforce, and 9 Division bent its right a little, placing a post at Peckham crater as a touch point with 19 Division. A difficult night withdrawal was made, which was completed by about 5.00am, but it was not without its scares. About 8.40pm the 9 Royal Irish Fusiliers reported that they were being fired upon from their right rear (by German troops who had broken through at Hill 63). While Wytschaete was still held, Messines had now finally and fully gone into German hands – and to make matters worse, 19 Division had lost touch with 25 Division to the south. It needed 108 Brigade to move several hundred yards and to thin out the line in order to regain contact.

Nowhere on this day was the enemy attack heavier or more successful than against 25 Division. Elements of 7 Brigade were still in front of and holding out in Ploegsteert Wood, with a main line of defence west of the wood. At about 3.00am two companies of 1/4 Shropshire Light Infantry of 56 Brigade had arrived to plug an 800-yard gap on the right of this line, south of Hyde Park Corner to La Grande Munque Farm. They linked up on their left with three companies of the 10 Cheshires, and the remnants of the 1 Wiltshires and 4 South Staffords. The fourth company of 10 Cheshires held the northern-most part of the 2,000-yard brigade line, up to the Douve. Behind this brigade was the now bare Hill 63, affording commanding views of the wood and down towards Ploegsteert and Le Bizet. Next 75 Brigade continued the line down from near La Petite Munque Farm past Romarin and Doudou Farm to link up with 147 Brigade about Nieppe. Hannay's command was temporarily swollen to include his own three battalions plus the 6 South Wales Borderers (pioneers), the 9 Cheshires from 56 Brigade, parts of 19 Machine Gun Battalion and assorted engineers and details. It was a small enough force to hold 3,000 yards of front, and had no reserve whatever.

An attack started early on the front of 75 Brigade but the front held as the defenders poured fire across the open, flat ground. German aircraft flew low over the lines, charting the positions of the British detachments, and at 10.15am accurate shell-fire presaged another assault. This fresh attack quickly broke the line around Romarin, splitting Hannay's command into two. Several attempts to counter-attack led to nothing but further losses. The survivors of the two battalions on the right (9 Cheshire and 8 Border) later withdrew towards Pont d'Achelles to maintain contact with 34 Division.

Opposite 7 Brigade the enemy was seen assembling in the Douve Valley at 8.00am, and here too, German aircraft reported the position. Some 3 hours later the attack struck under cover of terrific and accurate shell-fire. With 75 Brigade having been broken and pushed back, by 11.00am German infantry were firing on Hill 63 from the south. Hamilton-Gordon placed the 1/4 York & Lancasters of 49 Division, then west of Neuve Eglise, at the disposal of 25 Division to shore up the right of 7 Brigade, but it was unlikely to arrive in time to halt a serious attack. In consequence, at 12.30pm Brigadier-General Christopher Griffin ordered a withdrawal. By chance, the officers commanding the 1 Wiltshires, 10 Cheshires and 4 South Staffords had all gathered in the shelter of the Catacombs, to exchange information. They agreed with Griffin and decided to begin withdrawing at 5.00pm. However, the 1/4 York & Lancasters eventually arrived around 3.00pm, by which time the 1/4 Shropshire Light Infantry had held off the enemy and made a successful counterattack under Captain Henry Wace.[112] The situation for the most advanced posts beyond Ploegsteert Wood was becoming most precarious; they were ordered by 25 Divisional HQ to stand fast for as long as possible and then fight their way out, while the rest of the brigade retired some 3 miles to beyond Neuve Eglise. Few men got away from the posts. In view of the urgent and last-ditch nature of these orders the battalion commanders abandoned the orders for a 5.00pm withdrawal and instead prepared to hold on until at least 8.30pm. This action sealed their fate, for the enemy soon closed in on the Catacombs from the direction of La Grande Munque Farm and Red Lodge, capturing those inside, including all three officers.[113] During the evening the shattered brigade fought its way to a retirement on Neuve Eglise, as ordered by division. By day's end the 1 Wiltshires were down to just 70 men. Assistance for the sorely pressed division was now at hand, though, as 100 Brigade of 33 Division, on its way from detrainment at Caestre and Strazeele to its planned place of assembly on the Ravelsberg, was diverted and placed under the command of 25 Division at 1.00pm – another formation arriving before its artillery. The 2 Worcesters and 16 King's Royal Rifle Corps (KRRC) joined the line between 75 and 7 Brigades near Neuve Eglise during the hours of darkness.

The withdrawal from Armentières had inevitably mingled the units and troops of 34 Division, and some did not arrive on the general line of defence until dawn. Two German divisions (38 and 117) mounted an attack along the Nieppe road against the line held by 102 and 103 Brigades. The thinly held southern flank, running along the Bailleul railway, did not come under as great pressure, although it was pierced at one point, only for a counter-attack by half a company of the 1/4 Duke's and an assortment of some 200 men from other units to recover the situation. Incessant heavy shell and machine-gun fire was maintained on the divisional front but after an initial advance the German assault was not pressed home. Having lost heavily against 34 Division over the previous days, and wary of frontal attack, no doubt the Germans were expecting the division to have to retire in conformity with the units on either side as they were forced back. And that is precisely what happened. It was only when deep enemy advances were made on the left (through 75 Brigade) that the decision was made to retire the division through Nieppe to Steenwerck station. One officer of the 15 Royal Scots recalled seeing the five brigadiers in conference at the mill at De Seule, and thinking what a fine opportunity the Germans had to make a sensational capture.[114] The withdrawal through

Nieppe was made difficult by the presence of refugees, belatedly deciding to give up their homes to the enemy.

The story of the day between 34 Division and the right-hand flank of 50 Division grimly holding on to the Lys west of Estaires was one of unrelenting pressure and gradual withdrawal, in which all three divisions (29, 40 and 50) suffered heavy casualties. In the case of the latter two divisions, the terribly fatigued units were down to a very small scale indeed; all the elements of 40 Division north of the Lys amounted to fewer men than two full battalions. They were attacked by five divisions, of which one (11 Reserve) was completely fresh, with the main thrust being in the direction of the road from Estaires to Vieux Berquin. After early enemy gains at Lestrem on the front held by 51 Division, the remnant of 6 DLI manned the line of the railway to protect 50 Division's right from incursion. At much the same time a serious German attack on 5 DLI north-west of Estaires punched a hole between the two battalions, leading to the decision to withdraw towards Merville. By 2.45pm the enemy had reached Chapelle Duvelle. A counter-attack by just 100 brave men of 7 DLI was to little avail and 5 DLI retired on Neuf Berquin, where the men found they had a marvellous field of fire and held off large enemy forces until close-range artillery destroyed the posts. Around 6.00pm German infantry occupied Neuf Berquin, while 5 DLI dug in as best they could south-east of Vierhouck. The curious sound of singing was heard here; the enemy had discovered the wine cellars. Meanwhile 6 and 8 DLI were forced to evacuate even Merville and were now west of the town. The brigade ended the day some 3 miles back from its position of that morning. The experience of 149 Brigade was not dissimilar, losing Trou Bayard as early as 7.00am and leapfrogging rearwards as detachments were outflanked, almost surrounded but retired in the nick of time after doing as much damage to the enemy as they could. By the early hours of 12 April what was left of the brigade was on the line Vierhouck–Pont Rondin. There is little to add regarding the fate of 40 Division, which was forced back on Doulieu. Even the gallant 2 RSF found itself exposed and had to fall back on 29 Division. There was some relief in the shape of a 31 Division counter-attack towards La Becque, but in the scheme of things it made precious little difference. It was the end for 40 Division, at least, for it was relieved during the night. On its left 29 Division too had a stiff fight and retired on Doulieu, leaving 88 Brigade holding the line from Steenwerck station to Pont d'Achelles, where it linked up with 34 Division.

On the Lawe 55 Division once again held firm, the southern block to German ambitions as 9 Division had been to the north. It endured a morning bombardment of increasing intensity before an attack at 11.00am against 166 Brigade pushed back the division's left and opened, for the moment, an uncomfortable gap. A swift and effective counter-strike by the 1/4 South

Lancashires from Mesplaux and the 1 Northumberland Fusiliers from Les Facons recovered the lost ground. Later, reports of enemy troops massing behind Festubert were promptly addressed by British artillery, which destroyed the assembly in large part. Nonetheless the German attack came on and took Festubert East and Cailloux Keeps, both of which were recovered by counter-attack. Jeudwine had been right; his force could hold off the strongest enemy effort. The same could no longer be said of the overstretched 51 Division to their left.

Assaulted all along their line by four German divisions of LV Corps, with 1 and 8 Bavarian Reserve Divisions, and tiring after two days of continuous action, the Highlanders were forced ever backwards, despite being bolstered by the arrival of 8 and 16 Divisions. Finally, the extraordinary defence of Vieille Chapelle came to an end around 8.00am. With the British units on either side being pushed further west and away from the Lawe, the garrison not only faced continuous small arms fire and repeated infantry assault, but bombardment from field guns brought up to within 600 yards. Messages continued to come through from Captain James Christie and his dwindling detachment of 6 Gordon Highlanders and King Edward's Horse until the last moments. In those last desperate minutes he asked for advice on escape routes – but there was nowhere for them to go. Christie himself was severely wounded in an attempt to break out on his right, which seemed the more likely option. His last communication came through at 7.45am, after which the defenders were killed or captured to a man. Once the resistance from Vieille Chapelle was extinguished the attackers had an unhindered front along which to approach 51 Division; gradually the weight of numbers told and the British line was pushed back as first Zelobes and then Croix Marmuse and Paradis fell.

Among the early casualties of the day was Brigadier-General Beckwith of 153 Brigade, who went to hospital still suffering from the effects of poison gas inhaled during 'Michael'. His place was taken by Lieutenant-Colonel Louis Dyson of the divisional field artillery, who was perhaps shocked to discover that the brigade was now down to just 200 men. Things could have been much worse for the division but for the timely, if piecemeal, arrival of assistance in the form of the 1/5 Duke of Cornwall's Light Infantry (DCLI) and the 2/6 Royal Warwickshires of 61 Division, half of 39 Machine Gun Battalion and a company of 33 Machine Gun Battalion. They plugged a long gap on the left of the division that was opening up as 50 Division retired along the river, but soon began to suffer casualties. Behind the firing line a reserve was improvised of men from all sorts of units, with virtually no officers – 153 Brigade had none left at all. Volunteer officers of the Royal Field Artillery came to take command, establishing a line from Pacaut to Bouzateux Farm. The field artillery of 255 Brigade RFA retired to the edge of Pacaut Wood and 256 Brigade to near

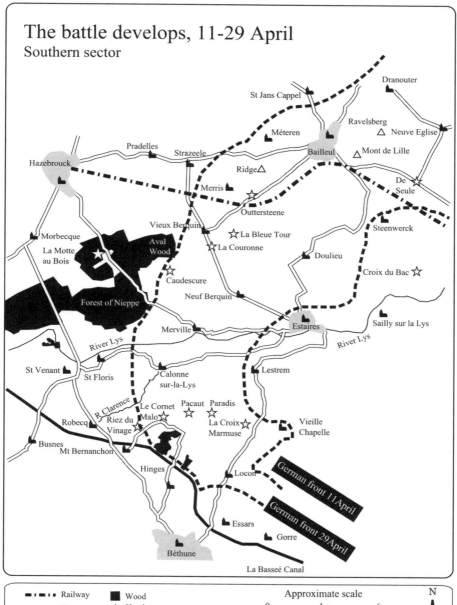

The battle develops, 11-29 April
Southern sector

Dranouter

St Jans Cappel

Ravelsberg

Méteren
Neuve Eglise

Pradelles
Strazeele
Bailleul
Mont de Lille

Hazebrouck
Ridge△
De
Seule

Merris

Outtersteene
Steenwerck

Vieux Berquin
La Bleue Tour

Morbecque
Aval
Wood
La Couronne

La Motte
au Bois
Doulieu

Croix du Bac

Caudescure

Neuf Berquin

Forest of Nieppe
Estaires
Sailly sur la Lys

Merville
River Lys

River Lys

St Venant
St Floris
Calonne
sur-la-Lys
Lestrem

R Clarence
Pacaut Paradis

Robecq
Le Cornet
Malo
La Croix
Marmuse
Vieille
Chapelle

Riez du
Vinage

Busnes
Mt Bernanchon

Hinges
Locon

Essars
Gorre

Béthune
La Basseé Canal

▪▪◼▪▪ Railway	◼ Wood	Approximate scale	N
Water	☆ Hamlet or	0 km 6	
Road	defended locality		

Le Cornet Malo, with guns firing over open sights as the batteries withdrew one at a time.[115] By the end of the day even these positions became untenable and further withdrawals were made to Riez du Vinage and Carvin, while 12 Australian Field Artillery Brigade came up in support at Calonne. The division was now being forced into a narrowing front, with the La Bassée Canal angling across behind the right rear.

Behind the fighting fronts, the day once again witnessed camps, dumps, engineers' stores and ammunition being abandoned after as much as possible was destroyed. Huge quantities of *materiel* fell into enemy hands, and stories began to circulate of parties of Germans enjoying the fruits of their captures rather than pressing on in the face of machine-gun fire. This was a repeat of their ill-disciplined (but entirely understandable) behaviour during 'Michael', and it was to dog the German command for the remainder of 'Georgette'. While the enemy drank, ate and were merry, many British wounded were got away from the field ambulances and clearing stations, thanks not least to ambulance trains which were kept running as close as 3 miles from German bayonets. Lieutenant-Colonel Cyril Howkins, Assistant Director of Medical Services and the senior medical officer with 61 Division, also had another and quite unforeseen problem to deal with. One of his Field Ambulances had taken over St-Venant's asylum. It

> appeared, when taken over, to be empty but about two days after we had settled down I had a message which ran, 'What are you going to do with the lunatics?' I found that there were nearly 1,000 lunatics who had taken refuge in the cellars because the place was, and had been, shelled. The matter was reported to the French authorities, who evacuated them by motor lorries.[116]

As more units of 61 Division arrived, they were ordered to take up ground north of an east–west line running through Paradis. Their left finally got in touch with elements of 50 Division on the L'Ancienne Lys stream. The remainder of 33 Division was also now fitting into place. The men of 100 Brigade went into reserve at the Ravelsberg. We have already heard how two of its battalions had been rushed to the assistance of 75 Brigade near Romarin. The other two brigades, 19 and 98, took up a line at Méteren and Strazeele. One of the units moving up was the 1 Queen's:

> During the night of 10/11 April we were roused from sleep in our billets, ordered to parade in full marching order on the road outside, and marched off in darkness to the railhead a mile or two distant, where we entrained for what was to most of us at the time, an unknown destination. ... we eventually arrived at Caestre, where we

detrained, marched up the road through Fletre and into a camp of huts about half a mile in rear of Méteren. . . . [We were] under orders to move at ten minutes' notice . . . [the] line apparently in rather fluid state, armed pickets [were] detailed to intercept anyone coming from the battlefield and ascertain their business. Méteren was under continuous shell-fire all night.[117]

The armed pickets were from the regimental police and the Provost Marshal's redcaps. With so many men lost and scattered, increasing numbers were now deciding to look after themselves and make their way to the rear, safely out of harm's way.

By now 33 Division was in position along the forward slopes of the very heights that Ludendorff had wished to capture on this day, a full 5 miles from the most advanced of his troops. The enemy, despite in so many cases having a significant manpower advantage, was certainly not having it all his own way. After three days of fighting, it was becoming evident that the lessons learned by those divisions which had experienced 'Michael' were being applied well. This was not a question of an army-wide dissemination of doctrine, but the application of hard, personal experience. Those reserves that were made available were not all pushed into the front line but were carefully positioned and waited for the enemy to come on to their guns; meanwhile stragglers were formed into useful composite forces, regardless of their own unit. But a habit was forming of retiring a good distance to safety whenever flanks looked like being turned, and such deep movement could not be afforded here. By day's end the enemy's progress had brought them to within 6 miles of Hazebrouck. Another two days like this, and the British army – indeed, the Allies on the Western Front – were in serious danger.

In London the War Cabinet met at 6.00pm in an atmosphere of considerable gravity. Not only was Haig's order now public but the Prime Minister had announced to the House of Commons that 100,000 miners would be called up from the already thinly stretched coal industry; the maximum age for conscription was to be raised to 50, and compulsory service applied to Ireland in the teeth of fierce nationalist resistance. The Chief of the Imperial General Staff Henry Wilson explained the military situation in France, saying that the Germans were making progress and Bailleul and Merville were endangered. It was important for the Cabinet to understand that with so few reserves available, although the French were now coming to British aid, the time could not be far away when Foch and Haig might be forced to withdraw Second Army from Ypres. But to where? It would probably be necessary to put into effect two schemes to inundate the area in front of Aire sur la Lys, Calais and Dunkirk by damming the River Aa and letting sea water in to the canal system at Gravelines and Dunkirk. The British army would hold fast behind the flood water, as the Belgians had done since 1914. Preparations had already been made and Haig had reported that the flooding could be complete within three days. By taking this action, a ribbon of water a mile across would hold the enemy away from the Channel ports and the British line would be shortened by 20 miles. There would be bitter, almost unthinkable pills to swallow: the blood-soaked and now iconic Ypres salient would have to be evacuated and the port of Dunkirk given up. The Belgians would have to comply and retreat from the line of the River Yser, and lose the last thin wedge of Belgian soil that they held. It was a gloomy prospect indeed, and inevitably some were looking for heads to roll. A note from the Liberal War Committee was read out, in which a case was made for sacking Generals Gough and Haking. Rarely can a strategic situation have been so misread and fingers pointed at the wrong men. Gough was soon sacrificed, terribly unfairly, for Fifth Army's withdrawal on the Somme. Haking, his cause no doubt helped by the headline in *The Times* of that morning, 'The Recapture of Givenchy', survived by the skin of his teeth.

Quietly, during the evening, Plumer called Hamilton-Gordon to authorise IX Corps to withdraw to a line from Steenwerck station to Wytschaete, and ordered the rest of his army to begin a shortening of the salient line around Ypres by drawing back from the current front line, leaving only outposts.

At GHQ Haig had further communication with Foch regarding the movement of French reserves. It was not encouraging. Simple calculation showed that if the enemy continued the offensive and achieved the rate of advance they had to date, the French could not arrive in time or in sufficient numbers to prevent the loss of Hazebrouck and the high ground. The consequences were too awful to contemplate. Uncharacteristically, Haig discovered the Nelson touch and issued a Special Order of the Day to all troops. After mentioning that the BEF had now faced no fewer than 106 German divisions since 'Michael' began, his closing paragraphs read,

> Words fail me to express the admiration which I feel for the splendid resistance offered by all ranks and our Army under the most trying of circumstances. Many among us are now tired. To those I would say that victory will belong to the side which holds out the longest. The French Army is moving rapidly and in great force to our support.
>
> There is no other course open to us but to fight it out; every position must be held to the last man; there must be no retirement. With our backs to the wall, and believing in the justice of our cause, each one of us might fight on to the end. The safety of our homes and the freedom of mankind depend alike on the conduct of each one of us at this critical moment.[118]

It is far from clear how many of the troops manning the machine guns along the front, or being blasted by shell-fire at Robecq as they carried the wounded to lorries, or carrying out the backbreaking work of shifting the guns for the umpteenth time, received this order. The ASC teams carrying ammunition up along cratered roads, or the Sappers preparing to blow up another bridge or rewiring the telephones as yet another headquarters had to move back, probably did not hear of it as they saw the darkening eastern sky lit by the burning villages and petrol dumps. Of those that did, reactions varied from the inspired to the cynical. At least one unit, knowing it was in the last line of defence with little behind it bar the sea, asked 'What ******* wall?' But perhaps the message was less for consumption by the men in khaki than it was for Foch, Pétain, Wilson and Lloyd George.

Chapter 5

'There is no wall'

12 April

South of Ploegsteert, three days of battle had brought the fighting well away from the old front. Estaires and now Merville and Robecq, all of which had managed to avoid serious damage up until now, lay in smoking ruins, as did the many villages and farms through which the German advance had taken them. Beyond was a pleasant country as yet largely untouched by warfare but being rapidly abandoned by its inhabitants. The area was still of the same flat, heavy type, criss-crossed by canals and ditches, but this would abruptly change as the advance approached Hazebrouck. To the north the long 50-metre high ridge running from Strazeele past Merris and Outtersteene to Méteren, Bailleul and the Ravelsberg could now be seen from the Neuf Berquin road. Between the Germans and the ridge the small and winding streams of the Bourre and Plate Becque presented an obstacle but nothing for which they were unprepared. It is, however, an area even today of few good main roads. With the exception of the road coming up from Estaires and through the Berquins to Strazeele, and that from Merville straight to Hazebrouck, all others are little more than farm tracks. The railway tracks from Bailleul and Armentières provided the only other solid route across the wet country but these were clearly of little value to wheeled transport and were oriented west–east, across the German line of advance. Beyond Merville and Calonne to the north-west and before Haze-brouck lay the thick Nieppe Forest, just coming into springtime green and cut through with straight 'rides'. In peacetime this was a most pleasant spot, much loved by the hunters of *la chasse*, keen to pot a hare or pheasant. Beyond the first acres of trees stood the magnificent chateau at La Motte, home to Ernest, Baroness de la Grange and her considerable retinue of servants, gardeners and handymen. Since the earliest days of the war the Baroness had played host to troops and was well on the way to earning the epithet the 'Mother of the British Army'. Her home had been handed over in part to various corps headquarters; the hamlet around the main entrance to the chateau was occupied by numerous signals and ancillary units, with the constant buzz of motorcycle despatch riders, staff cars and lorries. Many of the British high command had dined with the Baroness, admiring her cultured charm and beautifully appointed rooms, and there was little she did not know about the army and the war in general.

Away in Paris when the German attack began – at the very spot that she had believed vulnerable and had said so to John du Cane – the Baroness immediately feared for her home and pulled on every string and favour she knew in order to return, but to no avail. Among those she tried to charm was none other than Hereward Wake at the Supreme War Council. On the day she lunched with him – it was her birthday, 13 April – even Wake may not have known that La Motte had from 12 April been occupied not by the staffs but by the newly arrived troops of 5 Division, ordered by GHQ to hold it as a line of last resistance.[119]

At home, readers of *The Times* newspaper breakfasted over news of the conscription comb-out of miners and engineers; of a case of a butcher selling sausages contaminated with boracic acid, and a police raid on unlicensed gambling at the Windmill Club in London. Weary of war news, they may have missed the special correspondent's reports, hidden below calm headlines on page 7. Keener eyes would spot that the British had evacuated Armentières, 'full of gas'; that the Germans were at Nieppe, had gained the whole line of the Lys and were at Steenwerck but were being held on the Lawe and Messines Ridge. It was a remarkably accurate and candid presentation of the situation. Many British – and, no doubt, German – troops taking part in the battle would have valued such clear information. Rumours of the German breakthrough soon began to filter to the rear areas. Private 203756 Alfred Thomas and his chums of the 2/4 Oxfordshire & Buckinghamshire Light Infantry (OBLI) of 61 Division, on their way by train, had heard nothing. As far as they were concerned they were returning to a well-loved area to have a good rest. They were looking forward to 'our old billets at Riez Bailleul and Lestrem, and the "eggs and cheeps" of the little "dameselle who kept the chip shop in Laventie".'[120] Detraining at Steenbecque, where civilians were still about and the lights on at night, it came as a considerable shock to find as they moved up that people were fleeing and that 'stolid French peasants' were applauding them. As a line of lorries passed, the Army Service Corps drivers shouted down 'Fritz is over, boys. Good luck.' Everywhere they heard '*Allemands, ah, mon Dieu, les Allemands*'. The penny began to drop. When they reached abandoned Saint-Venant, it was clear that their chances of chips in Laventie were not too good.

Things were rather more obvious to those troops who were closer to the front. Private 68405 Joe Yarwood was with 94 Field Ambulance, one of the medical units of 31 Division:

> We went into action that night, but so far as our action was concerned we didn't know where to go, it was sort of wandering around aimlessly. We went into a casualty clearing station which was lying vacant. A lovely big hospital with wards, proper beds. There was a

piano in one of the nurses' quarters. All luxury. All this lot was going to fall into the hands of [the Germans]. We spent a night there and didn't do anything at all. Next morning one of our chaps was round scrounging and he found a quartermaster's stores intact. There was whisky, all sorts of luxuries lying there.[121]

Later in the day,

We were sending off the wounded. They would go off to a Casualty Clearing Station they know of. When they got there the CCS had hopped it. The whole thing was disorganised. Our chaps were throwing away their rifles at this time, making for Calais in large numbers, with the idea of getting back to Blighty. They were rounding them up there, equipping them with more stuff and sending them back into the firing line.

Joe had a 'sinking feeling, awfully sad' to see this. With the front being pushed back so quickly, it was obvious to all that organisation was beginning to break down. Some of it, at least, was due to open and easy access to abandoned stores: British troops soon engaged in the same activities as did the Germans just short distances away. Major Geoffrey Christie–Miller was with the 2/5 Gloucestershire Regiment of 61 Division:

On our way into this line we passed a dump of wine barrels left by the Portuguese Corps against the canal. It was a large dump and all were full. This naturally led to complications. During the night some of our men seemed to have found their way back to this and filled their water bottles. While the attack was going on I found a couple near the support line 'blotto'. We thought they had been killed but soon found it was the wine they were suffering from. We took advantage of a party of Highlanders bringing us ammunition and sent these men back on stretchers. Subsequently however this party found the same dump of wine and left our two men. They rejoined the same night. No one knew them and they could not be identified so nothing happened. The authorities handed this dump over to the APM who had the casks broached and when I next went past the field was swimming with wine. It seemed a pity the wine could not have been put under guard and issued to the troops.[122]

Passing through Saint-Venant after his battalion was relieved a few days later, Christie-Miller noted that the inhabitants had left so hurriedly that they could have taken little with them. 'We stepped straight into a town fully stocked with the world's goods.' His men found many useful things in the Portuguese stores, including the 'instruments of a brass band and last but not least a fully equipped set of baths'. It is not stated whether the Gloucesters, coming out of the line after losing 153 men, took advantage of either find.

Impatient to achieve the objectives set on 11 April, von Quast ordered his Sixth Army to continue to press on for the Strazeele–Bailleul high ground and to reach the La Bassée Canal. Meanwhile von Arnim's Fourth Army placed XVIII Corps, north of the Douve, on standby until X Reserve Corps had made further progress. The day proved to be one of tremendous success for von Quast, much less so for von Arnim. At 9.55am British GHQ issued instructions for the armies to hold on the line Hinges–Nieppe Forest–Bailleul–Neuve Eglise–Kemmel and to retire no more.[123]

Across the battle front the early fog soon cleared and this day became the first in which the air forces played a key part. The RAF mounted a relentless offensive against the advancing German army, not only by bombing the bridges and roads but by switching the scout (fighter) squadrons to a ground-support role. Many German histories record casualties and disruption caused by low-level bombing and strafing. Most British squadrons recorded an average of 5 hours' flying time for pilots, with many individuals in the air for 6 or more. The level of aerial activity can be judged by the fact that on this single day, more than 2,500 bombs were dropped, 114,000 rounds fired and 3,300 photographs taken. Naturally the German air force responded, not only attacking the ground-support aircraft but confronting higher-level British offensive patrols with groups of fighters. Observation balloons, pushed well forwards behind the advance as they had been throughout the battle, became the focus of much activity, with British scouts doing their best to bring them down and German fighters fending them off.[124]

On the British right flank 55 Division and 9 Brigade of 3 Division came under sustained shell-fire which lasted throughout the day but they did not face a general infantry attack. At 11.30pm an attempt was made against 166 Brigade but the German attack was held up in the fresh barbed-wire defences that the brigade had erected the previous night, and was cut down by rifle and machine-gun fire.

To their left 8 Brigade had relieved what little remained of 154 Brigade of 51 Division during the early hours, taking over the line from the Lawe south-east of Locon up to La Tombe Willot.[125] Their orders were to hold at all costs. It was, perhaps, not the best time for a new commander to arrive, but at 10.00am Brigadier-General Bertie Fisher took over, finding that his head-quarters was a barge, hastily moored across the La Bassée Canal near Long Cornet as an emergency bridge. As yet his brigade had faced no attack, although 1 RSF and 7 King's Shropshire Light Infantry (KSLI) were heavily bombarded during the morning. During this shelling, at around 12.50pm, Pont

Tournant, a swing bridge across the Lawe at Locon, was blown up. German infantry of 18 Reserve Division finally came on at 1.00pm. The 2 Royal Scots and 1 RSF, partly surrounded, found themselves having to fight their way out of Locon in small groups. XI Corps ordered the brigade to take up the line of the Le Hamel Switch, a trench running east–west to the south of Locon, and to hold on as best they could. To their north, in the area held by 51 Division, the enemy had made a spectacular breakthrough.

By the warmer, sunnier morning of 12 April 51 Division did not resemble even the under-strength formation that had moved into action three days earlier. Many of its battalions were down to very small numbers; there were parties of stragglers who had for all manner of reasons been split from their units, some of which were being reorganised behind the canals; and the men were dog-tired. At 4.45am a heavy trench-mortar and machine-gun barrage opened on the remnants of 152 and 153 Brigades holding the line at Pacaut. Patrols of the 2/6 Royal Warwickshires of 61 Division, caught out in no-man's-land between Pacaut and Paradis, did not send any indications of enemy attack; they were never heard of again. Some 15 minutes later infantry from 68 Infantry Regiment, of the relatively fresh 16 Division, advanced. British artillery responded but much of their fire fell behind the attackers, on the positions they had just vacated. By 5.15am the Battalion HQs of the Warwickshires and 1/8 Royal Scots, both in Pacaut, were surrounded. The Germans simply pushed resistance aside, the light machine guns carried by the forward units making defence impossible. Within half an hour they had reached Le Cornet Malo, some 2,000 yards from their start point. The advance was so rapid that the first 152 Brigade HQ on the eastern outskirts of Riez du Vinage knew was when German helmets appeared from the north-east. General Dick-Cunyngham and seven other officers were among those taken; Louis Dyson at 153 Brigade narrowly escaped a similar fate, having decided to go just a minute before.[126]

All night long 256 Brigade of the divisional artillery, together with 12 Australian Field Artillery Brigade, had worked to maintain harassing fire of 50 rounds per battery per minute. At 5.00am it had fired a concentrated bombardment on Paradis and the area of the church. They were fortunate, for being south of Haystack Farm at Carvin (1,300 yards east of Robecq), their guns were further away from the German infantry than were those of 255 Brigade at Riez du Vinage. As the enemy made such rapid progress, A and B Batteries of the latter brigade were hauled across the canal, losing many horses to machine-gun fire as they went. C and D Batteries remained, firing over open sights as the enemy closed. Sergeant L/13633 James Illidge, aged 29 and a former miner from Haydock, was the last man away.[127]

There were countless acts of great personal bravery during this action, most of which were never recorded. Second Lieutenant William McFarlane of D Battery was acting as liaison officer with the 6 Black Watch when his unit was surrounded north of Bouzateaux Farm. Sending back his horse and mounted orderly, he remained at the position and was last seen firing his revolver at the enemy.[128] There were stories of almost miraculous escapes. Captain Daniel McKelvey, the medical officer of the 6 Gordon Highlanders, was captured with his Army Service Corps driver Private M2/053918 Alfred Highmore, along with their Ford car. In the mist both managed to get away and back to British lines.[129]

With 8 Brigade having been ordered to stand on the Le Hamel Switch as a southern flank, 3 Division ordered 76 Brigade to the front to take up the line of the La Bassée Canal approximately from the Hingette bend as far as Robecq, where it would make contact with 61 Division. Other units and scratch forces were also positioned along the canal line: 7 Argyll & Sutherland Highlanders manned it from the Mont-Bernanchon bend to Robecq; 4 Gordons, 4 Sea-forths, 8 Royal Scots, 404 Field Company and assorted details held the north bank near Pacaut Wood; elements of 153 Brigade were around Les Amusoires, and a mixed force held the bridges at Busnes. Around 3.00pm the elements near Pacaut Wood were pressed back on Robecq. A small detachment of German soldiers crossed the canal near Mont-Bernanchon but confined their attention to looting some houses. They were driven off by artillery firing at just 600 yards' range.

Fanning on from Pacaut with great skill, the attack by the German 16 Division spread out and was joined to the north by 1 and 8 Bavarian Divisions. The 2/6 Royal Warwickshires (182 Brigade, 61 Division) were quickly overwhelmed and a remnant was fired on from Becquerelle Farm as early as 5.35am. The survivors joined the 2/7 Warwickshires on their left, which had been occupying the eastern bank of the Clarence, south-east of Calonne, since the previous evening. By 8.45am this battalion was also report-ing that its posts were being systematically driven in, and it had no touch with any British troops on the right. Holding on for the promised arrival of the 2/4 OBLI, the men learned that the 7 Gordons, which had been at La Cornet aux Loups, had retired across the Clarence.[130]

Behind this front the rest of 61 Division was doing its best to reinforce as quickly as it could. The fact that it was going into action again had come as an unpleasant surprise:

> It was understood that we were being sent north to detrain at Calonne and carry out our training in that area in reserve to Portuguese Corps which was holding our old line Neuve Chapelle–

Laventie. The news we received at our entraining point now completely upset these peaceful prospects. At first we got rumour and later in the day official information that on 9 April the Hun had attacked the Portuguese Corps, pushing back the line and had taken Laventie and was still advancing. . . . The time in bivouac at Hangest was utilised to get all fighting equipment ready and the officers got their revolvers, compasses, maps, tin hats etc out of their valises and all ranks made what small preparations were required for a return to war conditions. The journey was of the usual unpleasant description. Leaving Hangest about 6.00pm we reached Steenbecque about 5.00am [12 April]. The constant roar of artillery in the direction of Béthune and the fact that our route had to be diverted from that line owing to it being under fire provided evidence that something was going on. Our train was met by a staff officer from division with orders that all units as they arrived were to be pushed into the line in the neighbourhood of Robecq to hold the Clarence and Noc Rivers.[131]

The 2/5 Gloucesters were delayed for 3 stressful hours due to transport difficulties at the detraining point at Steenbecque, while 2/4 Berkshires and 2/4 OBLI went ahead of them.

During this time breakfasts were served, rations issued to companies and packs being dumped at the station. Eventually about 8.45am we got away and commenced our march to the line. Information was scanty but while going through Nieppe Forest a corps staff officer overtook us and posted us up as far as possible. It appeared that while we were marching from north to south on the Saint-Venant road there was no known British force between us and the enemy.[132]

When they reached Saint-Venant, brigade informed Christie-Miller that the Oxfords and Berkshires had the situation in hand and that his battalion should bivouac in a field near the canal. There it was joined by another 200 men, mostly boys straight out from England.

At 9.40am the 2/4 OBLI was seen marching up through Les Amusoires. For the 700 men who had joined the battalion since its costly engagement in 'Michael', of whom the majority were 18 years old, entry to the battlefield came as something of a drama. The burning of an enormous shell store at Robecq cemetery caused a few to hesitate – but then they pressed on:

News came to get into extended order. We spread out and . . . advanced in line for a good way, clambering over ploughed fields and through hedges. We halted on rising ground. Orders came: 'Dig in'.

The officers and sergeants came behind the line and said, 'The Bosche is advancing and will probably clash with us within an hour. Our information is that he has stopped advancing but is about to come forwards looking for resistance.'[133]

The battalion successfully linked up with the hard-pressed Warwickshires and pushed patrols across the Clarence. The men were not exactly unmolested but they did not encounter the stiff opposition that the older hands had anticipated. By mid-afternoon, after a sharp firefight in the area of Bacquerolles Farm, a more or less continuous line had been made although the enemy had at 10.30am crossed the Clarence by an undamaged bridge at Calonne. The situation was obscure for some hours. Lieutenant-Colonel James Wyatt of the 2/6 Warwickshires, out of touch by any telephone communication, decided to go and see for himself. It seemed that no one really knew the situation with any clarity:

> I therefore decided to form a mounted armed patrol and go forwards
> ... Accompanied by three grooms with their rifles, slung to start
> with but later carried at the ready, we set off at 2.00pm. We rode
> forwards persistently towards where I felt sure the front lines must
> now be, and we encountered the most conflicting statements from
> various bodies of our divisional troops whom we met with. At length
> we found ourselves in what had become divisional line, on the
> extreme right, as it turned out, of the divisional Front.[134]

XI Corps called through an instruction at 12.15pm that I Corps would now hold the line from Givenchy to the drawbridge south of Robecq, with XI Corps then taking the line on to Saint-Venant–Haverskerque–La Motte. On this new line, 61 Division would be responsible for the right and 5 Division, now moving up, for the left. This was broadly a restatement of the GHQ order to hold Hinges–Nieppe Forest.

Aerial reports came through at 5.35pm of enemy troops massing in Calonne, taking cover in houses there after moving up in broad daylight along the Lestrem road. Any British troops now to the east of the Clarence were likely to be outflanked. It was decided to withdraw and give the artillery a chance to destroy any German attack that developed from Calonne. At 8.10pm an order came through to abandon the river line and the Robecq–Calonne road but this was cancelled and amended by a later order, suggesting that a retirement be made to give the artillery a 'safe firing line'. This was essentially along the Clarence; by night the division had taken up its new line, with 182 Brigade being arrayed along the drainage ditch known as the Courant de la Demingue, parallel to and 1,000 yards behind that road.

To fill the gap between the right of 61 Division and 8 Brigade holding the canal line, a scratch force was formed and placed under Lieutenant-Colonel J.L. Fleming, the 51 Divisional Commander, Royal Engineers. The composition of 'Fleming's Force' is indicative of the highly mixed-up nature of forces holding this critical position. There were 100 men from various units of 152 Brigade, 200 from 153 Brigade, 250 men of A and C Companies of 11 Canadian Railway Battalion, small numbers of men from parts of some gas and machine-gun companies and 400 assorted drafts who had barely arrived. Not far away, the last 170 men of King Edward's Horse were ordered to the bridges south of Robecq in the early evening.

There is no question that the German advance was an extraordinary achievement, so rapidly and completely had it ruptured the British front and taken advantage of every gap it could find. But it failed completely to press on and exploit the initial success, and again the British found sufficient reserves and resolve to hold the line, if only just and at the cost of some ground. The German infantry were fleet-footed enough, at least until exhaustion set in. The problem was the transport, struggling as it now was to cross 9 miles of difficult ground and numerous barely bridged waterways; moreover, the German high command had simply not provided its army with any mobile means of exploitation: no tanks, no armoured cars, not even cavalry. Strategic decisions taken months, or in some cases years, before were now reaping a malevolent pay-off. For all the excellence of its tactical innovation in its artillery and infantry methods, the German army was rooted in the past, and without having mechanised it could not execute the devastating all-arms mobile warfare that Sir Douglas Haig would imitate at times later in 1918, and the German army itself would repeat on this very ground in 1940. Had there been a few squadrons of Whippet tanks in German hands at Paradis and Le Cornet Malo on the morning of 12 April 1918, the outcome of the Battle of the Lys might have been very different.

During the night German pressure forced 61 Division out of Merville, and troops crossed the Lys bridges into the town at about 4.00am. They continued to press westwards but without great effect as dawn approached. North of the river XI Corps now had all three decimated brigades of 50 Division holding the line, with the fresh 4 (Guards) Brigade, detached from 31 Division, on their left. Behind them, east of Aire sur la Lys, was 5 Division, newly arrived from Italy. In terms of manpower, this was stronger than other British divisions in France, as it had not yet implemented the reduction to three battalions per brigade. But nor had it yet formed a Machine Gun Battalion.[135]

Overnight 4 (Guards) Brigade had moved into position, deploying the 3 Coldstreams and 4 Grenadiers along a line running from L'Epinette (a large farmhouse surrounded by a moat) on the right and through Le Cornet Perdu, facing Vierhouck. On reaching this line, both battalions were ordered to extend a few hundred yards to their right. The official reports and archived copies of orders make their action sound all rather neat and tidy, whereas Captain Oliver Lyttelton admits that the brigade had no time or light in which to reconnoitre and followed de Lisle's anxious instructions to fill the gap and 'do something before morning'.[136]

As soon as it was light, the enemy opened heavy artillery fire and brought intense machine-gun and rifle fire to bear on any movement spotted. Infantry of the fresh 12 Reserve and 35 Divisions began to advance in large numbers at 8.00am. Even as they were coming on, brigade received orders, impelled by the news that Merville was now in German hands, to counter-attack in the direction of the town and to secure a line from the college and parallel to the Neuf Berquin road. The objective was to ensure no movement could be made along the road, and also to link up with men of 50 Division who were reported to be near Salt Farm and Les Pures Becques on the River Bourre. Patrols probed forwards and reported. Laying great emphasis on the occupation of Vierhouck and Les Pures Becques, both believed to be empty of enemy, the battalions, with two companies of 2 Irish Guards, began to advance at 11.00am, unsupported by artillery and without any machine-gun support other than their own Lewis guns. They were immediately met by a hail of fire that included field artillery firing in enfilade from just south of Pont Rondin on the Strazeele road. As men fell on all sides, the Guards somehow managed an advance of 400 yards, with the leftmost company under Captain Thomas Pryce engaging in hand-to-hand fighting for some houses at Pont Rondin. The trouble was, at the same time the enemy was advancing on either side and the two battalions found themselves in a deep promontory surrounded by a sea of field grey. The brigade now found itself holding a front of some 3,000 yards. By 3.00pm there was no sign of British troops on either flank; any men of 50 Division that had been there had vanished, although German attempts to advance north-west of Merville were halted by machine guns handled by 11 Tank Battalion with as many stragglers from 61 Division as could be found. The fighting continued in a pattern that was becoming almost a norm for this battle: localised attacks in which the Germans outflanked a section, platoon or company post; then a spirited counter-attack that won back the ground and made things secure for the moment; a further German attack and inevitable British retirement before being surrounded. And all the while, two sets of field guns were engaging at close range. As did so many others, Oliver Lyttelton would comment with admiration on the skilful tactical handling of the German machine guns. Gradually the Guards withdrew, particularly on their right, and made contact with the 31 Divisional pioneers, 12 King's Own Yorkshire Light Infantry (KOYLI), who had come up on their left. The remnants of 149 Brigade, which by day's end amounted to just 200 men – less than a company – also retired on this battalion, which was filling the gap between the Guards Brigade and 29 Division.[137]

As the Guards held off countless German efforts, 5 Division was on the move behind them. Having arrived in the area of Thiennes during the night (where gaggles of Portuguese were still on the roads), the division was placed under the command of XI Corps at 7.30am. Orders to retake Merville and establish two brigades east of Nieppe Forest reached Divisional HQ from Corps at 11.30am. 13 Brigade with 527 (2 Durham) Field Company was to pass south of the woods and 95 Brigade with 59 Field Company was to go through it. At the same time reports suggested that there were no formed bodies of British troops in front except 11 Tank Battalion at Le Sart. The GHQ 'stop line' order was then received, and as the positions to which the two brigades had been ordered were beyond it, the division cancelled the advance, but it was too late. The news did not reach the leading troops until 1.30pm, by which time they were approaching the eastern edge of the forest, having experienced only sporadic shell-fire and some aerial bombs as they moved up. Second Lieutenant Frank Glover of the 1 East Surreys remembered it well:

> About 3.00pm we had orders to take up positions immediately in the Forest of Nieppe. We arrived in rear (we were reserve) about 6.00pm and found the enemy had not penetrated the forest as had been expected and in consequence moved to a large clearing in the centre, south of La Motte. Everything was absolutely peaceful, no shelling and the houses left exactly as the inhabitants had hastily vacated them. All kinds of food had been left behind, while an empty Chinese Labour Company's camp opposite the houses we were in was filled with ordnance stores of all kinds and officers' huts with books and furniture.[138]

After some delay, First Army gave approval to hold the position gained; by then 5 Division was in contact with 61 Division and 4 (Guards) Brigade, and the area was as secure as it had been for quite some time. On the southern edge of the forest the 15 Royal Warwickshires captured a brickfield at Le Corbie around 6.00pm and defended it against a counter-attack. Meanwhile the 2 King's Own Scottish Borderers (KOSB) came up from the reserve 13 Brigade to take up the gap to the Lys. The direct road to Hazebrouck had been blocked.

In contrast, 12 April was a terrible day for XV Corps, which began it holding a front of some 8 miles with a jumble of formations. On its right, from near Vieux Berquin, was 29 Division, less its 88 Brigade and already tattered from previous days' efforts, holding the line to Doulieu. Then came 31 Division, stripped of its best fighting element, 4 (Guards) Brigade, and on the line almost to Strazeele, and finally the embattled 34 Division, propped up by 88, 74 and 174 Brigades covering the line from Steenwerck station through to Pont d'Achelles. The artillery support was similarly complex, with the guns of 38 and 57 Divisions still in place. Against this tiring force, six German divisions, including the fresh 81 Reserve Division which hit 86 Brigade, made the assault from early in the day. Survivors report that many observation balloons had been brought up, directing fire from almost above the heads of the defenders. By day's end this line had been caved in, and was now an ominous 3 miles nearer Hazebrouck. It was brought to a standstill only by improvised defence, enormous personal endeavour and the fact that 33 Division was already arrayed on the Merris–Méteren Ridge behind it.

Attacking unheralded by bombardment between 7.00am and 8.00am, German infantry quickly cleared Doulieu and poured volumes of fire west into 86 Brigade and east into 92 Brigade. By luck or design, they had pierced that most vulnerable of points, a junction between divisions. All units of both brigades suffered terrible losses, some from close-range artillery fire as the enemy brought field guns to within a few hundred yards. No story is more tragic than that of the 1 Royal Guernsey Light Infantry. Having gone into Doulieu 20 officers and 483 men strong, by the time they had retired and dug in on the railway south-west of Outtersteene, 9 officers and 220 men had become casualties, including the two company commanders, the RSM and two company sergeant majors. Most of the others would be similarly lost the next day. The Guernseys' gradual and leapfrogging retirement across almost 3 miles of flat ground, devoid of cover and swept by fire, was mirrored by the other units of 29 Division. Driven back by the enemy, advancing smartly along the line of the Méterenbecque, the division withdrew through Bleu on to Labis and Lynde Farms north-east of Vieux Berquin and there held the line between the Strazeele road and the Bailleul railway.[139] During these operations, and not for the first time, the figure of Lieutenant-Colonel James Forbes-Robertson, commanding 1 Border Regiment, stood out. His personal courage and the encouragement he gave to others did much to keep not only his unit but the entire force together. He seemed to thrive in such a situation. His brigadier would later recall,

> Forbes had been dull and morose all morning, but brightened up as things got worse. When they were really bad, he brightened up a lot, borrowed a horse (not his own, as he considered his old dun mare too good to risk) and said to one or two of his headquarters, 'The time has now come for me to take a hand'.[140]

Forbes-Robertson was awarded the Victoria Cross for his exploits and the citation is unusually through and descriptive:

> Through his quick judgement, resource, untiring energy and magnificent example, Lt.-Col. Forbes-Robertson on four separate occasions saved the line from breaking and averted a situation which might have had the most serious and far-reaching results. On the first occasion, when troops in front were falling back, he made a rapid reconnaissance on horse-back, in full view of the enemy, under heavy machine-gun and close-range shell fire. He then organised and, still mounted, led a counter-attack which was completely successful in re-establishing our line. When his horse was shot under him he continued on foot. Later on the same day, when troops to the left of his line were giving way, he went to that flank and checked and steadied the line, inspiring confidence by his splendid coolness and disregard of personal danger. His horse was wounded three times and he was thrown five times. The following day, when the troops on both his flanks were forced to retire, he formed a post at battalion headquarters and with his battalion still held his ground, thereby covering the retreat of troops on his flanks. Under the heaviest fire this gallant officer fearlessly exposed himself when collecting parties, organising and encouraging. On a subsequent occasion, when troops were retiring on his left and the condition of things on his right were obscure, he again saved the situation by his magnificent example and cool judgement. Losing a second horse, he continued alone on foot until he had established a line to which his own troops could withdraw and so conform to the general situation.

Such personal courage and excellence in battlefield leadership were key factors in the ultimate defeat of 'Georgette'.

On the left of 29 Division, the units of 31 Division suffered a similar pounding. Battalion diaries all mention how it was the unit on the left or right that retired first, never one's own. The action was confused and fast moving: it is apparent that the enemy first penetrated on the right at the junction with 29 Division and around the same time between the two brigades. Every officer and man of the company of 10 East Yorkshires that had been in contact with 2 Royal Fusiliers on their right became a casualty as German machine-gun fire hit them from front, right and rear. Retirement in such circumstances, readily ordered, is easier said than done. Many men, having lost their units and in most cases without officers, decided enough was enough and fled. Patrols sent out next morning from 33 Division to the south of Outtersteene found large numbers of wounded and unwounded men still in full retreat. But somehow a withdrawal was made by those elements that managed to stay together, in successive moves at a frightful cost in losses.[141] Some way behind the fighting, the transport men, headquarters troops, signallers, stragglers from 119 and 120 Brigades and others were collected into 'Details Battalions'. Comprising men from numerous different units and divisions, they provided an immediate reserve while 33 Division stood ready to launch a counter-blow, or if necessary to hold the GHQ line of resistance to the last man. By 6.30pm a reasonably continuous front was held between Vieux Berquin and Merris, but by then 31 Division had lost any semblance of coherent contact with 34 Division on its left, and a great gap had opened up that in the event would be filled by little more than eight machine guns.

Both 34 and 25 Divisions came under heavy attack from early in the day. Although the Germans wasted some effort in staging an attack on the already-evacuated Nieppe, they came on quickly to the weakened 88 Brigade holding the rightmost 5,000-yard line covering Steenwerck station and Pont d'Achelles. Hammered by artillery and infantry attack, the divisional pioneers of 1/2 Monmouthshire Regiment on the brigade's left came under great pressure and were cut off. One can only imagine the strain and fatigue felt by the men of this unit, who had dug four successive trench lines within the past day and were now holding on for their very lives. They were saved only by the arrival of the 1 Royal Newfoundland Regiment, moving up from reserve and carrying out two counter-attacks. A platoon led by Lieutenant Lorenzo Moore was surrounded after having held off the enemy and caused serious losses to those attacking. Among the casualties of the later counter-attack, around 6.00pm, was Captain Charles Strong, who died of his wounds at one of the Casualty Clearing Stations at Remy Farm near Poperinghe. He was a survivor, although wounded, of his regiment's most famous action, the disastrous attack at Beaumont Hamel on 1 July 1916.

By day's end the Newfoundlanders and Monmouths, the pioneers now being down to just 4 officers and 150 men after suffering the loss of almost 500, had withdrawn to a position at De Seule. Behind and on their left 75 Brigade and a battalion of 100 Brigade took the line up to Neuve Eglise after a hard day's fighting. Similarly 88 Brigade's 4 Worcesters and 2 Hampshires also came under sustained attack but managed to hold in the area of La Crèche. Against overwhelming odds, the brigade had made a stubborn stand and had withdrawn about a mile and a half.

Across the railway line, a prompt German morning advance had taken them well past Steenwerck up to Blanche Maison and Nooteboom. They had quickly taken advantage of the crumbling resistance of 93 Brigade of 31 Division and were in a position to threaten and pass the right rear of 101 Brigade. The position was a classic of infiltration tactics and of the inevitability of British reaction. Threatened on their flank by the Germans pushing into a weak spot (31 Division on its left, 34 Division on its right), the two British formations had no real option but to take self-protective measures and form a flank guard as best they could. Now 101 Brigade ordered the 11 Suffolks and 16 Royal Scots not to keep in touch with 31 Division at any cost, but to form a west-facing line. As the hours passed, this flank was extended almost up to Bailleul station by the addition of the 6 and 7 Duke of Wellington's from 147 Brigade. The German attack, suffering from enfilade fire from this line, nonetheless stuck to its north-bound course. The movement could be likened to the Germans having slammed open a pair of saloon doors, 3 miles across. As they passed easily through the gap and made for the high ground west of Bailleul and near Méteren, there was nothing to stop them other than the oddments of the Details Battalions, 19 Brigade of 33 Division and an extraordinary officer by the name of Lieutenant-Colonel Graham Seton Hutchinson.

Before examining how Hutchinson helped plug the gap, we should see how von Arnim's X Reserve Corps fared in its efforts to capitalise on the previous day's successes at Ploegsteert. The actions may be quickly summarised: they failed. Four divisions (31, 214, 31 Reserve and 49 Reserve) plus part of 17 Reserve launched no serious attack until the afternoon. Around 2.00pm, with the attack to the south against 34 Division making progress, infantry advanced against Hannay's 75 Brigade holding the Nieppe–Romarin line. The British force – which incorporated half of 33 Division's 100 Brigade – was forced to withdraw about a mile, principally to conform with the rearward move of 88 Brigade to De Seule. Elsewhere, 148 Brigade was forced back somewhat, as were the thin South African and 108 Brigades, but a counter-attack recovered their ground. The British line remained on the western slopes of the Messines Ridge and from Wytschaete northwards was largely unmolested. It was, to say the least, a disappointing day for Rupprecht's ambitions, other than the most promising breakthrough between Outtersteene and Bailleul – but in the event this would be halted too by small numbers of brave men.

Victor Fagence was bivouacked near Méteren with the rest of the 1 Queen's of 100 Brigade, getting a little fed up with enemy shells dropping close to the camp, when just after 1.00pm urgent orders came to move out and take up a defensive position of some 3,000 yards in length covering the village. The news was that 31 Division was reported to be retiring and the Queen's would move up to support it:

> The companies moved out at 1.15pm, C Company leading, the OC (Captain Cooke) being given direct orders by the Brigade-Major to take up ground with the right of the company at Hogenacker Mill,

the remainder deploying on a line facing ESE. B Company (Captain Allen) was directed to take up ground from the mill to the southern end of an enclosure, D Company (Avery) prolonging this line to the SW. These three companies were to be front line. A Company (Carpenter) was held in reserve. When it was our turn to move off, we marched up the road towards Méteren, and, upon reaching the point where the road curved to the left, we saw our Brigadier (Mayne) standing in the doorway of a house on the right of the road. Our officer gave the order 'Eyes right' and saluted. . . . a short distance on we met some horse-drawn limbers apparently coming from the front. The limbers were piled high with baggage, and a number of wounded men were perched precariously on top, with others (walking wounded) clinging to the sides and backs of the limbers to be helped along. The drivers were crouched low over the horses' necks, trying to whip their tired mounts to a canter . . . we continued marching, crossing the Bailleul–Strazeele road, a short distance further on came to a hamlet with a farmhouse on the left side of the road. We went through an open gateway into a meadow and about 500 or 600 yards away we saw German infantry debouching from a wood and advancing towards us. They evidently saw us at the same time and opened fire. We immediately received the order to deploy and take what cover we could, at the same time returning the enemy's fire. By this time the other three platoons of our company, who had preceded us from the camp, had taken up a position in a field of young green corn (about 6 inches high) and were engaged in firing at the enemy to check his advance, at the same time digging in with their entrenching tools, as and when opportunity permitted. They had, whilst moving into position, come under enemy machine-gun fire from the mill, but this had been immediately engaged and captured by Second Lieutenant Russen and eight men.[142]

Russen's encounter with the enemy took place on a promontory of high ground north-east of Outtersteene, an exceptionally important spot from which there are long views south across to the 3-mile gap through which the enemy was now pouring, and north to Méteren and Bailleul. Fagence continues:

Lieutenant-Colonel Kemp-Welch reconnoitred the flanks and found no formed body of British troops in rear of or on the right flank of the Queen's, and deciding that it was inadvisable to have a flank in the air between Belle Croix Farm and Outtersteene, he ordered B Company to find a defensive flank on the right, with one platoon

under Second Lieutenant Denny. The battalion was now strung out
on a front of 2,100 yards; no touch had been gained on either flank
with other British troops, while the sole artillery support was provided by two anti-aircraft guns. But the machine guns of two companies of 33 Machine Gun Battalion were disposed behind the
1 Queen's and rendered valuable service throughout the operations
that followed.[143]

During the afternoon and early evening the enemy attacked in waves several
times, but was stopped without difficulty and suffered many casualties. It was
the combined fire of 1 Queen's and the eight guns of 33 Machine Gun Battalion
that held the enemy, and it was probably thanks to Graham Seton Hutchinson
that the machine guns were on the Hogenacker position at all. I say 'probably'
only because the battalion war diary and published divisional history were both
penned by him; his autobiographical work *Warrior* also covers this action in
depth and paints a picture of a wonderful, bloody-minded and improvised
intervention. This author is prepared to believe that there is at least a strong
kernel of truth in Hutchinson's reports and memoirs. In essence, he took a
patrol on bicycles to investigate the disquieting news of an enemy breakthrough
on the front of 31 Division. Discovering hundreds of armed men running
away, lacking all order and organisation, he rallied a few to cover the casualty
clearing station at Outtersteene, which was still being cleared of wounded.
Commandeering first an ambulance and later a lorry, he loaded up with eight
Vickers guns, ammunition and teams and drove to the Hogenacker position,
where the guns were deployed, stretched out over 2,500 yards between La Belle
Croix Farm, the windmill and a steam mill on the edge of Bailleul. About noon
the lorry returned with more men of the battalion, who took up positions
spreading out towards Merris. Shortly afterwards, Fagence and his pals of
1 Queen's strengthened the force on the ridge and held it against sustained
attack.[144]

Gradually other units and groups of reorganised stragglers filtered through
to hold the Merris–Bailleul line. Walter Vignoles' 9 Northumberland Fusiliers
was one of those units sent to reinforce the critical area. It was a tense time,
broken for Vignoles by a somewhat comical moment:

> [At] 7.10pm brigade headquarters moved to a farm [Circuit House]
> near the Ravelsberg Road, which runs east to west on a commanding
> height overlooking the plain of the Lys. [Battalion] headquarters
> were established in a hutted camp on the reverse slope of the Mont
> de Lille, the men, headquarters and reserve company being sheltered
> in trenches originally dug for P&BT exercises. ... The CO received
> a message to report to 101 Brigade, the battalion being temporarily

lent to that brigade; there was a good deal of gas about, but it had cleared somewhat and, as it was very dark, masks had to be removed to see the way along the road, which was badly damaged, and across which trees had fallen as a result of shell fire. On reaching the head-quarters the party was received at the door, which had to be un-locked, in dead silence and was led, the guide taking the CO by the arm, still without a word being said, along a dark passage to a room at the back where two candles were burning. By this time we felt like a group of conspirators but the light explained the mystery; it was then seen that our guide, the Staff Captain, and all the officers in the room round the table were wearing their gas masks, reminding us of a group of Venetian Doges with their hoods over their faces, or the wolves in Peter Pan. The GOC (General Gore, a fine soldier who was killed a few days later) gave orders that the battalion was to guard the approaches on the western side of Bailleul.[145]

Elsewhere, actions of considerable strategic significance were beginning to take effect. Second Army took advantage of a quiet day, withdrawing most of its guns and infantry from forward positions in the Ypres salient. With the line shortening, 59 (2 North Midland) Division could now be released; it began to move south to strengthen IX Corps. The civilian governor of Dunkirk was requested to begin the process of inundating the hinterland; this can only have been authorised by Foch, but a later confidential report from John du Cane to Henry Wilson suggested that Foch was not altogether keen on the idea. He preferred to stand and fight it out.

> When a withdrawal behind the St Omer–Dunkirk inundations is suggested he replies 'Why lower the morale of your troops by such a retirement and let the enemy advance halfway to Calais without a fight? If you fight how many weeks if not months will it take the enemy to get to St Omer and how many fresh Divisions will he use in the process? Make him a present of nothing.'[146]

Foch also ensured that the movement of French reserves as agreed was taking place. By this time 133 Division had completed its arrival at Dunkirk and Maistre's Tenth Army was about to enter the British Zone; II Cavalry Corps had also begun its move northwards.

We should not forget at this stage the thousands of British and Portuguese soldiers who were now in enemy captivity. Most had yet to be shipped to Germany and were collected at points behind the old front line. Many would be shocked to find what they considered to be a lack of resources, organisation and, most importantly, food and medical care in the German-held area.

Captain Frederick Nattrass, a medical officer attached to the 2 South Wales Borderers, was captured between Sailly and Doulieu on 11 April and was kept by the Germans of *Sanitäts-Kompanie* 506 to attend the wounded in an old mill near the river at Sailly. He noted a 'complete absence of medical organisation. Large numbers of British officers and men were kept in order to carry in the wounded, but were not allowed to attend to any British casualties before the Germans were cared for.' The sheer numbers of wounded coming in made the accommodation in the mill inadequate, and Nattrass was surprised to see the use of improvised stretchers, and British bandages and materials. He would later report that British wounded were eventually placed in a barn with literally nothing to eat or drink and no further attention to their wounds for ten days.[147]

Skilled men were in short supply, and it could be argued that retaining Nattrass to assist the wounded was a humanitarian act. Not so for the hundreds, possibly thousands, of prisoners who were put on labouring work, unloading ammunition and materials from trains, clearing the battlefield for salvage, repairing roads and burying the dead. Frederick Horne was captured with some 200 of his pals of the 1/5 King's Own in the attack at Givenchy on the first morning. After spending the day being forced to carry in the wounded, he slept that night in Salomé church, where 'there must have been 400 to 500 prisoners, Portuguese and British, and the building was absolutely packed'. Next day and for several days he laboured at the railhead half a mile away.[148] Private 8825 John Capewell was one of the XI Corps Cyclists taken at La Couture on 10 April. Despite having received a flesh wound to his leg, he was added to a working party unloading shells at Salomé and kept there until he escaped on 30 April. He would later report that the church, still being used as a billet for the prisoners, was hit by British shell-fire on 27 April. Fourteen men were believed to have died and many were wounded. He also heard of twelve being killed when working at Festubert. Private 300431 John Dickson of 2 RSF also heard of the fourteen dead and said that well over a thousand men worked at the railhead. Another XI Corps Cyclist who worked at the railhead for six weeks, Private 10740 John Jones, gave the names of two men of his regiment who were killed by British fire on 8 May 1918.[149] Gradually, the numbers of prisoners were reduced, with most taken at first to the grim cavern of Fort Macdonald at Lille, which had been used for some time as the main prisoner assembly point for the Lens front. Some did not make it from there to Germany, for in the unsanitary conditions of the fort men are reported to have died of dysentery.

13 April

Despite all the German efforts, 'Georgette' had not as yet produced anything like a far-reaching result. Certainly there were promising signs of chaos and

Officers and men of 1/7 King's (Liverpool Regiment) in the line at Givenchy; their training played a large part in the successful defence. (*IWM Q10740*)

Men of 51 Division in a shell hole near Locon which they have made into a rifle pit. (*IWM Q6500*)

Portuguese prisoners giving up their gas masks. (*IWM Q55259*)

Two heavy German guns being drawn along the road by tractors. (*IWM Q55261*)

Private A. Smith, an 18th Battalion AIF Headquarters' observer, scans enemy territory from the camouflaged position of Ida Post in the Ploegsteert Sector in Belgium. While the picture was being taken, two Germans could be seen less than 400 yards away. Ida Post was typical of the forward positions on the Messines Ridge. (*AWM E01834*)

German troops halted in the Place de la Republique at Armentières. (*AWM H13255*)

Walking wounded coming back near Merris, 12 April 1918. (*IWM Q10293*)

Men of 2/7 Royal Warwickshires rescuing a bed-ridden old man in Robecq on 12 April 1918. (*IWM Q6511*)

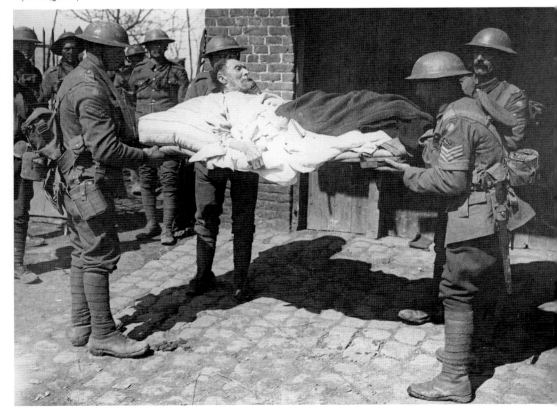

The German military cemetery at Sailly sur la Lys, close to their first bridgehead over the river at Bac St Maur. (*The author*)

Aval Wood, last resting-place of many who took part in the fighting around Caudescure. (*The author*)

On the Hogenacker Ridge, looking north towards Meteren. This important high ground was defended by the gunners of 33 Machine Gun Battalion and the infantry of 19 Brigade. (*The author*)

Memorial to 25 Division in the rebuilt town of Bailleul. (*The author*)

Once the Germans had reached this summit of the Ravelsberg they had perfect observation, making the continued occupation of Bailleul untenable. (*The author*)

From the Ravelsberg the importance of the Flemish hills becomes clear. Kemmelberg is the summit on the right. (*The author*)

From Brulooze crossroads looking north to the wooded height of the Scherpenberg. Along this road the Alpine Corps advanced, but the Germans were eventually brought to a halt, marking an end to the Battles of the Lys. (*Brian Morris*)

(*Left*) The French army memorial on the summit of Kemmelberg. (*The author*)
(*Right*) Still remembered. A photograph left at the grave of Second Lieutenant George Rumball MC at Outtersteene Communal Cemetery Extension in 2009, perhaps by a member of George's family. (*The author*)

collapse on parts of the British front, but equally the tactical objectives had not yet been met and resistance was stiffening. Transport and supply had given trouble almost from the start. There were instances of attacks not being pressed to the end and fleeting opportunities had been missed. Given that the whole strategic design of the offensives had been to exhaust and annihilate the British, was pushing more resources into the Lys operation the right thing to do, or should attention now be switched elsewhere? There was little unity of opinion among the German high command as to how best to proceed.

Ludendorff was leaning towards the launching of a number of relatively small attacks in other sectors in France. *General der Infanterie* Oskar von Hutier's Eighteenth Army was itching to renew the battle south of the Somme, not least to get them out of a tactical position in which they were uncomfortable. It also offered the compelling possibility of dominance or capture of Amiens. Second Army was planning for an attack on the Somme on 20 April and Ludendorff was also mulling over an additional operation north of the Somme towards Doullens, for which Rupprecht had initially shown support. But the Crown Prince, egged on by von Kuhl and Wetzell, was having second thoughts. The execution of a number of operations would be materially inefficient and the fact that Amiens was now defended by the French meant an attack there would not contribute sufficiently to the strategic destruction of the British armies. Rupprecht was privately questioning Ludendorff's strategic abilities, yet he too was wavering from principles by forgetting the maxim of concentration of force. He certainly wished to keep up the pressure in Flanders and was determined to keep Sixth Army moving. But he was also minded to launch converging attacks from Houthulst and Kemmel aimed at pinching out Ypres. If these did not gain far-reaching results, they would at least assist those elements of Fourth Army that were hung up between Wytschaete and Hollebeke. Prior to this the general direction of 'Georgette' had been north-west, aimed at securing Hazebrouck and offering the possibility of a turn to the south-west and the vital coalfields. The Ypres operations, which harked back to the *Hasenjagd* and *Waldfest* concepts and now went by the evocative name of *Tannenberg*, meant additionally attacking in a quite different direction. If these different movements succeeded, the British Second Army would have to give up Ypres and withdraw to the coast. This would be an enormous blow to British and Belgian morale. On 12 April von Kuhl issued the necessary orders, saying that any sign of a British withdrawal in the Ypres area should trigger the Houthulst and Kemmel attacks, noting that operations from the Kemmel area were necessarily dependent on the results of operations on 13 April which must seize the high ground at Neuve Eglise. It was going to be a big day.

The operational orders given to Sixth and Fourth Armies were almost a repeat of those of 24 hours earlier. The former would once again aim to seize the Strazeele–Bailleul high ground and to reach the La Bassée Canal. Fourth Army directed X Reserve Corps to make good the high ground from Neuve Eglise to Bailleul. Achievement of all of these would provide the springboard for a move on to Hazebrouck as well as the north-eastern attack towards Ypres.

Dawn once again opened misty across the entire front. Reviewing the line from on high, one would see some sectors that were clearly more strongly held than others. The southernmost area was solid: 55 Division still held on to Givenchy and Festubert, then bent sharply back towards and south of Locon. The village itself was in German hands, as was the entire line of the Lawe from there up to the confluence with the Lys near La Gorgue. Here 3 Division took on the line, bending around to cut across the La Bassée Canal at Avelette and up to Hinges. From there, 4 Division manned the line of the canal past Mont-Bernanchon until handing over to 61 Division near Robecq. The line then turned sharply to follow the north-eastward flow of the Clarence before bending north to cross the Lys in front of St-Floris. The division had been roughly handled but was sorting itself out and in reasonable condition to defend itself. Beyond it was 5 Division, the strongest element of the British front, holding the front face of the Nieppe Forest with detachments from 1 Australian Division and 4 (Guards) Brigade. The Guards' losses, physical fatigue and precarious position aside, all were confident and fresh. From Vierhouck up almost to Méteren, the situation was very different and much reliance was placed on those Australian battalions that formed a strong if thinly spread second line of defence behind a demoralised, often leaderless screen comprising an extraordinary mix of elements from 29, 31 and 40 Divisions and groups of men dug out from wherever they could be found. The men of 33 Division had secured the ridge of high ground in front of Méteren (the precise situation at Merris and Outtersteene being obscure for much of the time) and began to skirt round to the south side of Bailleul, from where the line was taken on by the shattered 34 Division. Bending northwards again and round to the south side of Neuve Eglise, the line was held by 25 and 19 Divisions. All three had of course been in continuous action since 10 April, with much of 34 Division having been engaged since the day before that. Reduced in numbers, tired and organisationally fragmented, it was a weak force indeed that held the ground on which hinged Rupprecht's hopes for an assault on Ypres. The front line had long since been pushed back from any area of prepared defences and where deep-buried cables allowed signals communications to continue. Haig's men were now fighting in the open, with scratch trenches, hastily erected barricades and the ruins of farm buildings the best cover they could hope for.

More worrying still was that for all the pinpoints of excellence that had been shown in defence – 55 Division at Givenchy, the Vieille Chapelle garrison,

2 Royal Scots Fusiliers, 34 Division escaping Armentières, 4 (Guards) Brigade – the fact was that many of the British units had crumbled after several days in action. Few war diaries or memoirs admit to weakness in their own unit, but frequently point it out in others. What the confident Australians found on taking up their positions fuelled every prejudice they might ever have held regarding British prowess. No one could tell them where any British presence was, or where the enemy were. As one who came to know them said, 'At any time they had a certain condescension for "Imperial Troops", a sublime assurance of their own self-sufficiency and a picturesque vocabulary in which they gave free expression to these opinions.'[150] In a difficult 7-mile night march in silence up through the north-eastern part of Nieppe Forest, Lieutenant William Joynt led his men of 8 Battalion to form posts whose fire would cover the two roads coming out from Vieux Berquin.[151] As it became light, Joynt's men saw they were overlooked by the stump of the tower of the village church – not a comfortable prospect should the enemy occupy it – but as yet it was quiet. Joynt had the opportunity to walk to the main road and look back on his positions. Satisfied that he had a good field of fire and reasonable prospects of holding against an attack, he became more conscious of what was going on around him. He noted the presence of civilian refugees, still shuffling along despite enemy gunfire; a detachment of Guards 'looking pretty done'; and then the stragglers – lots of them, from 29, 31, 40 and 50 Divisions. They were collected and added to the battalion's forward posts, 'where they did splendidly, but their own officers did not appear: where they were I don't know'. He went on:

> What English officers were there were useless. I did attempt to get some to work but gave it up. I 'collared' two English lieutenants and gave them each a sector, telling them 'Take charge here, collect all the men you can and fill a gap ...'. They started to do this but as soon as I left my sector to continue on my rounds they both cleared out.[152]

Joynt also recalled that the colonel of 1 Lancashire Fusiliers rejoiced at hearing that the Australians were to stand and fight, and remained with them until he had rounded up enough stragglers to mount a counter-attack during the afternoon. After being 'so disgusted with his officers and men who had retreated from their previous positions without orders', Joynt thought this brave man had 'vindicated the honour of his regiment'. Many of the junior leaders simply vanished, dead or alive, and in such circumstances it is hardly surprising that many men sought to get away rather than die or fall into enemy hands. Inevitably there are stories of men bolting, intent on reaching the coast, but the reality was that most stragglers just drifted away, dazed and hardly knowing where they were, let alone where they were going. Many were rallied by such individual acts of great foresight, courage and organisational talent, which managed to get many improvised units to fight and stand their ground.[153]

It was the higher formations that had struggled most of all in the last two days. Armies, corps and divisions did their best, very often with a complete absence of hard information and with their own headquarters and their units frequently moving, but their direct effect on the battle was small. The 'gilded staff' were not always held in the highest regard, even by those who were themselves in a staff role:

> First Army HQ seemed to think its proper role was administration. As to General Staff work, it confirmed and approved whatever was done or suggested by units in front. A case in point was the direction of 5 Division to the line St-Venant–La Motte on 12 April.[154]

The major contribution that any of them made was to deliver reserves, somehow, when they were needed. They also managed to maintain supply to the forward area, although many men got by at times on food and ammunition they found on the battlefield. The capabilities of the generals would face another stern test on 13 April. No fewer than 23 German divisions with a further 9 in support were about to attack 15 British and Australian divisions (of which 25, 40, 50 and 51 Divisions were exhausted and down to little more than cadres), plus the arriving French 133 Division and one brigade each of 6 and 59 Divisions moving up from elsewhere.

The story of the day focuses on the battles for the high ground on either side of Bailleul. South of the Nieppe Forest and north of Wytschaete there was no action that had any significant impact on the position, although heavy shell-fire fell once again and there were isolated infantry attacks that were held off. First Army's war diary records that 'the enemy relaxed his efforts' on that front. This was probably written with the benefit of relieved hindsight, for the Germans launched furious attacks along most of the front. The starting point for an exploration of events takes us once again to 55 Division, for during the night of 12/13 April they displaced the Germans and recaptured the tactically important Route A Keep.

Captain Joseph MacSwiney's X Company of the Liverpool Scottish was assigned to the operation, along with D Company of 13 Liverpools. Assembling at 11.00pm, both units quickly advanced under cover of a protective barrage. MacSwiney's group overwhelmed the small garrison holding some ruins 50 yards south of the keep itself; D Company did not enjoy such comparatively easy success, losing both its officers and some men in close in-fighting that lasted for almost 2 hours. Concerned that he was not in touch, MacSwiney went to reconnoitre, only to find his comrades without officers and grimly hanging on to only the southern edge of the keep. Sending a party back to collect boxes of hand grenades from the Tuning Fork, he organised the men of both units into a number of bombing parties, each under an NCO. Once seven boxes of grenades had appeared, these groups attacked up through the trenches of the keep and by 3.30am were able to report it clear of the enemy. A weak counter-attack was dispersed by machine-gun fire at 4.45am.[155]

Sergeant James Briggs of the Liverpool Scottish was assigned with Z Company to move up to the keep to relieve the detachment of 13 Liverpools:

> We had heard about this place before and weren't particularly keen to dash up there. However, it had to be done, so we stole off a very battered crew then, but as long as the food kept good we didn't mind. We took over from the 13 King's who seemed to be on the verge of collapse when we got there. They fled like rabbits when they saw us in the trench. What a desolate place Route A was that night. Dead of both sides lying all about. Reminded me of the crater at Hooge. An awful place, absolutely no movement whatever by day, and 'hold on at all costs' was the order given. The rations and rum (God bless the QM) were issued by night and barring an eagle eye watch by day, nothing happened at all. Well, our company were lucky for during the two days we were in Route A, he never bothered us except for an awful rattle of MG bullets just on the 'Stand to' in the evening.[156]

At 11.00pm the order came for the relief of 55 Division by 1 Division. No formation had done more to earn a rest.

The line from Robecq, along the Clarence to the Bourre, was held by 61 Division and part of 5 Division (13 Brigade and the right of 95 Brigade). The artillery of 5 Division, to which had been added LXXXIV Field Artillery Brigade and X Brigade of the heavies, covered the front. The sector was not an easy one to hold, being devoid of any cover other than hedgerows and flat to the horizon. They were subjected to almost constant attack during the day, in four waves, by three German divisions, the 16 Division, 8 Bavarian Reserve and 8 Division. These formations had also been in action for some days and were tiring, and were harassed during the night by British shell-fire aimed at the roads and tracks along which they would have to come. A German prisoner taken during the night admitted that troops were massing east of the Clarence for an attack in a north-westerly direction, but said there was difficulty in bringing up enough heavy artillery to support them. Here the day dawned clear but soon became dull and misty.

The enemy's attack towards St-Floris was covered by 184 Brigade. The brigade was repeatedly attacked, but it was clear that the Germans did not have their usual energies. The 2/5 Gloucesters near Cornet Malo brought the enemy move to an end through disciplined and murderous rifle and machine-gun fire. Major Geoffrey Christie-Miller was delighted:

> The night passed pretty quietly but at 8.00am things livened up on the whole front and in a few minutes information came in from the companies that they were being attacked. The morning was misty so the enemy got fairly close before they were seen. The attack made no progress on our front and did not seem to be seriously pressed on the front on our right. Soon after the attack the mist rose and revealed a light field gun which the enemy had brought up the road under cover of mist to within 300 yards. As soon as this was discovered two Lewis guns were turned on to it and three teams were brought up in turn by the enemy to serve it but could not do so. During the whole morning our support lines were heavily shelled. The satisfactory nature of this attack was that it was driven off by the infantry and very largely by rifle fire. As we were holding only small posts it was most reassuring to our new men who had just joined to find that the fire effect of a small party of men who kept their heads and used their rifles was able to stop an attack.[157]

During bouts of shell-fire in the afternoon, Battalion HQ was twice compelled to quit and take up temporary quarters in a neighbouring ditch. St-Floris village, which lay a few hundred yards to the right, came in for an unmerciful battering during the whole day: 'The sole occupants were, however, one OP and one water-duty man and such parties as had been sent to draw water – a duty that was performed without any undue waste of time. One or two old inhabitants refused to move.' Christie-Miller recalled one old dame who made it known she wished to stay put. Eventually military policemen of the APM's staff, on the instruction of the French Mission, carried her off, still protesting.

The rout of the enemy's attack lifted the spirits and gave great confidence to the large numbers of 18-year-old troops who were with the battalion. Just south of them, Alfred Thomas and his chums of 2/4 OBLI were in the thick of it too. Thomas recalls the arc of shells passing overhead and the zipping of machine-gun fire along the roads, and then came a memorable moment:

> The Sergeant calls 'Any signallers here?' I say 'I'm one and there's Bill Phillips over there', pointing to a sap further along. 'Get back to Bacquerolles at once – get Phillips and take him with you.' Ye Gods. Heaven! I signalled to Bill and sure enough he waddled over to

us, and we three threaded our way slowly and with great care to Bacquerolles Farm. At that moment a great shouting goes on up the right and suddenly a terrific burst of machine guns firing like hell amid the burst of shells. 'Here they come. Christ!' and 'Bill, shall we stop here?' We were by some willow trees and taking cover each behind a tree we waited. Presently we caught sight of men – a whole host of Jerries. 'Good God,' shouted Bill, 'they've got no guns, no steel hats!' They only had their kit and to our utter amazement the column was arriving more or less in formation. No guns, no hats. Just as they were. 'Surrender.' We stepped out of our ditch and covered them with our rifles. At their head came some of our chaps. 'Jerry napoo', they shouted.[158]

Now down to just 1,400 men, 182 Brigade lined the bank of the Courant de la Demingue south of St-Floris with the 2/7 Warwickshires stretching out to Calonne and along the road to Bacquerolles Farm. The brigade encountered little difficulty until a heavy attack began at 11.00am, holding with no great difficulty except for concentrations of mortar fire and fire from low-flying aircraft, which forced a brief withdrawal. The situation was restored during the afternoon, for very few casualties. Joined by 24 Entrenching Battalion and a draft of 300 men for the Warwickshires, the brigade enjoyed a quiet night. The remnants of 183 Brigade formed a composite battalion to cover Saint-Venant.

North of 61 Division, 5 Division covered Nieppe Forest along with four battalions of 1 Australian Division, strung out over a 6-mile front.[159] The two rightmost Australian units could see British troops in trenches just short of Merris. In his role as battalion intelligence officer, Lieutenant Frank Glover of the 1 East Surreys was in a perfect position to record the day's action. He left Battalion HQ at the hamlet of Pre à Vin (1,000 yards south of the chateau at La Motte) and during his absence it moved into the adjacent Bois des Vaches to take shelter from shell-fire.[160]

Enemy shelling commenced this morning, he having apparently got his batteries into position during the night. Our line runs in front of Bois d'Aval and the Bois Moyen and this afternoon I went up to see some of our companies who are digging some trenches on the eastern edge of the former wood. Wild reports concerning a breakthrough were prevalent and it afterwards transpired that 4 (Guards) Brigade who were in front had after three days' hard fighting been broken and they are said to have lost two companies in La Couronne. The DCLI and Devons on their flank were attacked all day, killed hundreds of Bosches but gave little ground. The Nieppe Forest is partially cleared of undergrowth and is intersected with long straight shooting drives; cowslips and other wild flowers grow in clusters among the turf, making the whole a delightful spot. Arriving back in HQ we were shelled and in consequence cleared to the fields. Returned for tea but were again strafed and proceeded to dig ourselves in the wood. I with my servant and Hawes built an excellent splinter-proof [shelter] and getting some bedding from the village we passed a good night.[161]

It was not just the 1 Devons and 1 DCLI that laid down impenetrable fire against the attackers. Four guns of 95 Machine Gun Company also kept the German infantry at bay during the morning. Two were located in upper rooms at Le Laurier chateau at the south-eastern tip of the forest, covering all approaches from Merville. The other pair, at Arrewage, caught lines of German troops in enfilade and stopped any serious attack on the 1 DCLI until Captain Herbert Hocking's A Company had to fall back on its left to keep touch with 4 (Guards) Brigade.[162] An insight into the terrific rates of fire can be gauged from the fact that the division was resupplied with two and a quarter million rounds of ammunition during the day, having almost run out since arriving on this front. Gordon-Hall thought that it could seldom have been equalled during the whole war. Certainly the volumes of fire brought to bear by 61 and 5 Divisions had halted the attack of 8 Bavarian Reserve, 8 Division and 16 Divisions. On the southern part of the front, it was turning out to be a most disappointing day for the German forces. North of 5 Division, however, the picture was rather different.

From about 6.30 am 4 (Guards) Brigade came under attack. Although 5 Division had been ordered to take over part of the Guards' front, this had not been effected by the time the German assault developed. The 3 Coldstreams still held the mile of front line from the L'Epinette/Arrewage lane junction up to Le Cornet Perdu, from where it was taken on by 4 Grenadiers another mile to a point 300 yards south of La Couronne. They were assisted in consolidating the line by 210 Field Company and 2 Irish Guards remained in close support. Taking advantage once again of the thick mist, the German assault troops brought light machine guns up very near to the Guards' line before attacking. For once they also deployed armour, in the form of an armoured car that drove up from Merville to the L'Epinette road junction and fired on the post there from just 10 yards' distance. The left and centre companies of the Coldstreams came under the heaviest pressure between L'Epinette Farm and Le Cornet Perdu. At one point men advancing through the fog shouted that they were from the King's Company of the Grenadier Guards; we must assume that an accent gave the game away for they were shot down by the Coldstreams. Small parties of Germans infiltrated between posts, but were ejected by a counter-attack mounted by A Company, Irish Guards. In this close in-fighting, the Coldstreams' Private 17800 Harold Jacotine, in the left-hand post of the centre company, found himself the last man alive of the garrison. He managed to hold on alone for 20 minutes before falling to an enemy hand grenade.[163]

While the Coldstreams were hanging on at Le Cornet Perdu, a serious problem had developed for the Grenadiers, which was all down to the enemy having shaken 29 Division out of Vieux Berquin. The Guards' left flank was open, and the enemy attacked not only frontally but from the left rear. An estimated two battalions of German infantry attacked down the lane from Bleu towards La Couronne, and suffered a bloody repulse at first. Two field guns were then brought up to point-blank range and proceeded to flatten the Grenadiers' shallow defences. The men of 12 KOYLI, just beyond La Couronne, were also now ejected under heavy trench-mortar fire, having held off at least four attacks since dawn. Captain Thomas Pryce and his men of 4 Grenadiers, who had been in close combat the previous day, found themselves surrounded and were shooting both ways, standing back to back in their trenches. On hearing of their predicament, brigade ordered a counter-attack to be made by the Irish Guards; on advancing, they too found themselves cut off by enemy coming at them from all sides and were hit by machine guns firing from Vieux Berquin. Just one NCO and six men made it through to Pryce. The tale of the next hours came back through a Grenadier corporal who escaped the holocaust. At about 6.15pm Pryce ordered his last eighteen men to carry out an heroic but suicidal bayonet charge. Surrounded, and with German troops closing in to 60 yards, it was either that or surrender. Incredibly, the charge succeeded, for the enemy were unable to fire effectively, knowing their own men were behind Pryce's thin line. The charge drove off the Germans and Pryce and his men retired to their original position. A second charge, in which the last seventeen men took part, was overwhelmed. The corporal who escaped – the only man to get away – managed to hide in a ditch, before making his way to the Australians the following night. Captain Thomas Tannant Pryce, 32, was awarded a posthumous Victoria Cross. The citation concludes: 'With some forty men he had held back at least one enemy battalion for over ten hours. His company undoubtedly stopped the advance through the British line, and thus had great influence on the battle.' They certainly did.[164]

The centre and right companies of the Grenadiers were down to a total of 26 unwounded men. A few survived and reached the Australian lines during the night. On the right equally tiny and ragged parties of the Coldstreams withdrew under cover of darkness. One wonders whether these were the Guardsmen seen 'looking pretty done' by Joynt. The Guards action was observed by the posts of 8 Australian Infantry throughout the afternoon. They would have seen few others: the brigade, in two days of fighting, suffered the loss of 39 officers and 1,244 men. Approximately 250 men were left. Not one Guardsman was reported as a battlefield straggler by the military police. By day's end the Australian screen, which had originally deployed behind the Guards and 29 Divisions, had become the new front line.

Given the terribly weakened condition of the elements of 29 and 31 Divisions holding the stretch from Vieux Berquin to Merris, it is perhaps not too surprising that a strong attack made by 12 Reserve Division eventually succeeded in pushing the line forwards by a mile or so. The German success here was at considerable cost, even from dawn when light from a blaze at the farm at Bleu illuminated the infantry assembly, bringing down fire from all units and the supporting 57 Divisional artillery. By 10.30am the attack had developed until the whole front was engaged and gradually the dispersed units were infiltrated. The various units gradually fell back on the Australian posts which brought the German attack to a halt, keeping the line more or less intact.

Some 13 miles north of Route A Keep, the ridge of high ground at Méteren was the key to both Hazebrouck and Bailleul. If the Germans could seize the latter village, through which ran the main road to Cassel and the coast, there would be no need for them to negotiate the Nieppe Forest for they could approach the town from the undulating slopes to the north–east. Bailleul itself could be easily outflanked on its west side and troops could then move smartly on Mont des Cats and Mont Noir at the western end of the Kemmel chain. This part of the line was held only by the battalions of 19 Brigade and Hutchinson's guns of 33 Machine Gun Battalion. The tactical disposition and fighting spirit of these units were key to what became an important repulse of German ambitions, though it certainly did not feel like that to Lieutenant-Colonel Martin Kemp–Welch during the night of 12/13 April. He was worried, and signalled to brigade to make the position clear. His battalion, 1 Queen's, was still holding the vital high ground around La Belle Croix Farm, south of Méteren, but was exposed to fire coming from the direction of Outter-steene. Other than D Company of the 5/6 Scottish Rifles forming a defensive flank on their left at Epsom Crossroads, there was no other defence and no sign of 22 Corps Reinforcement Company (of details) that was supposed to have joined them. Worse still, there was no sign of any artillery coming to their support and there was every reason to believe that this weak force would face a heavy attack in the morning. Victor Fagence recalled the sound of heavy German guns being pulled into position reverberating through a clear, still, starlit night, and the terrible loss suffered by the battalion when CSM L/8667 Maxwell Elderkin, passing among the men to give them encouragement, suddenly fell to a sniper's bullet. 'His body, with those of several others who had been killed during the afternoon, was carried back, sewn up in blankets and deposited on the rear bank of the sunken road where we were on guard duty.'[165] The Queen's gritted their teeth ready for the day ahead:

> With the coming of dawn, the enemy resumed operations. He commenced with a number of range-finding shells registering on our positions followed by a terrific barrage of whizzbangs, five-point-nines and (by the noise and size of some of the individual explosions) even eight-inch shells, interspersed with the dull 'plop' of gas shells. It was one of the most intense bombardments I can ever remember, made worse by the fact that there was not a single field gun at the back of us to reply. ... The houses close to our position on the sunken road received hits from shells and were set on fire, the thatched roofs blazing furiously. Then people came running out seeking escape from the inferno. There was very little we could do for them, as we were under orders to 'stand to' and be prepared to repel an enemy infantry attack which was momentarily expected. One old invalid lady was carried out in a chair by two of her friends, who asked for help. One of our officers, [who] could understand and speak French, asked them for a wheelbarrow which one of the Frenchmen produced. He and the officer hoisted the old lady and chair on to the wheelbarrow and the officers started to wheel her away to the comparative safety of Company HQ at the farmhouse. I never saw him or the old lady again.[166]

Having been under sporadic field gun bombardment since the early hours, the battalion confronted an enemy infantry attack in the fog – yet again it was a murky start to the day – which came on at 5.30am. Two lines of Germans in extended order were shot down by D Company, but it only led to further attempts under cover of machine-gun and shell fire. The Queen's inflicted heavy casualties on the attackers, with D Company alone claiming to have killed a hundred men, but eventually the pressure told. Fagence's platoon was sent to assist the Scottish Rifles:

> As we ran out towards the Rifles we had to cross a patch of ground that was almost devoid of cover, and in addition to encountering machine-gun and rifle fire, we were subjected to a barrage of minenwerfer missiles, but we were able to reach the position and strengthen them sufficiently to hold the line, at least for the time being. A Sergeant of 33 Machine Gun Battalion came up from behind with his gun and also rendered assistance.

For the men on the Hogenacker Ridge the morning proved to be a tough and strenuous time. Behind them, Division ordered forwards the two battalions of the reserve 98 Brigade (the third battalion was detached with 34 Division). The 2 Argyll & Sutherland Highlanders accordingly began to take up a position on high ground at Meulenhouck, north of Bailleul, and the 4 Liverpools dug in on the outskirts of Méteren. At about 8.45am some posts of the 1 Queen's B Company were overwhelmed when the enemy pressed on down the road from Outtersteene and along the sheltered valley of the Méterenbecque towards Belle Croix Farm, in rear of D Company. Their loss handed the crucial ground around the farm to the enemy. Two very gallant attempts, led by Lieutenant John Dickinson and Second Lieutenant John Corry, were made to recapture the farm but did not have the numbers and were driven off. Sustained bombardment and enemy attacks ground down the battalion, causing many casualties. Even though it was strengthened to some extent by the arrival of a company each of 18 Middlesex, the 2 New Zealand Entrenching Battalion and a gaggle of 11 East Yorkshires, the enemy attack forced the position back until by 4.00pm it ran forwards of the Brahmin Bridge–Gaza Crossroads lane. And then, with Méteren less than a mile away, clearly visible and with virtually no British reserves in between, the German attack dwindled to nothing. It was another moment when important results might have been achieved had the German attack been pressed with greater force and vigour. As it was, they had gained the high ground but had only effected an advance of some 700 yards. Fagence and his pals had earned a drink: 'One of our men discovered about a dozen cases of champagne ... we all helped ourselves to it, imbibing freely, some of the men even emptying water from their bottles and filling them up with the vinous liquid.'[167]

By evening the force holding Méteren finally had the benefit of artillery support. The guns of CX and CXII Field Artillery Brigades of 25 Division had travelled up by road from the Somme, and on arrival at Morbecque they were ordered to positions at St-Jans-Capelle.

The rest of Hamilton-Gordon's IX Corps held the sector that was becoming so critical to Rupprecht's plan for the attack on Ypres. Skirting around Bailleul, the line went up into the higher and undulating ground to the east of the town dominated by the Mont de Lille and Ravelsberg hills. To the east of these hills and south of Neuve Eglise was an area littered with the many camps, stores and dumps that had been established by the British army to supply the southern part of the Ypres area. There was severe fighting in this area on 13 April, and the trouble began with the early success of the German 214 Division's attack against the weak 75 and 100 Brigades holding the area along the Kortepyp road and east of Neuve Eglise. The men of 75 Brigade bore the brunt of this assault, which began at 5.00am without any artillery preparation and achieved complete surprise. Within minutes the lead parties fanned out to left and right, and also pressed on down the Waterloo Road leading to the Ravelsberg. We shall return to those detachments going left and centre, heading towards the rear of the left flank of 34 Division. On the right, first the 16 KRRC and then the 2 Worcesters found themselves being attacked from their right rear as the enemy also probed into Neuve Eglise. The King's Royal Rifles were quickly surrounded and effectively destroyed as a cohesive fighting unit although small parties held out throughout the day. The Worcesters, who also had to cope with a frontal attack by 31 Division, sent their reserve company to counter-attack and drive the Germans out of the village. They were assisted by 458 Field Company, and Neuve Eglise was cleared in a close-quarter fight. It was an entirely improvised and determined operation, about which the divisional staff appear to have known little. Major-General George Jeffreys of the adjacent 19 Division appears to have been better informed:

> 25 Divisional headquarters had rather lost touch with their troops in Neuve Eglise and I do not think they realised how gallantly and with what a considerable measure of success the latter were holding out. I had constant and excellent information from 4 KSLI (who by this time had reverted to my command) and who sent constant patrols into the village from the northern flank, keeping in touch with its defenders. I passed the information on to 25 Division, who were incredulous of its accuracy and at one moment would not believe that the Germans were in the village. Actually some Germans were in the houses but the bulk was still held by us.[168]

As parties of Germans evacuated Neuve Eglise, they ran into fire coming from the British front line, held to the north of the Worcesters by the 1/4 York & Lancasters of 148 Brigade. Every man was killed or taken prisoner. By 1.30pm, when 4 KOYLI and the 5 York & Lancasters of the same brigade had moved towards Neuve Eglise to assist the counter-attack and stand as a flank guard to the brigade, they were able to report it clear of the enemy. The situation in the area remained stable until early evening, when from around 6.00pm German pressure again mounted, this time driving the main body of the Worcesters back from the front line and into Neuve Eglise. Battalion HQ was set up in the hospice, a large building on the Dranoutre road, from where a defence was mounted that resisted numerous attacks through the night.[169] Touch was gained just south of the village with parties of 16 KRRC and contact was maintained with 148 Brigade to the north. But the British line disappeared on the right, where a 200-yard gap had opened up in front of the position held by 34 Division. Behind Neuve Eglise a mixed force had by evening taken up the high ground at the summit of the Ravelsberg and at nearby Crucifix Corner. Among the garrison were elements of the 6 South Wales Borderers, driven back by the morning's assault.[170]

After crossing the British defences along the Kortepyp road, 214 Division's left wheel brought them into contact with the rear of the left flank of 34 Division. The 23 Northumberland Fusiliers of 102 Brigade were holding the line to the right of 75 Brigade when the enemy struck and became embroiled in a hard fight for the rest of the day; they were joined by their sister battalion, 25 Northumberland Fusiliers. By 6.00pm the enemy had launched a fresh attack against the garrison of 22 Northumberland Fusiliers holding the De Seule crossroads, during which most of the battalion's officers at headquarters were killed by a single shell. The pressure of continual bombardment and infantry fire inevitably told on these units; the only immediate reserve, D Company of the Newfoundlanders, was rushed up and inflicted heavy losses by firing on enemy advancing in the open from De Broecken.

The main portion of 34 Division's front was assaulted by four divisions of II Bavarian Corps, which for the first time included the fresh Alpine Corps (which despite the name was effectively a division). Much of 34 Division, together with the two extra brigades which had found themselves within Major-General Cecil Nicholson's command, was thin in numbers and tired after continual fighting. A westward attack developed against the 11 East Lancashires – the old Accrington pals – and the 10 East Yorkshires of 92 Brigade holding a line from Lynde Farm in front of Celery Copse and around the east side of Merris, driving in the outposts and taking the latter village. There was severe fighting throughout the day here and to the east around Bailleul station and railway line, but little impression was made on the British position.

There was much discussion during the day, especially when it appeared that Neuve Eglise was falling, with regard to the risks involved to Bailleul and to the Messines Ridge. There was little prospect of strong reinforcement and prisoner identifications indicated the extent of the German concentration of strength in the area. The first two battalions of 71 Brigade, 6 Division arrived at Dranoutre at 6.00pm, but other than a mixed force of about 1,200 men plus 180 Royal Engineers, the Corps Cyclists and the XXII Corps Cavalry, there were no more. During the day the French 133 Division had arrived at Steenvoorde, and had already sent advanced units to Caestre, Fletre and Rouge Croix, and British cavalry also began to arrive at Blaringhem, but none of these were likely to be of immediate value should the German attack be renewed in the coming night. The decision was taken to withdraw to a geographically stronger line on the eastern slopes of the Ravelsberg and Mont de Lille. Orders were issued at 10.00pm: James Chaplin's 103 Brigade would hold the line from Breemeerschen (a hamlet on Waterloo Road) to Pewter Farm,[171] and 88 Brigade would then take the line round to Mont de Lille. Next 74 Brigade would carry on to the western slope of the Mont, from where 101 Brigade would stretch out to

Bailleul station and 147 Brigade carry on round to the steam mill and a connection with 33 Division. While this move was getting under way just before midnight, Brigadier-General Robert Gore was killed by the explosion of a shell in the cellar housing 101 Brigade HQ. This was a sad and significant loss, indeed. Gore was an experienced man who had been in command of the brigade since January 1916. He was replaced by Arthur Stephenson, of whose orders to 15 Royal Scots to halt the fleeing Portuguese we have already heard.[172]

During the night of 12/13 April a large gap of 1,200 yards appeared between 108 Brigade holding the south-west of Wulverghem and the garrison of Neuve Eglise but it was filled during the morning by the arrival of 178 Brigade. The situation at Neuve Eglise was most concerning to 19 Division as the ground there was key to its continuing ability to hold the line up to Wytschaete. George Jeffreys' headquarters was out of touch with 149 Brigade and 25 Division for long intervals, and he took steps to ensure the 8 Gloucesters were in a flank ready to repel any German incursion from Neuve Eglise; in the event this did not transpire. No attacks of any real danger developed against the divisional front, although shell fire was continuous and at times enemy forces were seen massing near North Midland Farm. This, together with news that two new German divisions had been identified opposite them, caused the divisional brigadiers to agree with Jeffreys to arrange a reserve line running from Spanbroekmolen via Spy Farm to Lindenhoek, linking up with the Kemmel defence force just behind it.

A day of unequal contest had ended with, in large part, a bloody nose for the Germans. Sixth Army had made not a dent in the British defences towards the La Bassée Canal and made precious little progress towards Hazebrouck; it had made minor gains of ground on the Méteren Ridge and overlooked Bailleul from the west, but no more. Fourth Army's furious attempts on Neuve Eglise had likewise been stymied in their main objectives, although their forces had made tactical gains and were now perilously close to the heights at Ravelsberg and Mont de Lille, which looked down on Bailleul from the south-east. It could only be a matter of time before Bailleul fell too. And then the way would be open to Kemmel and Ypres.

Chapter 6

'La bataille d'Hazebrouck est finie'

14 April

From their safe and plush base at Versailles, Hereward Wake and his staff of E Section of the British staff at the Supreme War Council were able to collate intelligence reports and make an objective appraisal of the situation in Flanders. Late on 13 April he submitted a paper which, after pointing out that the German attack had so far pushed a salient into British lines that had the effect of extending the front by 8 miles, suggested that

> The Germans will most probably use all available forces to continue their advance as quickly as possible with the object of seizing Hazebrouck and the Poperinghe–Cassel road, and cutting off the British north of Bailleul. They will count on the late arrival of British and French reinforcements, and on the decision to withdraw from the northern sector being too late. They may also attack from the north-east towards Béthune and Lillers with the object of turning the left flank of the troops holding Givenchy and south of that place. The date on which a further serious attack on the salient can take place is uncertain. The divisions present in line are probably worn out and will be relieved, while it will take two or possibly three days to deploy what is deemed to be sufficient artillery in the flat muddy country to support the attack. The Germans will not continue attacking, as they have done today, without artillery support, in view of the increased resistance met with.[173]

Yet that is exactly what the enemy intended to do, albeit with Ypres as the objective rather than the more strategic targets that Wake believed they would go for. By the end of 14 April, with Sixth Army's results having been so disappointing for the fourth day running, von Quast's Chief of Staff Lieutenant-Colonel Ritter von Lenz would have recognised the fundamental sense behind Wake's forecast. The transport and supply difficulties and the fact that attacks were now being made without sufficient artillery support short-changed the infantry and added up to failure. For another day of effort and losses, Sixth Army had achieved only a short advance near Méteren; elsewhere it had been repulsed and even lost ground. Fourth Army's influence in the battle rose as it shook the British out of Neuve Eglise and closed in on Bailleul. The results of this and the previous day swung the direction of the offensive inexorably from its original goals and increasingly towards Ypres.

Von Quast's single success derived from three heavy attacks delivered during the day by 81 Reserve Division at Méteren, although the orders for the day had once again also been to take the Nieppe Forest, Strazeele and Bailleul. The weather had taken a turn, for it dawned cold and very windy, with occasional showers from a glowering low cloud. This immediately presented the defence with an advantage. There was little chance of the Germans using concentrations of gas, and for once they could be seen assembling and advancing.

On the left of 81 Reserve, the German 42 and 12 Divisions for the first time faced 1 Australian Division, for the remnants of 29, 31 and 40 Divisions had now all withdrawn through the Australian outpost line. After their two days of valiant effort, a small group of 4 (Guards) Brigade men remained to fight with the Aussies, in position on the right (Verte Rue). Behind the line, the Australians' own artillery being still on the Somme, fire support was provided by the artillery of 24, 34 and 57 Divisions. The Australian line ran in front of the forest, curving up to the west of Le Paradis and Merris, to a touch point with 33 Division just south of Moolenacker on the slope down to the Méterenbecque. With the Australians enjoying good observation and broad, unhindered fields of fire, all attacks made against them, at intervals throughout the day, withered. The day started badly for the Germans soon after midnight when a 40-strong detachment of Infantry Regiment 141 (35 Division), making its way up a lane across the Australian front, was annihilated at 20 yards' distance by a Lewis gun post of 8 Battalion. Half of the group died and the rest fled, leaving six machine guns behind.[174]

The experience of 2 Battalion, Infantry Regiment 138 was typical of German fortunes in this area during the day as the attacking groups were lashed by shell and small arms fire. Attacking along the railway north of Le Paradis against 3 Australian Battalion, it was

> directed to move as a reserve to that [south] side of the village, to occupy with weak forces the gap to the left-hand neighbouring division and to secure the left flank. Hardly had this order been given to Hauptmann vom Hofe, than he was severely wounded in the immediate vicinity of 'Hohes Haus'. His adjutant, Leutnant Feick who was next to him, was hit by the same shell and killed. His shoulders and a small piece of his chest were all that was left of him. Hauptmann Giehler [officer commanding 5 Company] took over command of the battalion. Reserve Leutnant Bodsch, commander of 6 Company, was severely wounded in the stomach.[175]

The German attack suffered a severe reverse in this sector. To the east things went far better for the Germans at Méteren but even so they failed to make a serious impression on the desired capture of Bailleul. Beyond the left flank of 1 Australian Brigade, the line was taken up by 19 Brigade of 33 Division. Once again Victor Fagence of 1 Queen's describes in calm and measured tones the tense situation of facing the three strong attacks made during the day:

> At dawn the enemy launched very heavy attacks against our positions from the south-east and south of Méteren. A gap was made in the centre of the Queen's line covering the Méterenbecque; a second gap was made on the left of 5/6 Scottish Rifles covering the approach to Méteren from the east. Another gap was made between the right of the Queen's and the 1 Cameronians north-east of Merris. The enemy exploited these gains to full advantage, pushing forwards light machine guns with great rapidity.[176]

Although the enemy succeeded in taking the chain of outposts and thus advancing a few hundred yards, they were brought to a halt by fire in the third attack around 7.00pm. Their advance had also finally captured the steam mill south-west of Bailleul, and for a while 19 Brigade's left was threatened. In the afternoon came the welcome sound of British artillery beginning to open fire, even if they began by firing short as they ranged on uncertain enemy positions. Fagence believed it was the only occasion during the three days that he had been in the line that he heard or had any evidence of the presence of artillery support for the brigade, other than from two anti-aircraft guns. Its arrival was timely, for together with counter-attacks, including one made by 2 New Zealand Entrenching Battalion, it brought the German attack on Méteren to an end for the day.

Between the enemy attacks there had been some odd moments for Fagence and his pals, which serve to illustrate the confused and confusing nature of fighting in this campaign:

> For us in 12 Platoon several peculiar happenings took place. First at about ten o'clock in the morning a French civilian came riding up on a bicycle from behind our lines. [He] said he was on his way to fetch another bicycle that had been left behind the previous day [and was] allowed to proceed. [We] pointed out to him that Germans might be occupying the houses ... [we] conjectured he might be a spy. I don't remember seeing him return with any bicycles. Later on a German Red Cross ambulance came along the road from the direction of Bailleul. When it reached the crossroads it turned to the right and came a short distance down the road towards us, then stopped and

two men in German uniform jumped out from the side furthest from us and ran off back towards the crossroads through a gap between some houses and disappeared. We did not fire at them and no one went out to investigate, as we suspected it might be a trick of the enemy's to cause us to reveal our positions.

The Queen's were relieved by 4 Liverpool Regiment in the evening. It was an exhausted but proud battalion that formed up and marched out to Nooteboom, 370 officers and men fewer than had taken up positions on the Hogenacker Ridge three days previously.

On the Australian right lay 5 and 61 Divisions, covering the southern side of the forest and down the Clarence to Robecq. They faced 8 Bavarian Reserve, and 8 and 48 Reserve Divisions. Sustained German attacks against 13 and 95 Brigades of 5 Division came to nothing, being gunned down without reaching the British lines. Lieutenant Frank Glover of the 1 East Surreys even had time to note that his men 'salved a stove from a neighbouring camp ... the men continue to live amazingly well on the results of foraging expeditions ... a small deer killed by shell-fire in the wood was cut up, cooked and eaten'.[177] By no means were all British troops in the sector able to spend their time hunting for their dinner. Likewise 61 Division also came under constant attack and similarly cut down the advancing enemy. In between German assaults, Geoffrey Christie-Miller had time to reflect on the surroundings in which his battalion was now fighting. The position

> ran through water meadows and enclosures, well studded with farms, and immediately in rear of the front-line posts [ran] the Robecq–Calonne road along which were a succession of cottages and gardens. The posts were small ones and were mostly dug so close to the river that it was impossible to thicken the parapets. They were of the 'hip bath' variety and seemed incapable of being seriously improved. The conditions of this line were unlike anything we had yet experienced. There were of course no set trenches and no communication trenches. We were operating in a rich agricultural country which a week before had been fully populated. ... The processions of refugees were the most pathetic thing I ever saw ... [there were, from the farms] plentiful supplies of food for troops (chicken, eggs, vegetables, potatoes, decent claret) but sorrow at the desolation being wrought.[178]

Beyond 61 Division, 4 Division also faced plenty of German artillery fire but, with Sixth Army's attack having been directed against the forest rather than the La Bassée Canal, no sustained infantry threat. Their 11 Brigade took the opportunity to carry out an offensive operation to straighten out a problematic angle in its front line. The day before, patrols had ascertained that Riez du Vinage was only lightly held by the enemy, and a conference of battalion commanders at noon decided to mount this local attack. The idea was to recapture the village and establish a line of posts running from there to Carvin, to cover the eastern approaches to Robecq and the canal bridges near Mont-Bernanchon. The 1 Somerset Light Infantry and 1 Hampshires carried out the attack, crossing the canal quietly by footbridges from about 6.00pm. Once across, the assault teams took shelter while artillery shelled the village and any nearby locations where German reserves might be gathered. Resistance was at this stage negligible, although some casualties were sustained from a few salvoes of heavy German artillery. Exactly at 6.30pm the Somersets began to advance behind a creeping barrage, but were immediately pinned down by machine-gun fire. Advancing in short section rushes, and meeting a number of Germans who surrendered, the attacking parties entered and cleared Riez in severe fighting. A counter-attack from Pacaut Wood by a German company with six machine guns was repelled with heavy losses by 7.15pm and all of their guns captured. Among other booty, the Somersets recaptured an 18-pounder battery and a 4.5-inch howitzer battery that had belonged to 51 Division. The Hampshires had no problem in advancing 1,500 yards, meeting no opposition.

For the second day it was the German Fourth Army that launched the stronger attack. Some 10 miles north of Riez du Vinage, a force of nine divisions assembled for the assault to capture Neuve Eglise and the high ground east of Bailleul. Four of them (11 Reserve, 38, 117 and the Alpine Corps), plus another three in reserve (10 Ersatz, 32 and 235), faced the brigades holding out from Méteren round Bailleul to Mont de Lille. Still reorganising after their night withdrawal to the Ravelsberg and Mont de Lille, the much-reduced brigades of 34 and 25 Divisions dug in as best they could to face another onslaught. It was not long in coming, for the first assault took place as early as 2.45am. Unfortunately, 74 Brigade was still in the awkward position of being separated from its own division; it had 101 Brigade of 34 Division on its right and 88 Brigade of 29 Division on its left, all three being under the temporary command of Cecil Nicholson and manning the line that skirted the southern slope of Mont de Lille. Second Lieutenant Richard Ackerley, of 74 Brigade's 11 Lancashire Fusiliers, was lucky to survive the day:

> The enemy soon found out that morning that we had retreated. Having brought up a considerable amount of artillery by now they soon registered on the new line we were digging. They gave us a very hot time and caused a number of casualties but the men needed no pushing to dig faster and gradually we were getting well down.

During one heavy spell I was moving along to the right of the line, where I had a detachment, and stopped to have a chat with Captain Rufus of A Company where they had dug an HQ which was very deep. As the shelling was very heavy he urged me not to be a 'damn fool' but to stay with them until things calmed down. However, I was worried about my men as I had not seen them for the last hour and I decided to get on. They had had one or two wounded but were by now getting well dug-in and everything seemed to be in hand, so, after about a quarter of an hour, I started to go back to my main body. On going through the A Company section there was great activity among stretcher-bearers and a digging party. Poor Tommy Rufus and his sergeant major had copped a direct hit and been blown to blazes. So I was lucky again, as I had been about an hour earlier when supervising and urging on the digging-in and a shell landed at my feet splattering everybody with earth. It must have been a dud as when everything had cleared and the troops were frozen stiff expecting to have to pick up my pieces there I was standing up and shouting at them to b***** well get on with it, it wasn't a Sunday School party. That afternoon the shelling got worse and you felt as though you were being sniped at by shells but we were well dug-in and I amused myself by sniping at the Germans at about 800 yards' range as they were gathering at the foot of a hill for an attack, eventually made later in the day. . . . During this period the Germans attacked around dusk and managed to make an inroad to our defences but fortunately Second Lieutenant Ward, who was bringing up about thirty reinforcements from somewhere, took charge and made a counter-attack with great success, throwing the Germans out and pursuing them down the slope. For this action he received the Military Cross.[179]

The counter-attack led by Norman Ward was part of an action that also included 3 Worcesters, and took place after the third enemy attack of the day at around 4.30pm. Prior to this, 103 Brigade and the remnants of 7 and 75 Brigades, now organised as composite battalions, had withstood a similarly heavy attack on Crucifix Corner, 1.6 miles to the north-east of Mont de Lille. Walter Vignoles' 9 Northumberland Fusiliers were among the garrison, holding the left flank of 103 Brigade's position between Breemeerschen and the road to Neuve Eglise:

At 4.15am HQs and companies in reserve stood to and almost at the same moment the enemy opened a heavy bombardment of the forward positions; realising that an attack was about to take place they moved forwards as rapidly as possible in order C, HQ, D. As we reached the rear of the hill, wounded men were met coming back, who told us that the enemy had attacked in large numbers, and that fighting was proceeding; this was confirmed by the sounds of heavy rifle and machine-gun fire. A party of over a hundred men were moving away down the road towards the north, apparently without officers, while a group of six or eight of the latter were standing about in an aimless way having apparently lost their units. Their battalions were not known, and though some of the officers said they would come with us, we had no time to allot them special duties and they disappeared later. They were probably parties withdrawing from around Neuve Eglise, where they had no doubt been through very heavy fighting, and the incident is only mentioned to show how difficult it is to do anything with troops that have once lost their cohesion. Company Sergeant Major Hardman DCM led a counter-attack of B Company after Captain Patten was killed. He said, 'We've got to get the Bosche out, so this time we'll give a hell of a shout, and make him think there are more of us than there are.'[180]

The ruse worked and, as at Mont de Lille, the minor incursion that the Germans had made into the British positions was successfully ejected. CSM 41172 Robert Hardman was rightly awarded a Bar to his DCM for his work at Crucifix Corner. When the enemy had obtained a footing in posts held by his company, two counter-attacks had failed and all his officers were casualties, he led two more counter-attacks, at the last attempt driving the enemy out and restoring the position.[181]

A mile and a half east of Vignoles' men, the 2 Worcesters had somehow managed to survive the night under a continuous attack against their position in Neuve Eglise. The German 214 Division had also now been reinforced by the arrival of the fresh 11 Bavarian Division, although it took all day to haul the artillery of the latter into place. Under a rain of machine-gun and trench-mortar fire, Battalion HQ in the hospice gradually lost touch with the companies. Casualties were many, particularly from a German machine gun mounted just yards away at the crossroads and from trench-mortars plastering the area. The windows and exits of the hospice were continually swept by fire. Runners who tried to get to the scattered companies and to British troops further on the left were shot the second they emerged from cover; Second Lieutenant Anthony Johnson begged permission to go out through the curtain of fire in an attempt to make contact with brigade: he too was never heard of again.[182] Major Gerald Stoney placed a Lewis gunner in the top floor of the hospice and also directed snipers to known enemy positions, but against overwhelming numbers they could only achieve so much. Second Lieutenant John Crowe now volunteered to take a small party with a view to clearing enemy from the rear of Battalion HQ. On reaching the road a hostile party was encountered and driven off on to higher ground. Leaving two NCOs and five men to guard the road, Crowe set off with two men to work round the enemy's flank. At this moment Second Lieutenant Arnold Pointon, now joining the road party with other men from the hospice, opened fire in coordination with Crowe and advanced, driving the Germans further away with heavy casualties. Three enemy machine guns were captured too. An unnamed officer from VIII Corps School came through the fire into the hospice at about 11.00pm and was able to take a message back addressed to 'OC Troops, Dranoutre' requesting assistance. By 1.00pm a party of 9 Highland Light Infantry (the 'Glasgow Highlanders') had appeared, just in time to face a full-scale renewal of the German attack. At 1.45pm Stoney gave the order to evacuate: given the intensity of the German fire, it was almost a miracle that the entire garrison of about a hundred men escaped without loss, passing through British reserves on the railway in front of Dranoutre. This included some twenty to thirty wounded; only three severely wounded men had to be left behind. The Worcesters' recapture of Neuve Eglise and their brave stand there had held superior forces at bay for more than two days.[183]

While the Worcesters were holding on at Neuve Eglise, the British line developed a discontinuity in the same area, with a 2,000-yard gap. The line coming from Crucifix Corner passed to the north of Neuve Eglise and was manned by 178 Brigade, 59 Division. It was this line that Stoney and his men passed through when withdrawing. There was then a gap to the line of 19 Division, which started to the left of Neuve Eglise and bent sharply north-wards after passing in front of Wulverghem. With the Worcesters' defence ended and 25 Division attacked at about 4.30pm, George Jeffreys decided that his 19 Division would have to pull back on their right in order to close the gap and make contact with 178 Brigade. The effect was that by the end of the day the German effort had nudged the British line backwards and placed them in possession of Neuve Eglise, but it was hardly the breakthrough towards Kemmel that Rupprecht needed in order to launch his attacks at Ypres. One chief of staff, of X Reserve Corps, assigned the German failure to 'scandalously bad artillery preparations'.

Foch met with Haig at Abbeville at 11.00am. In addition to the respective chiefs of staff, the meeting was joined by Milner, who came especially from England. Haig opened by saying that he wanted the French to take a more active part in the battle because British divisions were fast disappearing due to wastage. Foch compared the situation with the British defence of Ypres in 1914; he reiterated again his maxims of 'never withdraw' and 'never relieve troops engaged in battle', but asked for proposals. Pointing out that the French reserves were too distant to be able effectively to oppose an enemy advance on Calais, Haig handed over a written request. In view of the condition of his troops, who had been continually engaged since 21 March, he requested Foch to direct the four divisions commanded by General Maistre to advance to the line Béthune–Lillers and for these to be followed by Micheler's Corps. Maistre's force should then be moved either to reinforce the British on the La Bassée Canal or in the Hazebrouck direction. Foch said he would consider it, once the present movement north was completed. For all Haig's protestations, and forgiving Foch for believing the German offensive had run its course, one must have some sympathy with the Frenchman's position. The Germans evidently had plenty more reserves (they now had 48 divisions in hand, more than at the opening of 'Georgette') and by no means were all positioned behind the Flanders front; Allied reserves were few, and no gamble could be taken that might leave them badly positioned. The enemy could strike anywhere from Arras down to Noyon. In the evening Foch wrote that one division of Maistre's would move north of Frévent (a day's move for infantry if they went by lorry) and he would ask Maistre to study a suitable position for another. Haig wrote that he thought Foch's arrangements were insufficient to meet the present situation. By this time Foch had already directed the Belgian army to prepare to extend their front down to Ypres to allow the British to withdraw some of their forces. This was in accord with a dialogue that Plumer had had with the Belgians, in which the latter agreed to ensure that 4 Division conformed with Second Army's quiet withdrawal to a shorter front. Plumer issued orders at 1.00pm for the line to be shortened by a retirement on to Kemmel–Voormezele–White Chateau–Pilckem Ridge. Outposts would be left in position and all arrangements carried out in as much secrecy as possible. Brilliantly conducted by the divisions holding the salient (from right to left 21, 49, 6, 41, 36 and 30, although most were incomplete at this time), the move wrong-footed the enemy when it came to their proposed attack. It also gave up virtually without a shot the ground over which so much blood had been spilt in 1917. One is forced to wonder what the Canadian Corps would have thought of that in October 1917, had they had the power of foresight.

Bailleul lost
On 15 April Bailleul fell into German hands, the British army retired from the Neuve Eglise high ground to the Dranoutre line, and the withdrawal in the Ypres salient was completed. On the very day that Foch announced that he believed '*La bataille d'Hazebrouck est finie*', there was another bout of hard fighting in Flanders. The original direction of Georgette had now been abandoned and in some ways Foch was quite right, as the German thrust on

Hazebrouck was certainly held up and conceivably finished. Rupprecht's attention was increasingly focused on Ypres and that meant that Bailleul and Kemmel must be obtained as a priority. The battle front was also inexorably narrowing. Although Sixth Army was preparing to go yet again for Méteren and Strazeele, it was not ready and other than artillery and some troop assembly opposite the La Bassée Canal, made no effort at assault. Fourth Army also left things alone from Wytschaete northwards and 9 Division experienced another relatively quiet day. It should not for a moment be thought that 'quiet' meant safe, even for the headquarters and other units some way behind the front. Private 42821 Alex Jamieson of 11 Royal Scots had been assigned as a runner working with the battalion signals section. In just such a quiet spell he was sent to take a message to huts at the foot of the Scherpenberg. He was glad to get away from battalion headquarters, which was in a huge dug-out, reached by entering a steep stairway from which sleeping galleries protected by gas curtains projected at different levels, with 'water dripping everywhere, pumps going continuously and an atmosphere whose smell I shall never forget and beggars description'.

> [The] 8-inch howitzers suddenly got the range of these huts and I found myself using my own field dressing on someone else's wounds! I still picture in great detail and lying on stretchers one man with part of a heel gone and in great pain, and the lumps of metal in another's bare agonised body, his groans stilled to complete silence when a Roman Catholic chaplain arrived; and the almost impossible task of collecting the remains of some who had been killed. We were glad to leave the Scherpenberg for a farm near a Casualty Clearing Station, and I recall my astonishment when I saw a nurse there and a strange feeling as I watched many sack–enshrouded bodies being carried out for burial.[184]

While the areas outside the main German attack came under sporadic shell-fire, great pressure fell on the 7-mile front from west of Bailleul to Wulverg-hem, although Bailleul itself was not frontally attacked. Fourth Army's *Generalmajor* Friedrich von Lossberg assigned the capture of Bailleul to the Guards Reserve Corps, newly arrived from the Eastern Front, which assumed command of 10 Ersatz, 32 and 117 Divisions.

The battalions of 176 and 177 Brigades of 59 Division had only just taken over a 6,000-yard line in the Bailleul–Ravelsberg area when the Germans struck again. They had been mauled during Operation 'Michael' and, like so many of the divisions hit on 9 April, were still assimilating large drafts of 18-year-olds and depot comb-outs. All of the divisions between Bailleul and Ypres were in a similar condition. Major H. Wilfred House and his 6 Wiltshires of

19 Division were returning to the line after his miraculous escape a few days previously. His testimony sheds some light on the state of these units:

> In due course we went back into the line and I certainly found it a heavy responsibility to be in command of a battalion [which] I did not know and whose officers I hardly knew. Luckily things went smoothly ... but after we had been in the line for a few days the Germans attacked and it was difficult to get these new young soldiers to understand how crucial the position was. They hardly seemed to realise that the oncoming Germans were the enemy; nevertheless we managed to beat them off and in due course were relieved.[185]

Not all of the newly arrived young men would live to tell the tale. No fewer than 352 men of the 2/5 Lincolnshire Regiment, hurriedly digging in as best they could on the forward slope from Mont de Lille to Feuter Farm would be killed, wounded or captured on this day. The battalion had relieved the shattered units of 88 Brigade only at 5.30am and set to digging a series of platoon posts, one every 400 yards, with more positions on the gentle reverse slope to their north. Behind them was the Bailleul–Neuve Eglise road running up and along the Ravelsberg Ridge. Within half an hour of the Lincolns' arrival, enemy patrols of X Reserve Corps began to probe their line and continued to do so for an hour, but all were driven off leaving casualties behind. The battalion also took in eight German deserters and they, along with the 4 Lincolns on their left around Breemeerschen and the battered Crucifix Corner, enjoyed the rest of a relatively quiet morning. At noon a heavy and sustained bombardment began and lasted for almost 3 hours, blasting apart and levelling the posts so recently dug. Around 2.45pm the bombardment became a barrage, behind which the German infantry struck, hard and fast. For a short while they were kept at arm's length but inevitably broke into the British posts in places. Counter-attacks by the 4 Lincolns and B Company of the 9 Norfolks of 71 Brigade on the left drove the enemy back, only for further German attacks to break in again. At 3.40pm an attack also developed on the right of the 2/5 Lincolns holding Mont De Lille. Around the same time enemy troops forced their way over the neck of the ridge at Lion Hill, breaking the line of the 4 Lincolns and getting behind the 2/5 Lincolns' left rear. From this point reports lose coherence as close in-fighting developed and the line fragmented. Detachments of 2/5 Lincolns were reported as being seen fighting to the last 'in a series of stands and retirements, in which hand-to-hand fighting was of frequent occurrence', while under heavy and close-range machine-gun fire others fell back to the north-east of Bailleul. Battalion HQ was forced to withdraw in a northerly direction to the right of Keersebrom, where it linked up with two companies of the 9 Northumberland Fusiliers. By day's end

X Reserve Corps had secured the high ground of Crucifix Corner and Mont de Lille and had gained dominant observation over Bailleul and the British defenders now pushed back on to the cemetery, the old Royal Flying Corps aerodrome and the asylum. Among the Lincolns' casualties was Lieutenant-Colonel Harold Roffey, who in 1911 had been awarded the Royal Humane Society Medal for saving three men from death by drowning.[186]

Behind 59 Division Cecil Nicholson's force of 34 Division and assorted brigades began the day well out of the range of machine guns, the depleted and tired units digging in on a discontinuous line 2,000 yards north of Bailleul. On the right was 147 Brigade, in touch with 19 Brigade holding the front north of Méteren, then came 101 and 74 Brigades with 103 Brigade on the left, in contact with 100 Brigade of 33 Division. Up on the Ravelsberg 88 and 102 Brigades had just been relieved by 59 Division. The afternoon attack and enemy break-in at Crucifix Corner caused these formations to be placed on alert. Once it was evident that 176 and 177 Brigades had taken a beating and were retiring on and even through Bailleul, Nicholson's force was ordered to throw out advanced posts to cover the withdrawal. With the exception of regiments of the French cavalry now beginning to arrive to the north, there was precious little by way of reserves. The North Staffords of 176 Brigade fell back through the ruins of Bailleul and took up a position to the right of 147 Brigade; the rest of the remnants of 177 Brigade lay east of the town. The 1/4 Duke of Wellington's was one of Nicholson's units that witnessed the retreat of British troops through Bailleul. Lieutenant-Colonel Richard Sugden was having none of it:

> At 7.30pm it was reported to me that large numbers of British troops were running down the road from Bailleul. I posted a machine gun [team] on the road and ordered them to fire high bursts in order to deflect them to our trenches and stop the Germans who were reported to be following. As the numbers were increasing I took 20 rifles, blocked the crossroads and told them that I should shoot down anyone who attempted to get past. I persuaded about ten of their officers to stand and fight, which they did most gallantly next day when the Germans attacked and were beaten off with heavy loss. I put two of these officers in for the MC.[187]

German patrols discovered late that night that Bailleul was empty of any serious force of British troops, and by 1.00am it could be said that it was now in German occupation.

On either side of the enemy breakthrough, British brigades swung back their flanks to form defensive lines and extended in order to keep in touch with those units that were falling back. In so doing, a tenuous but continuous line was maintained. On the right 33 Division's units at Méteren angled their line by manning a switch trench, linking what had been the front and support defences. Beyond the Ravelsberg 71 Brigade retired to the previously defined Méteren–Kemmel–Spanbroekmolen line, which existed rather more strongly on paper than it did in terms of any physical defences. Beyond it, 19 Division also complied with the order to withdraw to this line and was finally able to relieve 108 Brigade, which moved to La Clytte.

Facing the quietened Sixth Army, 4 Division decided to build on its previous day's success at Riez du Vinage by mounting a further attack across the canal to recapture Pacaut Wood. It was considered that this wood, which lay immediately adjacent to the canal, offered too good an opportunity for the Germans to mass troops prior to mounting a surprise attack across the water on Mont-Bernanchon. The troops of the 1 Somerset Light Infantry were still holding their positions in Riez when the battalion commanders of 10 Brigade were summoned to a conference at 9.00am to determine how to achieve their objective. While the conference was going on, news came that the artillery supporting 61 and 5 Divisions had broken up what appeared to be a massing of German troops in the area of Merville and menacing Bacquerolles Farm, which was not too far from the intended objective. It was determined that the 1 Royal Warwickshires and 2 Duke of Wellington's would clear Pacaut Wood and the buildings to the north, having crossed the canal and advanced behind a creeping barrage. They would also link up with the garrison of Riez du Vinage and capture the road to Le Cornet Malo. At the same time the 1 Hampshires would advance from the position they had already won and link up with an attack made by 2/4 OBLI from Bacquerolles Farm. By the time the conference broke up and preparations were made, it was well into the afternoon. A softening-up bombardment would open at 5.15pm and the assault companies must be in place by 5.45pm. The attack soon ran into difficulties, partly arising from the short time that many units had to prepare. The men crossed the canal in broad daylight by pontoon bridges near Pont d'Hinges as the creeping barrage opened, but in places the shells fell short, exploding behind the two left-hand companies of the Warwickshires. As they advanced it became apparent that there were far more enemy troops in the vicinity than had been envisaged, and both battalions became engaged in a stiff fight. The Duke's on the west side of the wood, in the gap between the cover of trees and the buildings of Riez, suffered severely from artillery fire. Two platoons of the Somersets, advancing as planned to meet up with them, were also cut down by machine-gun fire at a cost of 50 per cent casualties. The units consolidated on the east side of the wood, where they were unmolested during the night.[188] As they were doing so, 2/4 OBLI's attack at 7.30pm succeeded at first but was counter-attacked with some success; the 1 Hampshire Regiment attempted to secure a line 500 yards in front but, with the OBLI and Somersets struggling on either side, retired to their start point during the night.

The French II Cavalry Corps was now arriving in Flanders. By 8.00am 2 and 6 Cavalry Divisions were at Steenvoorde with 3 Cavalry Division north of Cassel. In addition, 28 Division was also now in the area, arriving on the cavalry's left, and 133 Division had completed its move to Caestre. The Corps commander General Felix Robillot had agreed with Plumer that 133 Division would begin to move to the Méteren front; on hearing of it, Foch refused, once again on the principle that 'relief is out of the question'. Robillot quietly agreed that the artillery of the British 21 Division, which Plumer had attached to Robillot as the latter had travelled without gun support, might be used there. During the night he also ordered two brigades of cavalry to Boeschepe and the leading elements of 28 Division reached the area of Westouter–Reninghelst.

Méteren and Wytschaete in enemy hands

The 15 Hampshires of 41 Division could hardly believe their luck. Going in for another tour of the sodden and shallow trenches at Passchendaele on 12 April, they did not suffer a single casualty until ordered to carry out their withdrawal at 3.00am four days later. In the salient this was almost unheard of. Frequent patrols had been sent out and reported no enemy contact at all. Each company left an officer and a Lewis gun section in place to cover any trouble while the rest of the battalion slipped away. Nothing happened; there was not even any shell-fire en route back to Ypres, although it seemed to some that German flares appeared to follow. It was apparent that the Germans were in complete ignorance of what was going on, and many a man breathed a quiet prayer of thanks for that. A prisoner had stated he was aware that the British contemplated falling back, but that was anyone's guess considering the gains the Germans had evidently made at Bailleul.

The German Guard Corps holding the salient had no intention of making trouble; quite the opposite. They were in an advanced state of preparation for a large-scale attack that was now planned to take place on 20 April, and had no desire to give the game away by losing prisoners in minor skirmishes or exposing new battery positions by firing. The main force was assembling in the area of Houthulst Forest, ready to strike south-westwards and cross the Yser canal. Coinciding with another large assault from Kemmel, this would squeeze the British out from Ypres and would represent an enormous tactical success, if not strategic victory. Eight divisions were being concentrated, of which four would make the attack with the remainder in support ready to take advantage of any breakthrough. There would be overwhelming artillery support from 79 field and 80 heavy batteries. Old lessons from Ypres, retaught in no uncertain terms on the Lys, dictated that while a breakthrough was possible using the infiltration infantry technique, it all came to little if the logistic support was not quickly put in place behind it. This was especially vital at Ypres, where the advance would have to take place for the most part across devastated and heavily cratered ground with virtually no roads. In retrospect the weakness again was that the German force had no mobile or armoured capability, short of two squadrons of cars.

The British deception could only last so long. During the afternoon German patrols from 58 and 236 Divisions discovered that all that remained in front of them was a few outposts and that the main British positions had been withdrawn. The Guard Corps had to react fast; the planned attack was brought forwards by three days to 17 April and all units worked feverishly to get everything into place. It was less clear whether a simultaneous attack could be launched from Kemmel. With the Germans now in occupation of Bailleul, the way was opening for a push on the western end of the Flemish hills and beyond to the Steenvoorde–Poperinghe road, the key supply route to the Ypres salient, just 8 miles distant. A strike north-eastwards along the road through Locre was also feasible, as was a northward assault from the heights of Ravelsberg on to Dranoutre and Kemmel. No advance from Bailleul was possible on 16 April. Every British gun – plus those of the French 28 Division at Mont Rouge – was turned on to the old town, bringing down those few buildings left standing after days of German bombardment. Bailleul was an inferno; no German units could safely negotiate it and few debouched to the north during the day. Those that did faced devastating fire from Richard Sugden's 1/4 Duke of Wellington's and other units of Cecil Nicholson's force of tattered brigades forming a line across the St Jans–Cappel road. Most of the men that were left in this group had been in constant action for days, some having been involved since the early hours of 9 April. The curtain of artillery fire bought precious time for the French divisions to complete their arrival and further reserves to be ordered to reinforce.

There was no widespread or large-scale action on 16 April, for the first time since 'Georgette' began. Most areas of the front came under continued shellfire and there were some minor local actions to improve tactical positions. Only in two areas were important results achieved, but even they were of a tactical nature in finally prising Méteren and Wytschaete from the British grasp.

A determined attack was made against Major-General Henry Tudor's 9 Division (whose command for the moment encompassed part of 146 Brigade and 62 and 64 Brigades of 21 Division), starting with a short but heavy bombardment with gas at about 4.30am. Attacking yet again in early morning fog, the enemy's thrust was directed on Wytschaete and the stretch of line running up to the Dammstrasse.[189] The field artillery, assisted by CLVI and CLXII Field Artillery Brigades of 33 Division, opened on pre-arranged targets but as

luck would have it the division had recently been switched from the command
of IX to XXII Corps and no arrangements were yet in place for support from
the corps heavy artillery. To some extent the German assault took advantage of
the gentle folds in the ground in this area. The garrison behind Wytschaete and
down to Spanbroekmolen, 1 Lincolns on the left and 1/7 West Yorkshires on
the right, quickly came under pressure and enemy parties broke into gaps in
the line. The British troops, those that could, retired westwards, leaving the
great 1917 craters at Peckham and Spanbroekmolen to the enemy. The high
lips of these craters offered great observation advantages in both directions and
were a sad loss to the defenders.

   On the left of Wytschaete, where the ground flattens out and the fighting
was across a series of old trench lines, the 1 East Yorkshires and 15 DLI of
64 Brigade and 5 Cameron Highlanders of 26 Brigade were able to stand their
ground. The trenches here had over the years developed into a most complex
system. Even the experienced East Yorkshires had difficulty when moving into
the sector a few days before, the guides provided by the outgoing unit having
got lost in the maze. The opening bombardment fell chiefly in the valleys
behind the front line, leaving the forward posts intact and on the alert. With
62 Brigade being driven back, the adjoining right platoon of D Company of the
East Yorkshires under Second Lieutenant Heaton Foster was overwhelmed,
every man being killed or captured.[190] Beating off three German attacks during
the day, the battalion turned back to hold on a south-facing defensive flank
from Somer Farm to Black Cot. On the left a minor incursion against the right
company of the DLI was ejected by a counter-attack by other elements of that
battalion and the East Yorkshires. By 11.00am the 2 Lincolns of the same
brigade had taken up a line some 1,000 yards west of Wytschaete.

   Down at Méteren, although the defenders were tired and few in number, the
position held was reasonably strong. In addition to the 5 Scottish Rifles on the
right and the 4 King's Liverpool on the left were some 18 Middlesex and Seton
Hutchinson's machine-gunners. Detachments of 5 Tank Battalion, less tanks
but manning Lewis guns, had also arrived to strengthen the force and 2 New
Zealand Entrenching Battalion was in close support.

   The various after-action reports give conflicting and mixed views of the
progress of the enemy attack. One thing is clear: it broke into the defences on
the left and quickly smashed the rest of the line. The Liverpools' war diary says
that C Company reported to Battalion HQ at 5.00am, saying that the Tank
Corps troops had evacuated the front line on the left without letting them
know. Conversely the tank unit's diary says that the enemy broke through
south of the Méteren–Bailleul road and that a flank was formed and touch
obtained with the Liverpools. Two platoons were at once sent forwards to plug
the gap, but did not succeed in reaching the broken position before the enemy,

in the shape of 96 Infantry Regiment, launched his attack in earnest. The Liverpool battalion suffered terribly within the next hours, 20 officers and 469 men becoming casualties; as the enemy charged forwards, a company of the New Zealand Battalion was surrounded and captured. This was the largest 'bag' of New Zealanders in a single incident in the war. In the midst of it all the Tanks' Second Lieutenant Fred Dawson and his teams kept four Lewis guns firing from shell holes at just 200 yards as the enemy came on time and again. Dawson had taken up the position during the night and the men had done their best to dig in and connect up the shell craters with the forward trenches, despite being under fire.[191] Counter-attacks mounted later in the day, notably by 1 Middlesex, were to little avail. Méteren had been lost and the Germans were consolidating in a strong position.

By 8.00am it had become clear to Henry Tudor, despite communications having been cut, that Wytschaete and Spanbroekmolen on his right had fallen to the enemy attack. After making arrangements for a counter-attack, he contacted Plumer later in the morning. He had by now also learned of the enemy's capture of Méteren. Plumer issued orders in conjunction with General Robillot for a counter-attack to be made by his strongest reserve, the French 28 and 133 Divisions. Foch too was decisive, sending a message to Robillot that it was time for the French forces to engage and 'to hasten to the battle'. First 28 Division would advance on the Messines Ridge with the objective of consolidating the Wulverghem–Wytschaete line, while 133 Division would assault Méteren with the objective of retaking it. The men of 1 Australian Division, on the right of Méteren, would be in support. Hamilton's IX Corps would arrange for other forces to link up between the two thrusts and would ensure that the Kemmel defences were secure. 9 Division would extend on the left of the attack by 28 Division, while 177 Brigade would cover its right flank. At the same time the French II Cavalry Corps would cover the western end of the Flemish hills, between Mont Noir and Mont des Cats.

There was much to do and the hours ticked by. With the troops gathering equipment and ammunition and deployed to their assault positions, Foch met with Haig and Wilson in Abbeville. Foch was becoming more alert to the potential of the German offensive and the need to bolster the British defences in the Flemish hills. He had already ordered another French division to move north and instructed that two of those divisions now near Amiens should move into the Tenth Army area. Haig explained what was happening in the Ypres area: that the withdrawal was completed but heavy pressure was now being placed on Wytschaete. He suggested that the inundation of the Dunkirk area should begin; in fact Foch had already given the instruction to dam the River Aa some days before. It was Wilson who was now most jittery, saying that a fresh water flooding from the Aa was insufficient and that Foch should also let go the salt water at Dunkirk. Foch then went to Cassel to meet with Plumer. After delivering an hour-long treatise on how best to defend Kemmel, he gave instructions for the French 34 Division, in Tenth Army and already within striking distance, to move by lorry to Steenvoorde.

As the generals were meeting in Abbeville, just after 5.00pm XXII Corps commander Lieutenant-General Alexander Godley learned that the French could not attack until 7.30pm. Further news then came, from various sources, which began to throw doubt on whether the French would attack at all. An advance was made in the southern attack, but only on a two-battalion front and it only reached the British front line. The two units, 32 and 116 *Chasseurs Alpins*, filled gaps in the line and extended during the night, taking over the whole Méteren front. The Australians advanced to extend up to the Méteren-becque as ordered and relieved the 5 Scottish Rifles by morning. As the war diary of 1 Australian Brigade reports, 'The French attack did not eventuate'; it seems that the French had received reports that Méteren was in British hands and had decided not to attack.[192] It was an ominous beginning to practical Allied cooperation in the battle.

The *Chasseurs Alpins* had no idea of the situation at the front, or whether there was a front, as they moved up. All they saw was the desolation of a ruined and abandoned landscape and all the evidence of a broken British army. Henry Vergnand was with 116 *Chasseurs Alpins*, on the march from Fletre and eventually taking cover at a farm near Méteren mill:

> On the road, we met isolated British soldiers, without arms, their uniform neglected, and on each side of the road military camps all completely open, deserted and abandoned. ... Whether there was really a gap in front of us no one could tell.[193]

Chapter 7

'Tannenberg'

The Germans were now fully aware of the British withdrawal at Ypres and intended to follow it up as quickly as possible, with the objective of hitting the enemy before he had settled into strong new positions. Second Corporal 103952 Harry Hopthrow was with the Royal Engineers of 30 Divisional Signals. He experienced what 'hitting the enemy' meant at first hand: 'It was an organised retirement. The enemy knew we were retiring and they made it as hot as they could – and it was bloody hot. It was a terrible battle. Our wireless station was shelled out on one occasion. I got very tired of life at that time. I used to write in my diary "fed up".'[194]

British morale at this point appears to have been very mixed; some men and units were exhilarated at having fended off a clearly stronger enemy, and the chief censor had noted a remarkably positive tone to the men's letters. Others were exhausted, like Hopthrow, and the sheer tension of day after day of fighting and the threat of death or captivity was grinding away at their nerves. The condition of many of the German divisions was not dissimilar, having now been in action for several days and being to all intents broken, and desperate for relief. One officer of the Royal Field Artillery, possibly of 162 Brigade in the Kemmel area, adds a note of melancholy:

> The fact that the fighting was in country which we had long occupied and among our standing camps had a curiously dispiriting effect. On our side there was frequent movement of small groups of our men walking aimlessly about, generally to the rear. The men seemed apathetic and weary, but were quite ready to go forwards to the line and on being told did so cheerfully. It was impossible not to feel that officers in the line knew little or nothing about what was going on. There was a considerable amount of material and stores left in the forward areas: Decauville railway engines and trucks, RE material, etc. Two 9.2-inch howitzers had been abandoned on the Wytschaete–Kemmel road near Maedelstede Farm. It was impossible to move them and they added to the forlorn and deserted feeling of the place.[195]

Morale was certainly slipping as far as Henry Wilson was concerned. The man who had bounced and backslapped around Versailles after securing his place at the table of the Supreme War Council was not finding life quite so enjoyable as CIGS. Foch was now taking a much more active role and 17 April would see him decisive and determined. Meeting Wilson at Blendecques in the morning, the Frenchman would not countenance Wilson's gloomy suggestions of deep withdrawal to the Dunkirk inundations. With Haig and Plumer's insistent voices ringing in his ears, saying that they believed Second Army was so exhausted that it was unlikely to be able to hold much longer, Wilson demanded more French reserves.[196] Having heard enough, Foch motored to meet the Belgian Chief of Staff Lieutenant-General Cyriacque Gillain and at 2.00pm had an appointment with Albert, King of the Belgians. The timing of the meeting could scarcely have been better planned, for it came as the Belgians were carrying out one of their finest feats of arms in the war.

Some of the troops who would take part on this day were not tired, for the launch of 'Tannenberg', the vital flanking operation north-east of Ypres that Rupprecht had brought forwards to exploit the British withdrawal, would be between fresh divisions. On the Allied side it engaged the Belgians, the army which had been earliest into action in the war when facing the German incursion across the Meuse at Liege in early August 1914. The German breach of Belgian neutrality, agreed by treaty, had been a strong factor in bringing Britain into the war. Entering the conflict with a small army of just six divisions and a number of fortress garrisons, the Belgians had fought like terriers in holding up the huge German advance but had inevitably been pushed aside. Falling back along the coast once it was felt necessary to abandon the last fortified zone at Antwerp, the Belgians fought a last stand along the River Yser and there held the enemy at the end of October 1914. The climactic battle on the Yser was every bit as violent and hard-fought by both sides as the First Battle of Ypres, with which it was concurrent. With the Belgian army desperately tired and having suffered serious losses, the battle was brought to an end by a brilliant piece of engineering. By precise management of the locks where a number of canals met the sea at Nieuport, the water levels were caused to rise in the hinterland. Belgian sappers closed off all possible leakage through the straight and high railway embankment that ran from Nieuport to Dixmude, and the rising waters inundated the land eastwards of the river and in some areas beyond it to a depth of several feet. The German force was now separated from the Belgians by a wide belt of water, and although both sides gradually took command of high buildings standing proud of the flood (which were used as observation posts and inevitably became easy, death-trap targets), the line remained as such for some years. Clinging on to the last vestige of home territory, the Belgians had stood mainly on the defensive ever since. Aside

from considerations of his army's ability to wage offensive war, King Albert
of the Belgians, who in addition to being monarch was constitutionally placed
as commander-in-chief of the armed forces, had no wish to squander his
limited force in costly operations that he did not believe would achieve decisive
results. By 1917 the Belgians had become remarkably self-reliant, supplied
by munitions and other factories they had set up in England, and actually
expanded as a fighting force by taking in men from the colonies, some who had
managed to escape via the Netherlands before the Germans electrified the
border, and from wherever Belgians came to play their part. They had stood on
the British left throughout the war, sometimes with French forces in between,
and often frustrating British attempts to subsume them.

On 26 October 1917, during the Battle of Passchendaele, French and Belgian
troops made a useful local advance north-west of Langemarck, crossing the
Maartjevaart Canal and capturing the ruined village of Merckem and the
De Kippe crossroads in front of it.[197] Some 3.5 miles to the east lay the large
Houthulst Forest, a vital spot in the German defences of the Ypres salient. The
five months since then had not been wasted but much needed to be done, and
the Belgian line was twice extended. In December 1917 the Belgians relieved a
French corps north of the British and in the crisis of 'Michael' relieved one of
Plumer's divisions to enable Haig to despatch it to the Somme. By April 1918
Belgian troops held the line from Nieuport to Langemarck. Much work was
expended on making the new front defensible; new trenches were dug, posts
built and wired in. The area did not have the benefit of wide inundations in
front of the line, but with the Germans demonstrating that they could suc-
cessfully cross several hundred yards of water, as they had done at Riga in
September 1917, it might have been of dubious value. Two tests came in
March 1918, when enemy attempts at Reigersvliet were beaten off.[198] The
Belgians readily appreciated the strategic significance of 'Georgette'. It would
not take much of a German gain in the Hazebrouck–Cassel direction, or worse
the Bailleul–Poperinghe direction, for the Belgian rear to be compromised.
Avoidance of encirclement would necessarily mean a withdrawal towards the
Channel ports. On 9 April King Albert agreed with his newly appointed Chief
of Staff that the army would retire on the Loo Canal if absolutely necessary but
the general principle should be to hang on to Belgian territory.

Von Arnim's force launched 'Tannenberg' against 7,000 yards of Belgian
line west of Houthulst Forest, on a front stretching from the Dixmude road
crossroads at De Kippe down to Langemarck. Three divisions made the
assault: from right to left the 6 Bavarian, 1 *Landwehr* and 58 Division. A
regiment of *MarineKorps Flandern* also took its place in the front line, opposite
De Kippe. This was a force of greatly mixed quality and experience. The
6 Bavarian Division was considered to be among the best in the German army,

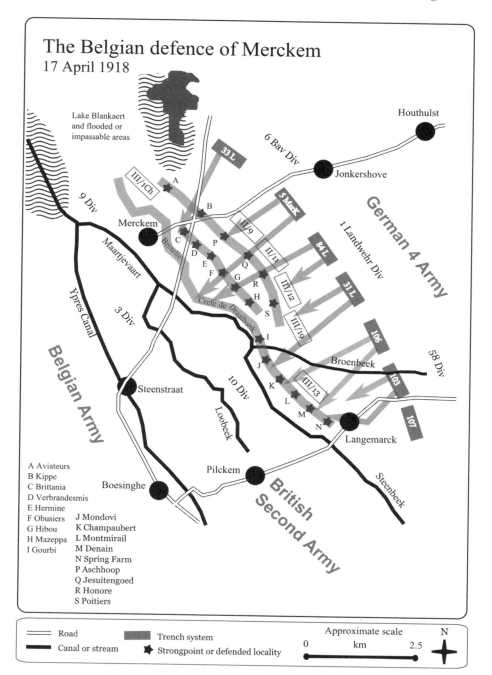

The Belgian defence of Merckem
17 April 1918

Lake Blankaert and flooded or impassable areas

Houthulst

6 Bav Div

33 L

III/1Ch

A

B

5 MzK

Jonkershove

German 4 Army

9 Div

Merckem

C

P

D

E

F

Q

II/9

III/11

84 L

1 Landwehr Div

R

III/12

31 L

G

H

S

III/19

I

106

Crête de Draaibank

Broenbeek

58 Div

Maartjevaart

Bruielle

Ypres Canal

3 Div

J

K

III/13

103

Belgian Army

Steenstraat

10 Div

L

M

N

107

Langemarck

Loobeek

Steenbeek

A Aviateurs
B Kippe
C Brittania
D Verbrandesmis
E Hermine
F Obusiers   J Mondovi
G Hibou   K Champaubert
H Mazeppa   L Montmirail
I Gourbi   M Denain
                 N Spring Farm
                 P Aschhoop
                 Q Jesuitengoed
                 R Honore
                 S Poitiers

Boesinghe

Pilckem

British Second Army

Road
Canal or stream
Trench system
Strongpoint or defended locality

Approximate scale
0   km   2.5

N

but it had only recently relieved 214 Division in this sector after action in 'Michael', where it suffered heavy casualties near Bullecourt. Conversely 1 *Landwehr* had spent all of its war in the east, being transferred to France only at the end of 1917. Manned by older troops, it was considered a mediocre division and was not one that would have been chosen to assault British or French positions. 58 Division was a Saxon formation that had been on the Houthulst front since October 1917. It had come back from Russia but prior to that had been involved at the Somme and Verdun.

Facing the onslaught were, from left to right, 9, 3 and 10 Belgian Divisions. Only the extreme right of the German attack, carried out by 33 *Landwehr* infantry against the crossroads, faced 9 Division. South of De Kippe 3 Division occupied two parallel lines of posts with a third entrenched line down to the Corverbeek. The forward posts – De Kippe, Aschoop, Jesuitengoed, Honoré and Poitiers – were trench works grouped around captured German bunkers. The second line posts – Britannia, Verbrande Smis and de l'Hermine, Obusiers, Hibou and Mazeppa Farms – were not so strong. Each regiment holding the front (9, 11 and 12 Linie) placed a battalion in the posts, with another behind it in counter-attack positions by the canal. Beyond 10 Division's area was in a much less advanced state of preparation, with a single chain of posts. Behind was the Steenbeek stream, flowing northwards from the British area, joining the Broenbeek in 10 Division's area and the Loobeek just north of the Dixmude road.

The German attack began earlier on the left than elsewhere, with 103 and 106 Regiments of 58 Division advancing at 5.45am. As they crossed the Broenbeek they were met by a hail of fire from the Belgian posts at Denain, Montmirail and Champaubert. A second attempt at 10.30am met with similar resistance. Only at a few places did German troops get into the Belgian posts, where counter-attack parties ejected them. No lasting inroads were made, while a battalion each of 13 and 19 *Linie* defended themselves with complete success against concerted efforts by seven German battalions.

The attack on the right and centre began at 7.30am with heavy shell-fire and gas aimed at the Belgian batteries across the Ypres canal, and concentrated trench–mortar fire against the forward posts. German infantry of 1 *Landwehr* and 6 Bavarian Divisions rose to the advance half an hour later. On their left 31 and 84 *Landwehr* Battalions met a similar fate to their comrades of 58 Division, being cut down by fire from Mondovi, Gourbi and Poitiers posts. The right of 84 *Landwehr* with 5 *MarineKorps* on their right managed to break through and between Honoré and Jesuitengoed posts, and were quickly followed up by two more battalions that overwhelmed the next posts and pressed on through to the trench line. 33 *Landwehr* also broke past De Kippe and captured the Britannia post. Orders were given by the Belgian 3 Division at 11.50am to prepare to blow the bridges over the Steenbeek, but in the event this was not required. The reserve battalions manning the trench line (known as the Bretelle at the north end and the Crête de Draaibank at the south) held firm and poured fire on to the German detachments that emerged. The enemy got in places to within 10 yards of the line – but no further.

The Belgians soon regained their composure, reorganising on and behind the trench line to launch a series of counter-attacks. As early as 9.45am 1 *Chasseurs* were pressing back and in conjunction with 9 *Linie* recaptured Britannia later in the morning, taking 100 prisoners and 10 machine guns. Local counter-attacks went on through the day until finally the entire position was back in Belgian hands by about 7.00pm. In this extraordinary and determined fight back, 20 German officers and 759 men were taken prisoner by the Belgians. The British Official Historian would later say that the 'palm of honour of this day must be awarded to the Belgians'. The northern element of 'Tannenberg', conceived in the Von Kuhl–Von Wetzell thinking of late 1917 and nurtured by Rupprecht and which had belatedly become a cornerstone of the Flanders offensive, had been utterly defeated.

At the same time as the Belgian troops were hammering at the enemy and clawing back to the old line, Foch left King Albert, having gained agreement that the Belgians would hold their line. He then went to organise the inundations at Dunkirk before finally meeting up with Plumer and Robillot. Foch was now in his element, laying down strategy, encouraging, demanding, cajoling. Within the previous 48 hours, he had come alive to the threat in Flanders, for all his Hazebrouck being 'finie'. Ordering two more divisions to move northwards, he restructured the French divisions into a new formation, the Detachment d'Armée du Nord (DAN), and placed it under command of Antoine de Mitry.[199] To Plumer and Robillot he laid down his plan: to hold the Flemish hills, recapture the lower slopes, then advance to regain Neuve Eglise, Bailleul and Wytschaete; to issue limited objectives each time and attack using weight of artillery rather than manpower; to get things moving immediately so that the enemy could not consolidate his newly won ground. He also insisted that they keep one French infantry division and one of cavalry as reserve, and that the British remnants should be reorganised but kept close by as emergency reserves.

Behind the lines as they now were, much work was beginning on creating deeper defences. As well as the inundations between St Omer and Dunkirk, several new lines were mapped out and construction begun over a belt several miles deep. There were stores and dumps to move, hospitals to relocate, headquarters to site, communications to lay out and test. The armies worked feverishly to get things done and for the Labour Corps and the hundred and one lines of communications and transport units there can hardly have been a busier period. It was also necessary to deal with the logistical nightmare that was the implantation of a large French force in the British area. New lines of supply meant much replanning of railway timetables, and the loss of some lines and shell-fire risk to others meant that options were fewer. To make matters worse, the French government was insistent that half of the railway capacity must be reserved for coal movements.[200]

The German 'Tannenberg' operations on 17 April also included an attack by Fourth Army on the Bailleul–Wulverghem front with the object of capturing Kemmel by working round the hill. At the same time an Allied counter-attack to recapture Wytschaete was also undertaken. This had begun the previous evening, when a planned joint attack by 9 Division, some companies of 39 Division and the French 28 Division had misfired with the French not yet being ready. At 7.30pm the 7 Seaforths advanced behind a creeping barrage and seized the ruined and cratered wilderness that was the village centre after coming up through Grand Bois, under fire the whole way. A number of enemy pill-boxes caused trouble, their machine-gun teams remaining until the last possible moment. On the outskirts of Wytschaete Captain Dennis Reid and CSM 4800 George Jeffrey led a party that rushed a pill-box, capturing its garrison of 14 men and five machine guns.[201] Intense fire from North House stopped the attack on its left flank and while 62 Brigade, moving up on the right, reached Petit Bois and Maedelstede Farm, they could not complete the recapture of the 1917 craters there. They had been badly affected by fire coming from Peckham and Spanbroekmolen, which would have been the French objectives. During the night the Seaforths were reinforced by 1, 2 and 4 South African Regiments (the latter being only some 250-strong), but no further advance was possible against severe enemy fire. An agreement was made for the French to attack Spanbroekmolen at 5.30am; according to 9 Division the effort was 'unexpectedly feeble'. A 200-yard advance was made, which was not enough to secure 62 Brigade's position. It was forced to with-draw to Lagache Farm. The situation in Wytschaete itself remained obscure throughout the day as close in-fighting took place.

Fourth Army's attack once again confronted 34, 25, 49 and 19 Divisions, all now much reduced in numbers. The whole area was bombarded with high explosive and gas during the night and from about 6.25am the shelling con-centrated on the front of 103 Brigade. British artillery responded, managing to maintain fire although many batteries suffered serious losses of men and guns under such heavy bombardment. No general infantry attack followed the enormous expenditure of shells but attempts were made on the front of 103 and 74 Brigades, both of which were beaten off with only the loss of a minor post. There were signs of a considerable assembly of enemy troops and by 9.45am

IX Corps reported that they believed a large-scale attack was developing on the front of 34 and 49 Divisions. If so, it never transpired. More serious was the German effort against 19 Division, holding 3 miles of line in front of Kemmel. All three brigades of the division were in the line, supplemented by 178 Brigade from 59 Division. Behind them the sides and summit of Kemmelberg were pounded by German artillery from about 6.00am, leaving the front line relatively unscathed. An infantry attack followed half an hour later; many men were instantly cut down by British fire.

Walter Vignoles' battalion was still in action and witnessed the arrival of the French artillery. He was the first to comment on the rather different methods employed by the French gunners:

> This day artillery support was very good, a number of French soixante-quinze batteries having arrived. The story goes that these batteries galloped into action, shouting 'Vive la France' and after one glance at an old 1/100,000 scale map, opened rapid fire. Certainly a considerable number of the shells dropped among our posts and it was some hours before all the batteries could be corrected.[202]

He was, later, more impressed with the French infantry:

> The 133 French Division relieved 34 Division on the night of 20/21 April, our headquarters being taken over by Le Colonel Borneque, 401 RI. The French troops were exceedingly smart and well turned out, and Colonel Borneque was aptly described by one of his own officers as 'un vieux guerrier'.[203]

While the French 75s were firing on the Northumberland Fusiliers, a weak spot on the right of 19 Division was quickly exploited by the Germans. Just one officer and 30 men of 459 Field Company had been ordered forwards during the night to fill a gap of 700 yards around Donegal Farm on the Lindenhoek–Dranoutre road. It appears that the weakness here was spotted in the initial German attempt to advance. On the renewal of the bombardment at 10.00am, Donegal Farm received the worst of it. After 50 minutes of screaming shell-fire, German infantry came forwards again, advancing on almost the entire front of 19 Division. The sappers, only the officer and eight men having survived the shell-fire, could do little and the position was soon in German hands. The 2/5 Sherwood Foresters and a company of 1 Leicesters were ordered up from reserve, but could not wrest the farm back and in consequence took up a line which bent back to Beaver Hall.[204] On their left the enemy also reached some former camp huts near Aircraft Farm, 800 yards distant and on the front held by 178 Brigade. Further north some enemy troops entered the trenches held by 56 Brigade at Lindenhoek but were ejected by counter-attack. These were, in the grand scheme, minor incursions. Given how important this operation was to 'Tannenberg', it had hardly made a dent, and even these gains would prove to be temporary. Three battalions of the French 99 Infantry Regiment also came from reserve; two relieved the Sherwood Foresters in the Donegal Farm–Aircraft Farm sector while the third remained east of Kemmelberg ready to reinforce at Lindenhoek. It has been suggested that the British line was so thinly held that the French had trouble in determining where it was.[205] During the night this regiment mounted an operation that recaptured Donegal Farm.

Sixth Army's attack west of Bailleul was also soundly defeated. The attack was presaged by shell-fire during the night, as far south as Festubert and Bellerive, but principally on the Merville–La Motte road and on the Allied front from north of Bailleul to Strazeele. There were several attempts by the German 12 and 35 Divisions to advance west of Merris against 1 Australian Division during the day, notably around 8.30am, 10.00am and 5.30pm. None succeeded and in their execution German casualties from artillery and fire from the Australian posts were severe. The attack by 81 Reserve and 38 Divisions against 98 Brigade north of Méteren met with little more success. The Allied force there comprised the three battalions of the brigade (4 King's Liverpool, 1 Middlesex and 2 Argylls) plus the French 32 and 116 *Chasseurs Alpins* and the Lewis gun detachment of 5 Tank Battalion.

It is apparent that little had been done to improve Allied cooperation or communication on this front during the night. The 1 Middlesex, having received RAF reports that the French had now advanced and were south of Méteren, sent patrols into the village. The reports proved to be entirely false: the patrol was fired on by German troops and Second Lieutenant James Adams was killed.[206]

Several German infantry attempts to advance north and north-east of Méteren during the morning were halted with heavy losses before a lull preceded another attempt at 6.00pm. The twenty gun teams of 5 Tank Battalion reported that enemy dead littered the ground in front of them. On this occasion a farm on the Flêtre road held by the French fell into enemy hands, but was recaptured by a counter-attack. Further reserves, notably 3 Australian Brigade and 102 *Chasseurs à Pied*, were brought into the rear of this area during the day.

It was all too obvious, even by noon, that 'Tannenberg', the German operation to destroy Second Army, had failed. There was only one conclusion to be drawn from the small impression made by the afternoon attacks and the bitter surprise of the Belgian counter-attack at Merckem. During the evening von Lossberg contacted von Kuhl. It was not possible to continue the offensive.

The German divisions of Fourth Army were worn out and in some areas were now in tactically difficult areas from which further assaults would be costly. Unless fresh divisions could be brought into play, Kemmel and the Flemish hills could not be won. Von Kuhl had no divisions to give, at least until 21 April. There was still the relatively fresh Guard Corps facing Ypres and IV Corps was also ready to try again at Givenchy. If they could achieve something on 18 April, the offensive would be worth keeping alive.

Chapter 8

The Death of 'Georgette'

Private 37665 Herbert Cooper was among the drafts of 18-year-old conscripts recently taken in by 1 Royal Lancaster Regiment to replace their losses earlier in the battle. It was his first time in the line, and he carefully noted the state of things near Riez de Vinage: 'hedges, bare, flat land . . . the trenches were just a mud ditch, not a real trench, and there were posts about fifty feet apart with a section of four or five men to a post'. At about 1.00am a violent German bombardment opened up and while it followed the pattern of concentrating on the gun batteries and rear areas, it was supplemented by trench-mortars firing on Cooper and his section in the support line. There were 'terrific explosions, whizzing fragments . . . I was quite afraid of those'. Then, at about 3.00am, nearby British field artillery began to retaliate. Cooper recalled the infantry SOS flares hanging in the air, provoking more German shell-fire. Rapid small arms fire to the front was ordered during darkness, but neither he nor his section could see anything. For those whose first tour of front-line duty this was, this was probably just as well, for the German Sixth Army was about to advance and had their destruction in mind.[207]

During the previous evening von Quast had formally called a halt to Sixth Army's attacks in the area between Strazeele and Bailleul. Intelligence reports had confirmed the presence of French troops near Méteren and the apparent impossibility of getting past the 5 and 1 Australian Divisions holding the line down to the Nieppe Forest discouraged further effort. To the south, however, his IV Corps was reasonably fresh after a week of comparative quiet on the Givenchy–Festubert front. It had learned a great deal about the British defences there during its torrid period of action against 55 Division and now, supported by IX Reserve Corps, would attack once again. Béthune was set as a deep objective beyond Givenchy and von Quast also targeted at least gaining a bridgehead over the canal at Hinges and Mont-Bernanchon. Henry Horne's staff at First Army HQ were well aware that such an attack was imminent and warned I and XI Corps to expect a German assault from Givenchy to Nieppe Forest.

The German guns opened fire as one at 1.00am, laying down a bombardment every bit as deep and severe as those experienced on 21 March and 9 April. Once again the shelling initially concentrated on the batteries, headquarters, dumps and roads behind the front and only later ranged on to the forward posts. On another cold and foggy morning, thick concentrations of gas soaked the entire area and men fought wearing masks well into the day. The shelling went on for some 7 hours on the front of 1 Division down near the La Bassée Canal, but slackened off after 4 hours north of Festubert, only for it to intensify just before the German infantry made their attack. The British field artillery was hard hit. Behind Givenchy the artillery of 55 Division had remained in place when its infantry came out for a well-merited rest.[208] Shell-fire continued to fall on the gun positions until about 4.00pm: 275 Field Artillery Brigade alone lost 11 guns and 2 howitzers, and 7 officers and 77 men on this day. Many battery positions and artillery headquarters were rendered untenable, forcing a number of moves to take place at the very time that the infantry needed maximum support.

Just after 8.00am, with visibility still only about 150 yards, German infantry advanced under cover of a creeping barrage. They were, as on 9 April, in overwhelming numbers, the troops of three divisions moving against 1 and 3 Brigades of 1 Division. The men of 1 Division did not have the benefit of knowledge of the ground, nor had they had the opportunity to rehearse their defensive measures, both factors that had been so crucial in 55 Division's defence of Givenchy. The right-hand companies of 1 Black Watch of 1 Brigade were quickly overrun by German infantry following very closely behind their barrage. Within minutes the garrisons holding Givenchy Keep and Moat Farm – both barely recognisable heaps of rubble – were engaged and suffered very heavy casualties. The attackers moved quickly to seal the entrances to the tunnel system, cutting off the reserves of A and C Companies and the counter-attack platoons that were sheltering in it. Yet somehow the few men holding Givenchy Keep held out, even though they were down to just nine men (they were later reinforced by Lieutenant Addison and six more troops). Moat Farm also held out against numerous German attacks, as did the companies on the left, facing northwards across the open ground towards Le Plantin. Enemy efforts against the 1 Loyal North Lancashires on the canal bank came to very little, with men being cut down not only by fire from the battalion but also by fire coming across the canal from the 2 Royal Sussex and 1 Machine Gun Battalion. There is also some evidence that the German artillery was firing short, killing men in Givenchy and affecting the route of reinforcements. By mid-day the attack on Givenchy had run its course. At a terrible cost in lives, the Germans had captured the crater field, saps and trenches east and north-east of the village but had failed to penetrate the line and were still an awfully long way from Béthune. The severity of the fighting can be judged from the Black Watch casualties of 15 officers and 366 men: more than half of its trench strength.

The fighting on the front of 3 Brigade was not dissimilar in that the German attack failed to achieve anything like a breakthrough, but a number of key posts were lost, notably the much-embattled Route A Keep. Major John Guild, second-in-command of the 1 Gloucesters, recalled that a German *Feldwebel* was taken prisoner near Cailloux Keep just before the attack. He had been out spotting positions for trench-mortars and provided much useful inform-ation about enemy intentions.[209] Knowing what was coming, the battalion officers ran through the arrangements and briefed the men, taking steps to evacuate prominent posts where they could. Although visibility was poor, the Gloucesters enjoyed excellent fields of fire and had plenty of ammunition. Some anxious hours were spent under the tremendous bombardment, being soaked in gas and the deafening noise of shell explosions being joined by that of falling buildings. At 6.30am the German gunners shortened their range and concentrated on the Village Line, the Tuning Fork and the roads back to Gorre. All communications were cut and both battalions in the line – the other being the 1 South Wales Borderers – relied on runners. When the German infantry advanced at 8.15am, the line of Very lights that they fired for com-munication to their own artillery gave the game away, and the Gloucesters opened fire. B and D Companies were able to report that 'the Huns were making no headway and the Old Braggs [the Gloucesters] had got their tails well up'. The trouble was that A Company at Le Plantin, where Le Preol Wood approached the front line, had a breach in its defences.

Sergeant 9359 Randolph Brassington noted in his diary, 'The initial bom-bardment was terrific and a section of about 80 yards of breastwork in front of Le Plantin was entirely demolished.'[210] By the time the enemy infantry came on, this gap had been opened to about 200 yards, cutting A Company in two and offering the Germans the opportunity to enter the line and roll it up. Enemy troops poured through the breach in the first rush, soon getting into the orchards and buildings of Le Plantin. To assist them, German field artillery brought up a number of guns to point-blank range to the south of Festubert. A flank defence was hurriedly organised by Lieutenant John Hall, the fire from which halted all attempts to put more men through the gap. Later Hall led a bombing party forwards, inflicted severe casualties and restored the line.[211]

A little to the north Festubert Keep was blown to pieces; of the small garrison, only eight men survived. Among them was 19-year-old Second Lieu-tenant Godfrey Hudson, who staggered back to Battalion HQ to report but was shell-shocked and incoherent. He was killed there by shell-fire.[212] Although the Gloucesters at the Cailloux North and South posts were causing mayhem to the German attack, parties filtered down the Route A track and captured the Keep. Of the South Wales Borderers' garrison of 70 men there, 50 had become casualties by the time the Germans arrived. From the Keep the attackers were in a position to fire on the left rear of the Gloucesters on the line down from Cailloux to Festubert. CSM 5820 William Biddle made the 1,200 yard journey, under shell-fire the whole way, back to Battalion HQ to report the situation and ask for help. There was little to give, except for a party of signallers, cooks, orderlies and batmen. They worked their way to the north end of Festubert and joined the defence. Biddle must have had a charmed life, for he made the trip to headquarters and back three or four times during the day when all other runners failed to get through. Among many incidents during the staunch defence mounted by the dwindling Gloucesters, a shell exploded in the dressing station, killing and wounding not only the medical staff but several men who had already been hit. The medical officer, Lieutenant Fairey, was among those affected, being buried by debris. The shell-fire and general situation at one point caused Lieutenant-Colonel John Tweedie to move battalion headquarters; all paperwork was destroyed and the last two pigeons released. The battalion sadly recorded that one bird flew towards the enemy, while the other was hit by a shell before it had flown 50 yards. It must have seemed a miracle that the Germans on the left suddenly gave up, for parties were seen retiring in disorder along the road to Neuve Chapelle. The South Wales Borderers, who believed they had killed or wounded a quarter of the attacking force in its efforts to press on to Loisne chateau, also began to report that the enemy seemed to have lost direction and men were seen wandering aimlessly around the battlefield. Soon after they too reported that groups of enemy were seen walking back in the direction of Rue des Chavattes. German troops who had been sheltering in craters and behind any cover they could find in no-man's-land also began to crawl or run back to their lines. The Gloucesters reported that they were shot down in scores as they did so. Few prisoners were taken; one man, a German American, turned himself in at Cailloux Keep, 'his hands in his pockets and a large cigar in his mouth, and announced to our nearest men that he was "thoroughly fed up".'[213] A combined party of 2 Welsh, 1 Gloucesters and 1 Cameron Highlanders finally cleared German snipers and detachments from Le Preol and reconnected with the garrison of Festubert. In all, 7 officers and 176 men of the Gloucesters were casualties of this action; the battalion was relieved by 2 Welsh during the night.

The shelling of 3 and 4 Divisions along the canal began at 2.45am, confirming what a number of prisoners had said about a forthcoming attack. As a result, 11 Brigade, the reserve unit of 4 Division, was ordered to move forwards just after 3.00am and 3 Division did the same by ordering 8 Brigade up 2 hours later. The working parties that 4 Division had out across the canal were prudently withdrawn, leaving only the machine-gun outposts on the north bank. The divisional artillery also responded to the German fire, putting a 5-minute burst on pre-arranged locations every 15 minutes.

The German 18 Reserve Division began to form up against 3 Division around 5.00am, but its assault was feeble and made no impression. It was withdrawn from the battle line next day. To the north of this, however, 4 Division faced a much sterner test. At about 4.00am the outposts of 10 Brigade's 2 Seaforth Highlanders, west of Pacaut Wood, were overcome. Few men got away to tell the tale. Pressing on to the canal, the Germans attempted to erect a pontoon crossing but were hit by strong fire from the 1 Royal Warwickshires. The attack was quickly abandoned, leaving many dead and 130 prisoners in the hands of the Warwickshires. By about 6.15am the infantry action was all over and the artillery fire died down by 8.00am, leaving the rest of the day quiet.

Ultimately 239 Division's attempt against 12 Brigade met a similar fate, but it had made a promising start when, after a severe bombardment, assault parties infiltrated into a gap between B and D Companies of the 1 Royal Lancaster Regiment between Pacaut Wood and Riez du Vinage. Turning south, they surrounded much of D Company from its left rear. Elements of B Company made a fighting withdrawal to the canal bank, but found on arrival that their bridge had been demolished. A few who could swim, and small numbers who were dragged across by rope, were the only men who escaped as the Germans advanced. The rest were killed or captured, including Company Sergeant-Major 5824 Victor Batty, a regular Boer War veteran with 20 years' service.[214] On the battalion's left C Company held its line while the remainder of the battalion fell back through Riez du Vinage. Herbert Cooper was among the men withdrawing. He recalled being told that his platoon had been surrounded and to make for a small house. It turned out to be already packed with British troops, whom Cooper thought were waiting to give themselves up. Gradually things quietened. The men did not surrender and the enemy did not approach the house, although there was much firing during the day. At 8.15pm 2 officers and 100 men were organised and counter-attacked through Riez du Vinage behind a barrage, recapturing their original positions. The German attempt to cross the canal had been held.

Most of 61 Division's front to the north of 4 Division was not heavily shelled, with the exception of the area held by 184 Brigade. Special targets were Bacquerolles Farm and the Brigade HQ in St-Venant asylum, both of which came under fire from 1.15am. German infantry quickly seized White's Farm, just 400 yards from Bacquerolles. A section of 20 men of the 2/5 Gloucesters under A Company's Sergeant 240397 Edward White was ordered to retake it before a larger-scale attack developed. They did so with alacrity, killing more than their own number of enemy and taking 17 men prisoner. Other than for a minor advance south of Bacquerolles Farm, in which the Germans established a new machine-gun post, the attack on 61 Division came to an end until

8.15pm, when the divisional artillery broke up what appeared to be an assembly for a further attempt.[215]

Some 30 miles to the north Fourth Army's efforts against the Belgian–British line in front of Ypres came to an ignominious end. Ordering 6 Bavarian, 58 and 83 Divisions to renew the attack, von Arnim had decided that should insufficient progress be made, the offensive would cease until all preparations had been completed for a fresh assault at Kemmel. That sector was now changing hands. Just before midnight on 17/18 April Plumer confirmed that de Mitry's DAN would assume responsibility for the Kemmel front at mid-day on 18 April.

During the night the Belgians side-stepped to relieve 30 Division and the left of 36 Division, and they would face the brunt of any fresh German effort, but no meaningful attack developed. The Bavarian Division was not sufficiently composed after its setback against the Belgians to go in again, and 83 Division was delayed in reaching its deployment area.

The remainder of the British line did not face concerted attack but the whole area remained under shell-fire for several miles to the rear of the front line. Lieutenant Archibald Macgregor was a Royal Engineers signals officer attached to 27 Brigade HQ. His experience of the day was not untypical of that of men behind the line:

> Ryan had acquired a Triumph motor bike. I no longer had the illicit 2.75hp Douglas that I used at the end of the Somme retreat. I don't remember what became of it. Ryan and I were left at Spoil Bank until it was taken over by Captain Skinner (12 Royal Scots) as a Company HQ. Then, after daybreak, we both got away on the Triumph, I being on the carrier. It was a ghastly experience of bone-shaking vibration on the shell-pocked pavé roads. Brigade HQ had moved to the Scherpenberg ... where we found them in a collection of Nissen huts between the hill and the road to the north-west. At breakfast I learned from Oddie that a shell had recently landed on one of the Nissen huts, killing three senior officers – one the Staff Captain of 26 Brigade – and a padre. Hardly had we finished breakfast when we heard a dreadful crash nearby. Rushing out we found a HV (high velocity) shell had landed on one end of a Nissen hut where some of the Signals Section were asleep. Three of them had been killed and two badly wounded. While we were getting the bodies and wounded removed another shell landed and wounded Ryan, hit by a fragment. He was taken to a CCS and we never saw him again. I did not see him, but think he was hit in the foot. This was very bad luck for Ryan, but fortunate for me, as I inherited his Triumph bike. We got

the Signal Office transferred to a tunnel in the hill which was already occupied by 26 Brigade and some Frenchmen. The transfer was a nerve-racking business as HV shells, unlike the more common run of shells, gave no warning of their approach – they just burst. Slower shells could be heard approaching and one could usually judge how close they would be on landing, and, if necessary, fall flat (and the flatter the better!). Later in the day Hall, the Staff Captain, and I went to look for a suitable new HQ at a safe distance from Scherpenberg. Hall selected a farm (we were in almost undamaged country) a little to the north-west of the road. The farm was abandoned and shut up, so we proceeded to break in by way of a shuttered window. We found ourselves faced by an enormous hound, which seemed larger than a Great Dane!! However, he proved quite friendly, so all was well.[216]

For the German high command, 18 April was a moment of vital decision, taken in an atmosphere of deep disappointment. 'Georgette' and 'Tannenberg' had now both failed in their objectives and the spectre was raised of the Flanders campaign being dragged into the awful attritional fighting of past years. The French had attacked on this day on the River Avre down near Amiens and there was a serious possibility that German momentum and initiative were being lost. Sixth Army was now reporting that it had not the resources to break through to Béthune; Fourth Army believed that 'Tannenberg' was an overstretch and represented a risk now that German troops were in tactically inferior positions in many places. Ludendorff tended to agree. Operations were closed down on the Sixth Army front: 'Georgette' was over. 'Tannenberg' likewise was called off but orders were given for one more operation. One key spot, the Kemmelberg, remained almost within reach, and it could, if captured, not only greatly improve the tactical situation for the Germans but could yet bring on a British collapse at Ypres. Von Arnim was ordered to make full preparations for the assault, to take place on 25 April.[217]

Chapter 9

Kemmelberg

25 April – Feuerwalze

Late on 18 April, having not yet heard the full story of the debacle of the failed attack against the Belgians, Ludendorff agreed with von Kuhl and von Lossberg that the Guard Corps would continue its offensive against Ypres and that XVIII Reserve and X Reserve Corps would capture Kemmelberg. Overnight the situation became clearer and early next morning the Guard Corps operations were called off. Only local adjustments would be made, with the objective of occupying the bank of the Steenbeek. This decision meant that, for the while, Ypres was safe from attack from the north and east. Not so Kemmelberg, for von Lossberg ordered three of his divisions to move from the Ypres salient down to join the force that would mass for the attack now fixed for 25 April. These were 13 Reserve, 19 Reserve and 233 Divisions. These relatively fresh formations would join another eight divisions and make full preparations for the capture of the Kemmel massif and, if possible, to cut the Poperinghe–Ypres road beyond it. Once that was achieved, the British and Belgians would have little choice but to evacuate Ypres and the Guard Corps would then advance to complete the capture of the town.

Today's battlefield visitor to Ypres, having moved a little way from the increasingly built-up town and down to pleasant Zillebeke or St Eloi, will see Kemmelberg from a distance of 5 or 6 miles. It is a whale-backed hill, the only really noticeable high ground to the south. By the time the traveller has moved a little closer, perhaps to Wytschaete, Kemmelberg looms above. From far to the south the picture is similar. Kemmelberg is easily visible from Alfred Hull's trench raid position way down at Fleurbaix and from most points on the Lys battlefield. There is nothing like it in this flat country as far south as the Vimy and Lorette Ridges some 25 miles from Kemmelberg. It is dominant, making for a difficult tactical situation for the German forces now at the foot of the slopes and their irrepressible desire to capture it. Before the war the hill's tree-shaded lanes, winding their way to the belvedere look-out tower at the summit, made for a pleasant afternoon outing. By April 1918 it was riddled with dug-outs and deep shelters and the tower had long since been fortified as a key observation post, but the wooded and country aspect remained. After the German attack the hill resembled the all-too-familiar

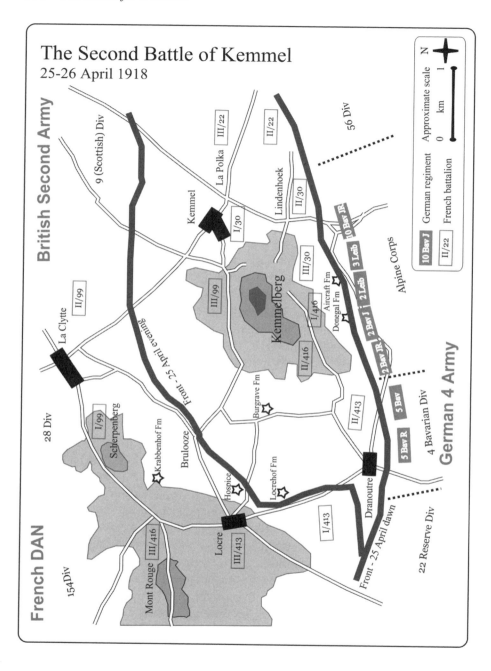

The Second Battle of Kemmel
25-26 April 1918

landscape from Passchendaele: crater after water-filled crater, endless mud, and the sad remains of tree trunks stripped bare of branches and foliage. The former belvedere was reduced to a pile of bricks and concrete barely as tall as a man.

The French front line now ran (from left to right) from the northern bank of the River Douve just south of Dranoutre, then along the Wulverghem road past Brain Cottage, Donegal Farm and Aircraft Farm, turned to the south of Lindenhoek and then ran along the Spanbroekmolen road. The German front complied with the French, but at all points was on marginally lower ground. Their entire front was overlooked from the heights behind the French front, with the summit of Kemmelberg, just half a mile away, being some 150 feet higher than the general lie of the front line. Kemmelberg is broadly oval-shaped but has a secondary peak on its south-west face; this height, which is about 50 feet lower than the main peak, is known as Little Kemmel and the higher summit as Great Kemmel. The south-eastern face slopes down to a plateau which stretches out through Lindenhoek towards Spy Farm and Vroilandhoek. Von Lossberg wished XVIII Reserve Corps to mount a preliminary operation to capture this plateau, since enemy troops on it could fire down and in enfilade across the German front at Aircraft and Donegal Farms – in other words the key central sector for the attack on Great Kemmel itself – and this possibility simply had to be eliminated. Initially he believed this should be done two days before the main attack, but resistance from the corps, which truthfully believed that preparations would be incomplete and that it would signal to the Allies that an attack on Kemmel was imminent, persuaded him instead to bring the capture of the plateau into the main attack but starting just 15 minutes earlier in that sector.

Ludendorff came to the Fourth Army planning conference on 21 April. Among the details to emerge, X Reserve Corps was ordered to undertake a small preliminary operation to capture the Hille Farm–Scantling Farm Ridge. This was another tactical improvement before the main assault, removing the possibility of enfilade fire coming from this slightly higher ground which is south-west of Dranoutre.

The German preparations for the attack were once again prodigious: 290 artillery batteries, of which 128 heavies and super heavies were hauled into position, together with enough ammunition for a sustained heavy bombardment; eleven divisions of infantry took their places and a fleet of 318 aircraft gathered at nearby fields. Despite the disappointments of recent times, as the days went by morale began to improve; high command was confident. On 22 April Rupprecht ordered that if the Kemmel attack went well then advances on the left and right shoulders of the attack front should follow. With Sixth

Army also being advised to maintain pressure on Givenchy and Festubert, the tempo once again began to increase as the hours ticked down to zero.

In the intervening 'quiet' period, the weather had turned colder and there were occasional snow flurries. The operational tempo died down considerably, although there were some localised actions. De Mitry set about reorganising the various divisions and corps now making up DAN. Under General Charles Nollet, XXXVI Corps now comprised 34 and 133 Divisions, with 2 Cavalry Division in reserve. Robillot's 2 Cavalry Corps was given command of 28 and 154 Divisions in the vital Kemmelberg sector, with 3 Cavalry Division in reserve. De Mitry, headquartered now at Esquelbecq, retained control of 39 Division and 6 Cavalry Division. Foch finally replied to Haig's request for three more divisions, and while explaining that this now added up to a requirement for eight, he believed he had delivered six and the Belgians had also enabled one British division and brigade to be relieved. In other words, Haig now had seven divisions and a brigade in reserve. The fact that these formations had been all but destroyed and amounted to very little by way of fighting power was glossed over. Foch also wrote to Wilson to enquire about the possibility of using British marines to defend Calais; the timing was not good, for the Admiralty was about to launch its surprise attack from the sea at Zeebrugge and gave a firm veto to Foch's idea. Petain was ordered to release some more divisions from the south, to move generally in the direction of the Somme and to support any action in the Arras area. He was less than impressed with this continued frittering away of French arms, especially when confronting a possible enemy attack on the Somme or Montdidier. Haig remained exasperated, thinking that Foch was acting in a piecemeal, rather than strategic, fashion. Cracks were beginning to show in the unified Allied command, and further German assaults could only propagate them.

Haig and Plumer were mulling over the best way to defend the north and to maintain touch with the Belgians should the enemy renew their attack on the salient. Despite building deeper defensive lines and placing reliance on salt-water inundations, they agreed that the best way to proceed was an active defence; taking action to restore the line and capture Wytschaete, Spanbroekmolen, Méteren, the ground forwards of the Nieppe Forest and, later, Neuve Eglise. The time would come when these operations came to be, but that would turn out to be some time in the future after many more thousands of Allied lives had been lost to the German offensive.

At this time a new system of warning of hostile attack made its appearance in Second Army. The codeword 'Alpha' was a precaution for 'Beta', which signalled that the enemy was expected to attack. The latter would trigger all moves and preparations for the defence scheme, and in many cases meant that men were positioned in places of safety when the German shell-fire started. It was not necessary to issue detailed orders at this late stage. Garrisons of front-line posts would be thinned out to a minimum and all the reserves, engineers, pioneers, transport men and details would take up positions in trenches and posts echeloned in depth. By the time the enemy came on he would be facing a prepared defensive system several thousand yards deep. It was not quite Jeudwine's inspired 'Bustle', but it saved many lives and helped inflict defeat on Ludendorff's offensive.[218]

Heavy shell-fire was a daily occurrence on the whole front during the lull but nowhere more so than in the Nieppe Forest and Kemmel areas. There were many local actions too. On 19 April 4 Division mounted an attack to improve the tactical position at Riez du Vinage. Undertaken by the 2 Essex, it was immediately effective but fighting continued until 23 April. Next day the 1 Northamptonshire Regiment recaptured ground lost on 18 April at Givenchy; the 1 South Wales Borderers also prised Route A Keep out of German hands, only to have it taken away from them on 22 April. Two days later 55 Division had occupied the line again and promptly regained the Keep, once again employing the Liverpool Scottish. The Australians twice attacked at Méteren and 4 (Guards) Brigade went into action at Beaulieu Farm. Robillot's Cavalry Corps completed the relief of IX Corps by 21 April, giving the British 19, 25 and 34 Divisions a respite for the first time since 'Georgette' began. On the Kemmelberg front the German 22 Reserve Division captured Hille Farm, while a French attempt to improve its position at the Lindenhoek–Donegal Farm sector did not succeed.[219]

It was quite apparent that the Germans were going to attack Kemmel; only the date and time were unknown. Air reconnaissance reported artillery being massed on the Kemmel front and specific infantry preparations were spotted near Dranoutre. On 24 April the Alpine Corps had been identified, signalling their move from north of Ypres. A prisoner taken by 9 Division told of the forthcoming attack; all units were placed on the alert but other than making sure their dispositions were wise and that ammunition and reserves were ready, there was little to do but wait for the onslaught.

On the German right XVIII Reserve Corps had four divisions in the assault front (7, 13 Reserve, 19 Reserve and 56 Divisions) and X Reserve Corps on the left had three (Alpine Corps, 4 Bavarian and 22 Reserve Divisions). The attack frontage ran from the Comines Canal down to Haegedoorne, with the dividing line between the two corps running from Wulverghem to the east of Lindenhoek. The first objective set for this force was to reach a line running from the southern end of Dickebusch reservoir along the Vijverbeek to Paul Burgrave Farm and on to the northern edge of Dranoutre.[220] As the main force pressed on in the centre, flanks would be held from the reservoir to Lock 8 on the Comines Canal and along the line from Krabbenhof Farm (north of Locre) to the Scherpenberg hill and Reninghelst. The reserve divisions (3 Guard, 233, 214 and 10 Ersatz Divisions) would then leapfrog through and push on 4 miles northwards to cut the Poperinghe–Ypres road west of Vlamertinghe. This required the capture of Kemmelberg and, on the right, an advance down the valley slope from Wytschaete and up the opposite side to Vierstraat and beyond. This area was covered by enfilade fire from the hill and was well within British artillery range from the batteries arrayed along the Ypres–Vierstraat–Kemmel road and the Ypres–Dickebusch–La Clytte road beyond that. It was an ambitious plan but with the powerful force assembled and the parlous state of the opposing British divisions, it was one that seemed feasible as long as French resistance could be overcome. The French position, despite the clear advantage of holding Kemmelberg and being able to shelter reserves behind it, was not at all easy. In particular, the front line was close to the hill and gave no room for tactical withdrawal without losing it. There was no 'battle zone' here unless one was prepared to sacrifice Kemmel, and no one on the Allied side was. For the French 28 Division in particular, it was another case of holding the front to the last man. The French divisions were comparatively fresh, but it should be borne in mind that 28 Division had been one of the formations affected by mutiny following the April 1917 offensive on the Chemin des Dames. As late as January 1918 there were incidents of men singing anti-military songs at their officers and attending anti-patriotic talks. Although the fragile state of the French army's morale had been kept strictly secret, and was unknown to the majority of British and certainly the German commanders, in retrospect there were questions about their will to defend against overwhelming attack. Without doubt, the French troops provided a clear answer.

With little room for manoeuvre behind them, the French divisions manned the forward zone in strength, with troops either in the front line, in close support positions behind on the forward slope of Kemmelberg or just beyond the summit. From right to left two battalions of 413 Regiment held the Dranoutre line, with the third in reserve at Locre; one of 416 held Donegal Farm–Aircraft Farm with another on Little Kemmel; then two battalions of 30 Regiment took the line on through Lindenhoek with the third behind Great Kemmel; and finally two battalions of 22 Regiment went on to the junction with the British 9 Division near Spanbroekmolen. Relatively small deeper reserves – two battalions of 99 Regiment of Infantry and one of 416 – were arranged and positioned at La Clytte and behind the Scherpenberg and Mont Rouge.

Precisely on time at 2.30am on 25 April the German guns opened up. The pattern was now that familiar from 21 March and 9 April: employing high explosive laced with prodigious quantities of poison gas, the artillery targeted the Allied batteries, roads, dug-outs, headquarters and communications. It was, as before, instantly effective in destroying the Allied ability to command and communicate, and had a serious effect on its artillery. Once again the area was blanketed in fog, made even thicker by the smoke and dust thrown up by the bombardment. For 2 hours the shells rained down on Kemmelberg and beyond; it was, as men had experienced before, a continuous, inhuman, pulsing roar of explosions that were impossible to distinguish. No words could factually describe such a phenomenon. Descriptions of such drumfire ascribe to the bombardment a living quality. Peter Ingwerfen said it 'growled, cracked and roared, hissed and burst, as though a primeval giant danced'.[221] Below it, French and British troops died in their hundreds, and thousands of others quaked in the dubious safety of their dug-outs. A half hour's pause was then followed by another hour of destructive fire on the French and British front lines, with shells also continuing to sweep the rear. At 5.45am on the left and 6.00am on the right the firing switched to a creeping barrage behind which the German infantry could advance. The 15-minute difference was to allow for 56 Division to capture the Lindenhoek–Vroilandhoek plateau before the Alpine Corps and 4 Bavarian Division on their left rose to join them in the assault. During the morning they carved three serious breaches in the defences and were well on their way to their objectives. One commentator used a metaphor of the French drowning in the flood of the German assault.[222]

The experience of the French units holding the Kemmel front was similar to that of the dazed British and Portuguese units in the fog of 9 April. Captain Rolland, commanding 9 Company of 30 Regiment to the right of Lindenhoek, reported:

> The first waves of enemy having been sighted in the smoke, my two sections in the front line open fire. The enemy stops and installs machine guns. A gun battle ensues between the sections. I send many red rockets to call our artillery barrage but there is no response. Shortly after I saw the enemy advancing in the *thalweg* to our left in the area of 11 Company, threatening to take in the rear my two reserve sections. Some men make to escape, but are killed or captured, and these sections were particularly suffering from the bombardment, for I have seen, subsequently, no man leave the trenches.[223]

On the German right parties from 88 Regiment had crept out into no-man's-land and taken up positions in shell holes while French heads were being kept down by the barrage. On the signal they quickly advanced, surprising the garrison of French 22 Regiment, and infiltrated into weak spots. Stiff machine-gun resistance in some posts meant that the French front line was not completely in German hands until 7.00am. The junction with 9 Division was broken through, and La Polka and Kemmel village encircled and eventually captured.

Rolland's 30 Regiment was similarly attacked, by 3 Leib Regiment and 10 Bavarian Jäger of the Alpine Corps, in the centre of the French line. Here the assault units made full use of trench-mortars and flamethrowers in their advance, and parts of the front ruptured very quickly. The French garrison near Spy Farm appears to have been badly knocked out by the bombardment and a breach into its line soon developed. By 7.30am the Germans had got behind the survivors fighting from the forward posts and were advancing up the hill.

> Seeing as we were so completely surrounded, the sections attempted then to escape in small groups. Some men were stopped by me near the command post and continued the fight. I tried to encourage my little company, saying that the counter-attack will come [and] rescue us. But the enemy waves unfurl increasingly dense on each side and in the end overwhelm our small group. During my journey through enemy lines [into captivity], I heard the explosion of five or six rounds of French 75s.[224]

The men of 416 Regiment, holding Aircraft and Donegal Farms, had all of their machine-gun posts destroyed by the bombardment, although, as in other sectors, some posts held on and fought most bravely despite being surrounded. Germans were now pouring up the hill. The troops of 1/30 Regiment, held in a counter-attack position to the north-east and down a steep slope from the peak of Great Kemmel, took up their planned defensive positions by 7.00am. Although to some extent enveloped before they could mount a concerted counter-attack as a unit, many elements provided fierce resistance to further German penetration. In particular, 3/99 Regiment, holding the summit, had been badly affected by the bombardment and could barely summon up enough men for a serious defence. Around 8.10am 2 Company of 10 Bavarian Jäger Reserve under Leutnant Arns captured the ruins of the belvedere. Many French detachments were captured in the warren of dug-outs as the German advance moved on down the northern slopes. Perhaps naturally, some German detachments also veered left, following the high ground.

At the same time elements of 2 Bavarian Jäger had reached to within 200 yards of the peak of Little Kemmel, by way of a sunken lane behind Aircraft Farm, whose garrison had been killed by the shell-fire. Here, however, 2/416 Regiment, which had been held in reserve just over the hill, mounted a stiff resistance and carried out two counter-attacks, both repulsed. Gradually the garrison holding Little Kemmel was reduced and eliminated; the defenders were now under fire from Grand Kemmel, attacked frontally by 2 Bavarian

Jäger, and now in flank by 2 Bavarian Jäger Reserve, which had advanced to the west of Donegal Farm and turned inwards. The final resistance, at the very entrances to the dug-outs, was around 11.45am. At about the same time the survivors in a key command post located in a British tunnel (long since out of communication except by pigeon), being used by 30 and 416 Regiments and various other detachments, were forced to surrender. It was over. The unthinkable had happened. The capture of Kemmelberg was a superb feat of German arms, certainly to be ranked among their finest exploits of the war. Some 8,200 prisoners, 53 artillery pieces and 233 machine guns fell into German hands.

To the French right the Germans exploited a large gap that had opened up as 4 Bavarian Division infiltrated up the Hellebeek Valley east of Dranoutre. The French 2/413 Regiment on the west bank soon lost touch with its left-hand neighbour 416 Regiment, cutting 154 Division in two. Turning left and right as they advanced, the assault companies soon encircled and destroyed the French front-line posts. Around 9.30am 6 Company of 2/413, which had been kept in reserve and held the Brulooze–Dranoutre road, mounted a counter-attack which slowed the enemy advance but ultimately proved fruitless. Despite strong resistance from 1/413 in Dranoutre, the way was now open for a German advance on Locre, Brulooze and the Scherpenberg, and the slopes of Little Kemmel were gradually cleared of resistance.

With reports showing that the attack was apparently proceeding according to plan, by 9.00am von Lossberg was pepping up both of the corps for the continuation on to the objectives, and telling the Guard Corps to get ready for an advance on Ypres. Kaiser Wilhelm II was already claiming victory by 11.30am, saying that the battle was over: 'We have the hill.' In contrast, Ludendorff remained nervous of counter-attack and von Lossberg consequently instructed his units not to go too far forwards without suitable artillery support. There was little chance of an immediate counter-attack in strength, for there were no formations of suitable size within striking distance. But during the day there were disconcerting air reports of Allied columns on the move; an intercepted British wireless message revealed that a stand would be made on the line La Clytte–Vierstraat, and prisoners talked of reserves in the Poperinghe area. Von Lossberg instructed the corps to prepare for counter-attacks and to bring forwards the second-line divisions. It is perhaps inevitable, given this caution but also as units became terribly intermingled by fighting through the craters and dug-outs on Kemmelberg and lost communication with increasingly distant command posts, that the advance on Scherpenberg should slow.

The shock of the loss of Kemmelberg caused friction, fright and a certain amount of denial on the Allied side. Brigadier-General William Monkhouse, commanding 19 Divisional artillery in support of the French front, lost a number of his guns when the German infantry advanced so rapidly:

> The Germans actually arrived among the guns of 87 and 88 Brigades [RFA] before they could be seen and my men took them on hand to hand, and in some of the batteries removed the breech blocks and were able to hide them so as to prevent the Germans from using them. .... An airman flew over us and dropped a message, 'We have retaken Kemmel.' By this time the fog had cleared. I could see the top of the hill covered in French soldiers. It appears that when the Germans attacked, the French got into the tunnel which had been made for OPs through the hill. The Germans drove them out and stuck them on top of the hill to prevent our shooting at it. Arrived back at French Divisional HQ, I report 'Mon General, Kemmel est perdre.' With his head in his hands he remarked, 'Mon General, c'est un accident, mais ce n'est pas – pas un accident – tres grave'! As from the top of the hill one could see the coast from Ostende to Dunkirk, I agreed to differ.[225]

The capture of Kemmelberg was a sweet and encouraging moment for the German high command. A real bastion of the Allied defence had fallen. At 2.30pm von Lossberg ordered 10 Ersatz Division forwards to continue the push, and by 3.15pm was telling the Guard Corps that it was almost sure that Ypres would be evacuated. This was not to be, although by day's end the German advance had met and surpassed its objectives on the Kemmel front. Dranoutre was captured and the line pushed forwards almost to Locre hospice and across to Brulooze crossroads. However, on the German right, it fell far short of the initial objective.

On the left of the French the troops of 9 Division held the front south of Eikhof Farm on the Dammstrasse and had been joined by Lewis gun detachments from 5 and 13 Tank Battalions. When the Germans attacked, the division had all of its brigades in the line.[226] The sector next to the French was held by 27 Brigade, from Lagache Farm to Black Cot, then the line was taken on by 146 Brigade to North House, then by 64 Brigade to Dome House, and finally by 26 Brigade to Eikhof Farm. On the far right 12 Royal Scots held a 2,000-yard line adjacent to the French 22 Regiment. Behind the front the division had taken the opportunity to strengthen the Vierstraat and Cheapside lines, although work had been hampered by heavy shell-fire falling on the whole area between 18 and 24 April, which was manned by the reserve battalions of each brigade. Confronting the division were more than three German divisions: from the British right to left, they were part of 56, 19 Reserve, 13 Reserve and 7 Divisions.

Divisional communications were soon broken by the German bombardment and once SOS rockets were seen on the French front, the few reserves available were ordered to stand by at Vierstraat and Cheapside. The enemy's assault hit the right of the division at much the same time as the French 22 Regiment, and the 12 Royal Scots came under extreme pressure from their right and then, as the attack developed, from their right rear. Every trench-mortar and a number of the battalion machine guns had been destroyed by the shell-fire, and the rightmost company was soon surrounded and the men killed or captured. By 7.00am the 6 King's Own Scottish Borderers in the Vierstraat line were also being engaged by elements of the German 88 and 78 Reserve Infantry. Soon afterwards a message confirmed that enemy troops were just 300 yards from Siege Farm, well over a mile north-west of Lagache Farm – a testament to how quickly the German infantry could move. The rest of the Royal Scots continued to fight from their original front, attacked from front and flank, until at 8.30am the few remaining men slipped away to the Cheapside line. Next in line to the Royal Scots, the 1 East Yorkshires encountered small parties of Germans coming over Black Cot Ridge from about 7.00am. Battalion headquarters was soon surrounded and cut off from its forward companies; Lieutenant-Colonel James Coles organised his staff and details into two groups of about twelve men each, who fought the enemy off for nearly 2 hours, sniping at them as they appeared over the ridge. By 8.30am German machine guns had arrived, covering an advance down the slope past Petit Bois and Wytschaete Woods. The remnants of the battalion were obliged to retire as best they could towards Vierstraat; in doing so only 3 officers and some 30 men escaped. Coles was among those killed.[227] The 6 King's Own Scottish Borderers lost almost all of its two forward companies and battalion headquarters in the same engulfing advance. The remnants of this unit also moved to the Cheapside line and there held on, joined by the 9 King's Own Yorkshire Light Infantry, the tank Lewis gunners and companies of 11 Royal Scots, 9 Durham Light Infantry and 8 Black Watch. This gradual increase in strength on the line enabled it to be stretched out and held to La Clytte, and the Black Watch and King's Own Scottish Borderers mounted some successful counter-attacks, taking between them more than 120 German prisoners.

Archibald Macgregor had been sent out from 27 Brigade HQ to repair the line to the Advanced Report Centre at Siege Farm, encountering as he worked some of the King's Own Scottish Borderers withdrawing to Cheapside:

> About this time I saw Corporal Bishop and Sapper Young coming across a field north-east of the road – they had been manning the Siege Farm Report Centre. Bishop said they had just managed to get away before the farm was overrun, bringing what instruments they

could carry and destroying the rest. Then, to my horror, I saw some KOSB straggling back along the road (some French poilus were also doing the same). The KOSB arrived in ones and twos. I made them fall in beside the road as they arrived, until there were a dozen or more, including a sergeant wearing the ribbon of the DCM. I think this encounter must have been about half a kilometre or a bit less, towards Beaver Corner from Millekruis. The men were dazed-looking but quite docile and in no way panic-stricken. At the time, of course, I did not know what an ordeal the KOSB had been through. I had seen some people beside farm buildings a bit north-east of the road, so went across with a view to putting the KOSB under the command of an officer there. I don't remember who these people were, but a major who appeared to be in charge simply would not pay the slightest attention to what I was saying – he just kept looking through his field-glasses. So I returned to the KOSB and decided there was no alternative but to lead them forwards myself until we encountered the rest of their battalion. This prospect scared me stiff, as I had no training in infantry battle tactics. Then, to my extreme horror – this was NOT 9 Division behaviour – I saw a KOSB officer (a second lieutenant) strolling back. Horror or not, it was indeed a great relief to me! I stopped him, told him I was one of 27th Brigade STAFF (which of course I wasn't technically) sent forwards to find out the position, informed him that I had seen a message saying the line was holding and ordered him to lead the KOSB stragglers back to the line – and off they went! I remember there was a dead Lewis gunner on the road not far away; I should have ordered the officer to get the gun and ammunition, but didn't do that. He would have done it himself if he had had any guts. Fortunately, I did not know the man. He survived. I saw him once in Edinburgh.[228]

Half of the 7 Seaforth Highlanders had only just arrived at the hutted Surrey Camp (near the southern end of Dickebusch reservoir and on the German objective line) after being relieved, when they suffered casualties from the bombardment at 2.30am. They were now in reserve for 26 Brigade, holding the line north of Wytschaete, and joined the defence of the Vierstraat line before going into deeper reserve near Ouderdom once things had settled down. The enemy attack broke just as heavily on the 8 Black Watch and 5 Cameron Highlanders holding the front line. The remainder of the Seaforths, C and D Companies, were in close support. The outposts of the Cameron Highlanders in the area of the Dammstrasse were obliterated by the shell-fire; the main body, holding The Mound–Piccadilly sector, came under strong infantry attack but held it. The two companies of the Seaforths extended a flank as planned, connecting up with 9 Scottish Rifles in the Vierstraat line. They had a grandstand view, as the British and French positions on their right gave way, of enemy transport and guns coming over the Wytschaete Ridge and up the Vierstraat road unmolested and unhindered. Messages sent to the artillery, delivered by runners who had to negotiate a long and terribly hazardous trip, brought no response.

About 2.00pm touch between the Scottish Rifles and Seaforths was lost, forcing the latter to form almost a right-angle-shaped defence around Piccadilly Farm. It was an extraordinary situation, maintained through two concentrated bombardments in the afternoon, until a withdrawal was ordered at 7.45pm. It was enough for the day, ensuring that the enemy intentions in the Vierstraat–Dickebusch area were frustrated. Some ground had been given up, but nowhere near sufficient to force Plumer to think about evacuating Ypres. Brigadier-General John Kennedy was in command of 26 Brigade and accurately summed up the day's fighting in this area:

> If this stubborn defence had not prevented the enemy from widening his gap, the results might have been disastrous to the Ypres salient. The taking up of a defensive flank by the Seaforths under the conditions of the battle was itself an operation of which a well trained regular battalion might have been proud – it was carried out by a Kitchener battalion which had a few days earlier absorbed large drafts of 18-year-old boys.[229]

In addition to the staunch 9 Division and the improvised French defence, the German attack was slowed by incessant British and French artillery fire on the slopes down from Kemmel to the north. As the infantry pressed on, once again the weakness of German transport and logistics would mean that artillery and engineering support dwindled, with guns unable to move forwards to maintain a creeping barrage and the destruction of Allied strong-points. One commentator saw the effect at close hand:

> I was stationed in Advanced HQ close to the French artillery for some time near Poperinghe. Their enthusiasm was remarkable. They seemed to fire almost without intermission. And at times the enemy guns were more haphazard in firing than was usually the case. Back areas were shelled indiscriminately and with very questionable success. No doubt the situation was as dark, if not darker, to them as it was to us.[230]

Muddled and delayed orders to the Alpine Corps also led to a slowing momentum: the situation was not perhaps quite 'dark' among the German commanders but the fillip of taking Kemmelberg was certainly tempered by disappointments elsewhere. Orders were given to reorganise and start again at 8.00am.

The next day Haig met with Plumer and his excellent chief of staff, Major-General Charles Harington, at Cassel at 1.30pm. He noted in his diary,

> The French 28 Division did not fight well. We all thought Kemmel almost impregnable. Yet the place was abandoned after 2 hours' fighting. General de Mitry commanding the Cavalry Corps in Second Army had to employ French cavalry to collect the French fugitives from Kemmel, and prevent a rout. What Allies to fight with![231]

26 April

Plumer had been pressing de Mitry to counter-attack to regain Kemmel from mid-afternoon on 25 April, but, just as on the German side, communication delays and units not being ready led to a delay until 3.00am. The French 39 and British 25 Divisions were added to Robillot's corps and took up a position facing Kemmelberg and Kemmel village respectively in order to undertake the operation. On the flanks the French 154 and British 49 Divisions would also undertake covering operations. Orders filtered down to the British brigades by 8.25pm and small patrols went out under cover of darkness to ascertain exactly where the enemy front now lay. As the assault units moved up to their places of assembly, it began to rain. Exactly at zero hour, it turned into a downpour that soaked the men and turned the churned battleground quickly to notorious, glutinous Flanders mud. The Kemmelbeek and Vijverbeek, which were the initial objectives on the front of 25 Division, swelled and presented a serious hazard to the assault. To compound things, once again a thick fog descended in the early hours. Field artillery support was to be provided by the guns of the British 38 Division and those of the French 154 and 39 Divisions; the latter, though, had not completed assembly by zero hour. This no doubt contributed to what was reported to be a very feeble creeping barrage, behind which the infantry were meant to advance at the slow rate of 25 yards a minute. The thinness of the shell-fire had an unusual effect, in that the enemy did not believe it to presage an infantry attack and were surprised when it came on. Unfortunately this proved to be just one component in an attack that soon went wrong and caused unnecessary loss of life.

On the left of the main attack 74 and 7 Brigades of 25 Division struggled to keep up with even this slowest of barrages and soon lost its protective cover. Nonetheless they pressed on, incurring only moderate casualties, and were on their first objective by 4.35am and 5.00am respectively. The 3 Worcesters and

9 Loyal North Lancashires of 74 Brigade, after overcoming enemy machine-gun posts and stiff resistance at RE Farm, pushed on through the ruined Kemmel village and engaged in house-to-house fighting. Companies of the reserve battalion, 11 Lancashire Fusiliers, were ordered up to close gaps that were appearing on the left and a small party under Second Lieutenant Maurice Walker advanced well beyond Kemmel. But it now became increasingly obvious that the French division and 7 Brigade had not kept up on either side and that 74 Brigade was advancing into a deepening salient. Walker's group held its position for an hour before he decided to withdraw, and by 9.30am he had joined the rest of the brigade which had now regrouped on the railway line crossing the La Clytte road, north of the stream. In making the withdrawal, the units suffered heavier losses than in their original advance but they dug in and held the position. The brigades took many prisoners from the German 56 Division, who were reported to be of poor morale but better than average physical specimens.[232]

Unfortunately 7 Brigade's attempt to advance from the Vijverbeek was hampered by 49 Division on its left not making progress, with enemy fire from front and left causing casualties and disruption. All three battalion commanders were hit, their places being taken by junior officers: in the case of the 4 South Staffords, a lieutenant. This brigade also withdrew, suffering casualties as it did so.[233] The attack by 49 Division was a shambles of late orders and of touch being lost between battalions. Crucially, while 7 Brigade was advancing, on their left the 1/4 Duke of Wellington's halted – as told they should when they lost contact – on the Cheapside line, leaving 7 Brigade completely exposed and inevitably affecting 74 Brigade alongside.

On the right the assembly of the French 39 Division was also late and ragged. It did not begin to advance until 3.30am and ran immediately into devastating fire from the Alpine Corps units holding in front of Kemmelberg. By 8.15am it had been ordered to hold on to the small gains it had made and to dig in. It had, at least, added some strength to the scattered and thin line of French detachments that were in the area, having retired from the Kemmelberg fighting only hours before.

The Allied counter-attack made little impression upon von Lossberg's preparations for the renewal of the attack at 8.00am but when it was added to the logistical disorganisation resulting from the previous day's fighting, it helped ensure that the advance of the Alpine Corps and 56 Division amounted to very little. The German artillery bombardment did not open as ordered, and units were still sorting themselves out when they should have been advancing. When the fog eventually lifted, troop assemblies were hit by Allied fire and went to ground. It was on the two flanks of the attack that more intensive and successful action took place: on the French right 4 Bavarian Division attacked at Locre, where there was to-and-fro fighting throughout the day, during which the hospice changed hands twice. At day's end it was once again in French hands, although nearby Locrehof was lost.

On the left the German 13 Reserve and 7 Divisions renewed the attack on the British line from Vierstraat to the Comines Canal. The latter division quickly broke through the outposts on both banks of the canal, reaching the spoil bank some 1,000 yards into the British position on the south side, and attacking the Bluff on the north. Losses to the garrison, made up of the 16 Manchester Regiment (30 Division) and the 39 Divisional Composite Battalion, were severe. Elements of the reserve 2 Bedfordshires and 1 West Yorkshires were rushed to the key Bluff position, and intense fighting went on for several hours before the Germans finally captured the height.[234] The assault by 13 Reserve Division between Vierstraat and Voormezele fell on the tired 26 Brigade, which was about to be relieved, and more elements of the 39 Divisional Composite Battalion. Fighting was also severe in this sector, intensifying at around 2.30pm when a terrific bombardment heralded a renewed infantry attack. At great loss to both sides, the only German territorial gain was of part of the outpost line from Voormezele to the Bluff.

In the middle of the day things had looked very black to Plumer, and with Haig's endorsement of his authority to withdraw from Ypres should it become necessary, Plumer's decisions were vital to the outcome of the day. If the Bluff fell, the way was open to a short advance on Ypres; if the enemy also pushed on from Kemmelberg, Second Army was in serious danger of envelopment. Plumer disposed his reserves during the day to ensure that the line could be held in front of Ypres as far as possible, but also forestalled an enemy advance after the fall of the town by manning defensive lines through Brandhoek and Vlamertinghe. He did so at the very time that Foch was imploring Haig not to consider a withdrawal from Ypres; the Generalissimo even offered – perhaps threatened is more accurate – to travel to the area if Haig felt he could not conform. During the afternoon Haig met with Henry Wilson and Lord Milner, making it clear that they must persuade Foch to allow the replacement of all British troops between Méteren and the Belgians by French ones. In conjunction with de Mitry, Plumer's staff organised further lines of defence, as far back as Abeele and Boeschepe well to the west of Poperinghe. Plumer also took steps to withdraw deeper into the Ypres salient during the afternoon, leaving only a thin outpost screen on the Pilckem Ridge. The British army was now holding on, almost literally, to the ramparts of the old town. Foch ordered Petain to send more artillery and aircraft to Flanders and handed control of the French 31 Division to DAN.

As it became evident to Fourth Army that its troops had not yet broken through at the Scherpenberg or Ypres, von Lossberg decided to postpone further action until 27 April. Arrangements were made to bring three extra divisions to the front in order to press on. Interestingly, XVIII Reserve Corps demurred at this order. Believing they needed more time to reposition the artillery, bring up ammunition, relieve tired units and generally get organised, they requested a delay of an extra two days.

The last day

No major action took place while Fourth Army gathered its strength for another assault, but the whole area remained on the alert with much artillery fire and gas bombardment. Down at Festubert, Route A Keep was once again the scene of fighting, with this time the victors being the 1/5 South Stafford-shire Regiment. The 10 East Yorkshires, rebuilt after their near-destruction at Doulieu by the receipt of large drafts, also mounted a successful action at La Becque. There was also a good deal of localised fighting for tactical advantage at Voormezele and Ridge Wood. More high-level discussion also took place, during which Foch and Clemenceau firmly rebuffed the idea of retirement to the Dunkirk inundations and insisted that the Flemish hills be held. There would be no voluntary retirements, the French and British divisions would stay in close touch and the Channel ports would be held.

As both sides took advantage of the lull to change a number of divisions holding the line, it is necessary to briefly review the situation prior to describing Fourth Army's assault. The front now ran from Méteren across the north of Bailleul, where it was held by the French 34 Division almost as far as the Douve Valley. On their left came 154 Division, still holding the Locre sector, and then 39 Division taking the line on to La Clytte. Behind this French-held sector were the western peaks of the Flemish hills: Mont Noir, Mont Vidaigne, Mont Rouge (marginally the highest at 460 feet) and the Scherpenberg. The British sector had no such natural defence behind it; the ground runs flat to Dickebusch and beyond to Poperinghe and Vlamertinghe. It was now held by a series of brigades, not necessarily under command of their original divisions: from right to left they were 75 Brigade along the Kemmelbeek, then 147, 148 and 28 to Vierstraat; 89 Brigade held the line from in front of Ridge Wood to behind Voormezele.[235] From here a main line of resistance was held by 110 Brigade almost to the Comines Canal, from where it was picked up by 18 and 16 Brigades around Ypres itself. These brigades also threw out an outpost line in front of Voormezele and arching round to the western edge of Zillebeke reservoir. Time also gave the opportunity for more artillery to be brought up. Guns were arrayed in depth along the shallow valley of the Grootebeek running south-westwards from Vlamertinghe. Every means of concealment was used and most batteries did not fire to register. They remained unsuspected by the enemy until it was too late. Most of all, the day would mark a significant victory for the gunners and for the Army Service Corps and Royal Engineers who quietly went about their business of supply and signalling.

Facing the 10-mile Allied line was a force of eight German divisions with a further five in close support. On the right 236 and 7 Divisions stood north of the Comines Canal, with 13 Reserve and 36 Divisions opposite 110 and 89 Brigades down to Ridge Wood; 233 Division faced the remainder of the British-held line; then came the Alpine Corps and 4 Bavarian Division, still in place after the capture of Kemmelberg, and finally 22 Reserve Division south of the Douve. All of these formations were identified by prisoners and the increasing number of German deserters who crossed no-man's-land. The situation on the German side was not entirely happy, the assembly being constrained again by lack of transport and this time a shortage of gas shells. The work of the Allied artillery in firing on roads and known positions took its toll, disrupting the work of assembly and causing losses prior to the assault. It was clear that the Allies were expecting something and for once the attack would be made without the benefit of fog, for the day dawned cloudy but perfectly clear.

The action, as ever, opened in darkness at 3.00am with a heavy bombardment on the Allied positions but in this instance it was not the paralysing high-explosive shelling of before, but mainly of gas. After 2 hours the guns directed fire for 40 minutes on the Allied front from the Douve to Zillebeke. While the Allied artillery responded on the German front and known battery positions, the gunners along the Grootebeek held their fire. Their moment came at 5.40am when the German infantry began to advance.

Fourth Army's tactical objectives were the line Ypres–Vlamertinghe–Reninghelst–Westoutre–Mont Rouge, with aspirations once again to cut the main Ypres road beyond and force a withdrawal from the salient. At no point did the advance remotely achieve this. After a day of severe losses, the only German gains were another bulge into the Allied line in front of the Scherpenberg and a minor advance near Voormezele, both positions being on the flanks of the attack. In the centre the assault met with a bloody repulse. It had walked into a trap: dismay and death came early to this assault, as the British artillery – completely unexpected – opened up, laying down a curtain of fire on no-man's-land and the German front-line system.

The primary German gain near the Scherpenberg began with a rapid advance by the Leib-Regiment of the Alpine Corps in the area of Fairy House and the Brulooze crossroads, in which two companies of the French 156 Regiment were overwhelmed. Things had not been helped by the regiment carrying out an adjustment of its company positions during the night, which was only completed late and under the German bombardment. The strength of the German force had been whittled away by French fire, with many Germans losing their lives, particularly in front of Butterfly Farm and the railway line at

Pompier. The loss was to prove decisive. The German break-in, between Fairy House and the Hellebeek stream, was exploited by a swift movement towards the 'col' between the Scherpenberg and Mont Rouge, 1,200 yards distant, at which was a road junction known as Canadian Corner or Hyde Park. The now-familiar tactical doctrine was followed as detachments fanned out on both sides of the breach, wiping out the French detachments holding the front lines by attacking from the rear from about 8.00am. The reserve sections of 6 Company fell back towards the Scherpenberg, joined by the reserve 5 Company, and took up a defensive position at the sunken crossroads some 600 yards north of Brulooze and east of Hyde Park. On their right 9 Company in reserve, which had been in the small wood at La Couronne and holding another sunken crossroads behind it, suddenly found itself under attack. Within minutes the two sides were engaged in bayonet and hand-to-hand fighting in the wood, from which few Frenchmen escaped. The remnants of 9 Company withdrew northwards and gained touch with what was left of the rest of 156 Regiment, now holding a south-facing line from 200 yards north of Fairy House across to 200 yards north-east of Hyde Park, with the summit of the Scherpenberg just 300 yards or so behind. From this strong position it was able to pour machine-gun fire on the attempts of Leib-Regiment to advance to Hyde Park and eventually made contact with 154 Regiment on the Mont Rouge. Mown down by crossfire in these last yards of the slopes, the Germans could advance no more. On the right parties pushed through Locre and Krabbenhof Farm towards Mont Rouge, but a similar gradual gathering of French reserves and a number of localised counter-attacks halted any further advance. During the afternoon the French divisions mounted further attacks that drove the Alpine Corps back down the slopes and out of most of Locre. In the early hours of 30 April the rest of the village and the hospice were secured.

The situation between the two hills appeared most critical to the French command during the morning. De Mitry ordered his deep reserves, 27 and 32 Divisions, towards the area by 8.00am and by 10.00am 31 Division was preparing to make a strong counter-attack. It would not, thanks to tenacious fighting by the reserve units on the slopes, be needed. Only 10 minutes beforehand the British 25 Division had received the alarming message from the French 39 Division that the Germans had captured both Mont Rouge and Mont Vidaigne; they passed the news on immediately to XXII Corps. Plumer and Haig heard within minutes; a message also came from Foch himself that the Scherpenberg had fallen to the enemy, prompting Plumer to prepare the order to evacuate Ypres. Haig's Chief of Staff, Lieutenant-General Herbert Lawrence, proved imperturbable, suggesting to Plumer that while GHQ had no more reserves to give him, he should wait for clarification of the situation, and remarked that things were never as bad as they might seem. It was good advice: a fresh message came from the French at 10.55am, contradicting their original statement. Arrangements that had already been made by 25 Division to form a defensive flank were cancelled (although it took a while for it to be communicated to all units) and Plumer never did have to make the headlines by quitting Ypres.

The effect of the German attack against the British sector south of Voormezele can perhaps best be judged by the fact that the war diary of 25 Division says 'all quiet by 12 noon'. The assault had been little short of disastrous. Machine-gun and trench-mortar posts that had escaped the relatively short and patchy bombardment opened up as soon as the German infantry showed themselves; they were joined by the guns along the Grootebeek. British reports talk of the Germans being in massed formation, with bayonets fixed, echoing the tactics – and casualty rates – of earlier years. 25 Division alone repelled four distinct attempts to advance. In places, notably on the front of 89 Brigade, where the German bombardment had been heavy and accurate, there was a harder fight in which casualties were great but no inroads were made into the British line. XXII Corps found that it did not need to call on its reserves. The German artillery livened up again about 5.00pm and some efforts were made to renew the attack but with the same effect.

By 7.00am reports from the forward units gave the impression to von Lossberg that the rate of progress was slow and that Allied resistance was proving stronger than expected. In mid-morning he discussed the situation with Ludendorff and both concluded that the action should probably be broken off. Orders for the 5.00pm attack were given, but in the event the efforts were weak and halted by determined Allied fire. At 10.20pm, after discussion between Ludendorff, von Kuhl and von Lossberg, orders were given that the offensive would not be resumed. The Battles of the Lys were over.

Chapter 10

Retrospective

I see the English press is beginning to talk as though we had won a great victory, or at any rate as though the danger were over. Oh Fools and Blind; the Hun offensive is only just begun, and we must be prepared for another equally violent offensive. The 'Morning Post', I think, had a heading: 'German *defeat* on the Lys', which is really about the limit!

Captain Harry Graham, 40 Division staff.[236]

There is no doubt that the Allies inflicted a serious defeat on the German army in Flanders in April 1918. The von Kuhl/von Wetzell logic of applying the accumulated German strength to destroy the British army was abandoned. Never again did Ludendorff launch a major offensive solely against the British, for all attentions now began to turn to operations against the French. Not until 1940 did German forces strike again in Flanders, although there was a serious plan and preparations made to do so – Operation *Hagen* – from May to July 1918. On 30 April, and indeed for many weeks afterwards, the German army had the scale and capability to launch several more major offensives and Allied commanders remained wary of their intentions well into August, by which time the initiative had swung the Allies' way. A terrible irony is that when the Germans struck in force on the Chemin des Dames on 27 May 1918, at the very centre of the attacked front were a number of British divisions that had been so badly mauled in Flanders that they had been sent there to recuperate.

The defeat in Flanders was of a strategic nature; time, men and resources that the Germans could ill afford to lose had been squandered. No strategic goal had been achieved. The territorial gain had served only to extend the line being held and to place the German army in a tactically difficult salient. It is true that the British had suffered severe losses and several divisions were completely or temporarily disabled, but Allied resources had not yet been so badly injured that their defensive ability had been crippled. Of itself, failure on the Lys and in the Flemish hills was not sufficiently damaging to cause Germany to give up, but in combination with ultimate defeats on the Somme, Marne and Metz it contributed significantly to a collapse of morale and fighting capability.

Tactically the German offensive had superlative elements, notably the ability to squeeze infantry into gaps, employ light machine guns with great effect and to exploit the breaches by fanning out and destroying resistance on either side. The effect of deep artillery fire, neutralising the Allied ability to respond at the vital moment and causing huge disruption to command, control and supply, was, in the early phases, of supreme importance. But by no means were these tactics universally applied and the threat and performance of ordinary 'trench' divisions was nowhere near that of the 'attack' formations. Throughout the battle, for every nimble group of *stosstruppen*, the defenders encountered massed groups of infantry and in many cases inflicted the same grave proportions of casualties that had been the case since 1914. The British, and later the Allies, began to learn to deal with the German tactics in 'Michael' and continued the development process in 'Georgette'. They were given breathing room to do so by Germany: the fact that the German forces were largely unmechanised and were suffering from a shortage of horses took away mobility and any ability to exploit breakthroughs made at the sharp end. By the time they had gathered their strength for a renewed attack, the Allies had prepared themselves to defend again.

Operationally and strategically, the German high command made a significant contribution to its own defeat. The force assembled was not as strong as that for 'Michael' and was not given time to make sufficient preparations. Divisions were kept in line, hammering away for too long, day after day, without respite. The attack frontage became narrower from 12 April onwards, and operations were broken off increasingly quickly when there were many instances where one more determined push might have brought results. Most crucially, the initial north-west thrust towards Hazebrouck was abandoned and attention moved to Ypres, just at the time when the brilliant strategic prize of Hazebrouck was within reach. This decision cost Germany the battle. While Plumer came close to giving the orders for a complete and humiliating withdrawal from Ypres, it is doubtful in retrospect that even such a retirement would have led to a British or Allied collapse. If the goal of the reorientation of the German offensive was the strategic encirclement of the British and Belgians, pressing them back towards the coast and Dunkirk, it would have taken a larger and much more mobile force than Ludendorff had available in April 1918.

The British in Flanders can be accused of complacency in that the defences had been allowed to deteriorate in the very sector where untried or tired formations were sent to hold the line. It was asking for trouble. The doctrines of zone defence were not yet applied and in some corps were insufficiently understood; there was confusion about whether positions should be elastic and ground could be given up, or whether a line should be held at all costs. It is not possible to do both of these things. With the exception of 55 Division's stand at Givenchy, where tactics had been defined and practised in advance, the Allies were forced to improvise once the original line had been pierced. German delays after 18 April offered the opportunity for a more considered reorganisation, which, coupled with a much greater emphasis on holding a line with no voluntary retirement, brought Fourth Army to a standstill.

When the German offensives began, the British army was in the process of a considerable reorganisation, not only moving to a three-battalion brigade structure but dealing with the concentration of machine-gun companies into battalions. The Lys gives little opportunity to assess the genuine operational and tactical impact of these changes. The improvised nature of the defence meant that units rarely fought as such, with battalions being split into companies and companies into platoons that were often sent to different places or commands. Where they did fight as a unit, the machine-gun battalions were a great success, offering the opportunity to concentrate fire where it hurt. Many brigades fought almost as independent commands; no doubt there was many a time when a brigadier-general would have given much for a fourth battalion in reserve, and certainly the smaller formations meant that individual units and men would remain longer in the front line than was good for them. The army was well served by its unglamorous backbone during the battle, and the fact that it could do so is testament to Haig and the hard work by many in developing the army's capabilities in these areas since 1915. The supply, transport, administrative, medical, training, ordnance and other services rarely let down the units going into action.

It is an interesting academic exercise to reflect on how the battle would have played out had the advice of the Supreme War Council been adopted early in the year. A single strategic front, with a well-deployed general reserve commanded by a central body with no national interests at play, is intellectually strong. One wonders to what extent the reserves would have been rushed to oppose 'Michael', perhaps playing into von Kuhl's hands and leaving the Lys even more exposed than it was. In the event Foch's instructions brought sufficient reserves to bear in Flanders, even if it was hugely exasperating to Haig and Pétain. In this author's opinion, Foch's influence on the battle was a key factor in the defeat of the enemy. His firm and oft-repeated doctrines brought a nervelessness, a steel, to high command, where all too often Haig and Wilson were looking at withdrawal and a demand for more and more men. In such a situation someone had to draw a line – and Foch did so.

But neither the German shortcomings nor Foch represent the central reason why the Battles of the Lys were won. Countless were the occasions where positions were held, or delay and loss inflicted on the enemy, simply through personal bravery and a bloody-minded will not to be beaten. The telling of this story has hinged upon many tales of individuals doing extraordinary things; they are but a tiny proportion of the whole. The battle was won by the many thousands of junior leaders, NCOs and men, a proportion of whom were just 18 years old and in action for the first time, coping with improvised circumstances and doing their bit. Those who survived would form an experienced and capable backbone to the Allied victory of later in the year.

Appendix I

Phases of the Battles of the Lys

In 1921 the Battles Nomenclature Committee reported on its definition of the phases making up the Battles of the Lys and those formations that took part in each:

The Battle of Estaires, 9–11 April 1918
First Army
    XI Corps
        3, 51, 55 and 61 Divisions
        2 Brigade
        2 Portuguese Division, 3 Brigade of 1 Portuguese Division
    XV Corps
        29 Division less 88 Brigade, 31 Division, 34 Division less 102 Brigade, 40 and 50 Divisions, 74 Brigade

The Battle of Messines, 10–11 April 1918
Second Army
    IX Corps
        9 and 19 Divisions, 25 Division less 74 Brigade
        62, 88, 100, 102, 108, 147 and 148 Brigades

The Battle of Hazebrouck, 12–15 April 1918
First Army
    I Corps
        4 and 55 Divisions
        3 Brigade
    XI Corps
        5, 50 and 61 Divisions
    XV Corps (transferred to Second Army at noon on 12 April 1918)
        29 Division less 88 Brigade, 31, 33 and 40 Divisions
        1 Australian Division
        Composite Force comprising personnel from II and XXII Corps Schools, 2 New Zealand Entrenching Battalion, two companies of 18 Middlesex Regiment and the XXIII Corps Reinforcement Battalion

The Battle of Bailleul, 13–15 April 1918
Second Army
    IX Corps
        19, 25, 34, 49 and 59 (2 North Midland) Divisions
        71, 88, 100 and 108 Brigades
        South African Infantry Brigade

The First Battle of Kemmel, 17–19 April 1918
Second Army
    IX Corps
        19, 25, 33, 34, 49 and 59 Divisions
        71, 88, 89, 108 Brigades
        Wyatt's Force
    XXII Corps
        9 and 39 Divisions
        62 and 64 Brigades

The Battle of Béthune, 18 April 1918
First Army
    I Corps
        1 and 4 Divisions
    XI Corps
        61 Division

The Second Battle of Kemmel, 25–26 April 1918
Second Army
    XXII Corps
        9, 21, 25, 39 and 49 Divisions
        71 and 89 Brigades
French Détachement d'Armée du Nord (DAN)
    II Cavalry Corps
        3 Cavalry Division, 28, 39 and 154 Divisions
    XXXVI Corps
        2 Cavalry Division, 34 and 133 Divisions

The Battle of the Scherpenberg, 29 April 1918
Second Army
    XXII Corps
        6, 21, 25, 39 and 49 Divisions
        89 Brigade
        South African Infantry Brigade
        French Détachement d'Armée du Nord (DAN)
    II Cavalry Corps
        2 and 3 Cavalry Divisions, 39 and 154 Divisions
    French XXXVI Corps
        34 Division

Appendix II
Place-names

This list gives the modern Flemish equivalents of the French language place-names of 1918:

Brulooze	Bruiloos	Mont Vidaigne	Vidaigneberg
Dickebusch	Dikkebus	Neuve Eglise	Nieuwkerke
Dixmude	Diksmuide	Nieuport	Nieuwpoort
Dranoutre	Dranouter	Poperinghe	Poperinge
Hogenacker	Hogenakker	Reninghelst	Reningelst
La Clytte	De Klijte	St Eloi	St Elooi
Locre	Loker	Vlamertinghe	Vlamertinge
Merckem	Merkem	Westoutre	Westouter
Messines	Mesen	Wulverghem	Wulvergem
Mont Noir	Zwarteberg	Wytschaete	Wijtschate
Mont Rouge	Rodeberg	Ypres	Ieper

Notes

1. Lloyd George, *War Memoirs* (London: Odhams, 1936).
2. Hansard, 19 November 1917. Lloyd George had tried once before to place a British army under French command, when he subordinated Sir Douglas Haig to Robert Nivelle in early 1917.
3. NA, CAB25/127, Supreme War Council: British Secretariat: Papers and Minutes. Paper titled 'Historical record of the Supreme War Council of the Allied and associated nations from its inception on November 7th 1917 to November 12th 1918, the day after the signature of the Armistice with Germany, together with a note as to its role and work subsequent to that date.' Although the paper appears to have been assembled and edited by the head of the SWC Secretariat, Major (Temporary Lieutenant-Colonel) C. Lancelot Storr, parts of the text are taken from earlier work written by Leo Amery.
4. NA, CAB21/91, Formation of Supreme Inter-Allied Council. A paper written by Leo Amery, dated 21 November 1917.
5. Britain, France, Italy and the United States of America. The political participation of the Americans was weak throughout. President Woodrow Wilson did not attend the Sessions himself.
6. NA, CAB21/91, Proceedings of the Army Council, 12 November 1917, and War Cabinet reply three days later.
7. NA, CAB21/91, Formation of the Supreme War Council, discussion of the proceedings of the 237th Meeting of the Army Council four days earlier; War Cabinet 275, Minute 14, dated 16 November 1917.
8. *The Times*, 10 November 1917, p. 7.
9. *The Times*, 12 November 1917, p. 9
10. *The Times*, 12 November 1917, p. 9. Among the 'certain amateur strategists' were Lloyd George and Churchill.
11. Lloyd George, speech made in Paris on 12 November 1917, quoted in *The Times* on 13 November 1917, p. 7.
12. Wilson to John du Cane, 9 July 1918. IWM, Wilson correspondence, 2/36/4.
13. NA, WO158/57.
14. The National Archives holds many examples of papers submitted for consideration at this time, in CAB21, CAB25, WO32 and WO158. The Wake papers at the Northamptonshire Record Office also contain a selection of analyses.
15. NA, WO158/57.
16. NA, WO158/58.
17. Marshal Foch, *The Memoirs of Marshal Foch*, trans. Col. T. Bentley (London: William Heinemann, 1931).
18. The War Office reported that there were more than 607,000 A-grade British soldiers at home on 1 January 1918 but a large proportion of these were 18-year-old conscripts still in basic training. The law at this time did not permit overseas service before the age of 19. In

addition, more than 850,000 officers and men were serving in theatres of war other than the Western Front.

19. NA, WO158/72.
20. NA, WO158/57.
21. Gough, Gen. Sir H., *The Fifth Army* (London: Hodder & Stoughton, 1931).
22. The Rt Hon. Leo Amery, *My Political Life*, Vol. 2, *War and Peace* (London: Hutchinson, 1953).
23. Examples include Bruce I. Gudmundsson, *Stormtroops Tactic: Innovation in the German Army 1914–1918* (New York: Praeger, 1989); Robert T. Foley, 'Institutionalised Innovation: The German Army and the Changing Nature of War 1871–1914', *RUSI Journal* (April 2002) and Timothy T. Lupfer, *The Dynamics of Doctrine: The Change in German Tactical Doctrine During the First World War*, Leavenworth Papers No. 4 (Fort Leavenworth, Kansas: US Army Command and General Staff College Combat Studies Institute, 1981).
24. NA, CAB45/177.
25. Haig's diary, TS version, and also NA, CAB45/183. Wilson had already replaced Robertson as CIGS when the latter resigned, holding firmly to his principles and the belief that dual control of the army would lead to disaster.
26. Bugnet, Maj. Charles (ADC to Foch), *Foch speaks* (New York: Lincoln MacVeagh, 1929), p. 242.
27. NA, WO158/60.
28. NA, WO158/28. In his diary on 5 April Haig wrote that he thought the French were thoroughly tired and they had no intention of attacking as a way of helping the British.
29. NA, WO158/72.
30. NA, WO95/295.
31. NA, WO157–85, First Army intelligence reports.
32. George Brüchmuller developed new approaches to the use of artillery during his time on the Eastern Front. Giving each battery specific fire plans, the tactics were to hit the enemy with a surprise deep bombardment that concentrated first on its artillery, headquarters, roads and communications before adding fire on the front line that would be assaulted. The attack by the Eighth Army at Riga in September 1917 was in effect a dress rehearsal for 'Michael' and 'Georgette'.
33. NA, WO157–487, XV Corps intelligence reports. Prisoners stated that the tanks had been south of the area of 42 Division, which places them near Aubers.
34. NA, WO157–487, XV Corps intelligence reports. A prisoner belonging to 102 Infantry Regiment, captured on 3 April, stated that morale in his unit was low. Two Poles of 141 Infantry Regiment, taken on 12 April, reported that they had to move up to the line through dead bodies and smashed transport, destroyed by British harassing artillery fire on 7 April.
35. NA, CAB45/125.
36. IWM, 4258, sound recording by Stephan K. Westmann, a medical officer attached to an infantry assault regiment.
37. NA, WO157–487, debriefing of Polish prisoners of 35 Division.
38. NA, CAB45/123, First Army report GS1167, 6 May 1918.
39. NA, CAB45/122.
40. NA, CAB45/125.
41. NA, CAB45/123.

42. NA, CAB45/124, Brigadier-General Robert McCulloch, commander XI Corps Heavy Artillery.
43. Second Lieutenant Henry Pickering, who had been in charge of the Barnton posts, committed suicide on 9 March 1918. He is buried in Gorre British and Indian Cemetery.
44. NA, CAB45/122, in which Brind also refers to Jeudwine as 'General Judy'.
45. NA, CAB45/123 (Glover). It had initially been intended that 166 Brigade should move to the north of the 55 Division front in order to relieve a Portuguese brigade. As events were to prove, the fact that it did not do so was fortuitous.
46. NA, CAB45/122 (Beckwith and Brind) and CAB45/178.
47. NA, CAB45/180. At the age of 25 Briggs was already a veteran, having gone to France with the battalion in 1914. He came through the battle and the rest of the war unscathed.
48. NA, CAB45/178.
49. Meade was among the dead and is buried in Guards Cemetery at Windy Corner. Jeudwine unsuccessfully recommended him for a posthumous Victoria Cross.
50. *London Gazette*, 28 June 1918, p. 7618. Joseph Collin VC is buried in Vieille Chapelle Military Cemetery.
51. Newman was no stranger to the front line. He had already been awarded the Military Cross for rescuing two men, both of whom subsequently died, from a gas-filled dug-out. His activities on 9 April led to a Bar to his MC. The citation reads: 'For conspicuous gallantry and devotion to duty. While an intense bombardment was on this officer made his way to the trenches, three miles under heavy fire. He was captured by the enemy, and escaped. He was continually going about in the open under fire of all kinds, tending the wounded and organising parties of prisoners to carry them away.' *London Gazette*, 16 September 1918, p. 10899.
52. *London Gazette*, 28 June 1918, p. 7618. John Schofield VC is also buried in Vieille Chapelle Military Cemetery, very near Joseph Collin VC.
53. NA, CAB45/122.
54. NA, CAB45/124.
55. IWM, Private papers of E.M. Summers, 74/7/1.
56. *London Gazette*, 8 May 1918, p. 5556. Richard Masters landed in France in February 1915. He had already been awarded the Croix de Guerre and had recovered from a wound to his knee sustained in November 1917. He survived the war.
57. NA, CAB45/123.
58. NA, CAB45/123.
59. From his autobiographical work, *A brass hat in no man's land* (London: Jonathan Cape, 1930).
60. NA, CAB45/122. This problem continued throughout the day. Frederick Bewsher, GSO2 of 51 (Highland) Division, and Horatio Berney-Ficklin, Brigade Major of 152 Brigade, both recorded that their battalions had difficulty in distinguishing Portuguese from German troops, as they advanced from reserve positions and encountered troops coming towards them.
61. IWM, private papers of Lt Alfred Hulls, 03/57/1. Hulls spent the rest of the war at Pforzheim POW camp. 'Poor old Teddy Groves', 25-year-old Second Lieutenant Reginald Edward Groves from Plumstead, has no known grave and is commemorated on the Ploegsteert Memorial.
62. NA, CAB45/123. There are indications of some delay to the orders being given for 120 Brigade to advance, which may have had serious consequences.

63. IWM, 80/14/1, private papers of Cecil Eric Lewis Lyne. Lyne was awarded a Bar to his Military Cross for this action.
64. Jackson had only been in command of 50 Division since 23 March, Carter-Campbell since 17 March.
65. Captain George Cardew MC of 4 Devonshire Regiment, attached to 6 DLI, was killed later that morning. He has no known grave and is commemorated on the Ploegsteert Memorial.
66. There are unconfirmed stories of Portuguese troops taking the parked bicycles of the Cyclist Battalion to assist their retirement.
67. NA, CAB45/123. Captain F.I. Gerrard, 7 Black Watch.
68. NA, CAB45/122.
69. NA, CAB45/125. The GSO3 of XI Corps, and formerly of King Edward's Horse, Lieutenant-Colonel George Russell believed that 'but for this [transport] blunder' 152 Brigade might have been at Croix Marmuse at 10.00am rather than 11.40am. Although the advance of the Scots was taking them into unfamiliar territory, the fog was beginning to lift; one also wonders at the need to wait for guides to come back from La Couture and Huit Maisons. Two of the great 'what ifs' of the battle.
70. Milhais was eventually cut off and spent several days – most accounts say three – alone and living off food and water he found on the bodies of dead comrades, while he continued to operate a number of guns, known to the Portuguese as 'luisinhas', scrounging ammunition. A British officer, whom he found and saved from drowning in a swamp, reported his actions and Milhais was decorated with the military *Ordem de Torre e Espada*, Portugal's highest award for valour. He was the only soldier to win this award during the First World War. His battalion officer said to him, 'Your name is Milhais but your value is a million men [Milhões]'. The nickname stuck, and he was known as 'Mr Million' thereafter, his family even taking the name.
71. No. 2008 Private Albert Hartle was awarded the Military Medal for his actions, one of many honours earned by the King Edward's Horse on 9 April. Among them was no. 775 Sergeant Reginald Ewbank, who was recommended for the Victoria Cross but was eventually awarded the Distinguished Service Order. His citation identifies his action as being 'when the troop officer and senior serjeant had become casualties in hand-to-hand fighting. Although attacked by the enemy in force of about fifteen to one, he organised the defensive flank and held it for three hours. He showed magnificent courage and initiative in dealing rapidly with a succession of situations, each of which was critical.'
72. NA, CAB45/123.
73. Military Cross citation, *London Gazette*, 16 September 1918. Mackersy survived the war and returned to his home in Canada. He went on to become the first President of the Canadian Imperial Bank of Commerce.
74. An example is 255 Brigade RFA, which took over such a store at Le Cornet Malo.
75. The weather prevented flying again during the mornings of 10 and 11 April.
76. NA, CAB45/124.
77. NA/CAB45/125. Lieutenant-Colonel Edward de Renzy-Martin, commanding 11 Lancashire Fusiliers.
78. For no reason that the author could find, and thus presumed to be an error, some histories and maps refer to Le Séquenteau as Sequemeau. The ammunition shortage affecting 10 Ersatz Division was reported in *Die Bayern*.
79. Christie was a former ranker who had landed in France as a sergeant of the battalion in November 1914. He was commissioned in September 1915.

80. A heavy gas bombardment was also laid on the extreme southern flank of the German assault area, southwards of Annequin.
81. Despite the name, which harks back to the Middle Ages, Fort Rompu was a small village with no significant defences useful to 101 Brigade save for some very small posts along the Laventie road.
82. IWM, 77/3/1-3, private papers of Walter Adolph Vignoles.
83. NA, WO95/198.
84. NA, CAB45/122. Brigadier-General T. Astley Cubitt of 57 Brigade was the man who foresaw the potentially lethal traps for his men. He would later come to believe that he lost the equivalent of at least a company of each of his battalions in these deathtraps, which were built before 19 Division moved into the area.
85. NA, CAB45/123. Hamilton-Gordon was of noted melancholy disposition and was known in some circles as 'Sunny Jim'. The commander of 19 Division, former Grenadier Guardsman George Jeffreys, wrote of the marked difference between him and Plumer. The latter found an opportunity to visit Divisional HQ each day and 'it would be hard to exaggerate the good that these visits did in cheering us all up, giving us information and creating an atmosphere of confidence and encouragement. The personality of the IX Corps commander was a very different one. He too spent considerable periods in my headquarters but he always appeared to be in a state of gloom and depression.'
86. In view of the uncertain situation on the right, Divisional HQ had arranged during the night for the 6 South Wales Borderers (divisional pioneers), three Royal Engineers field companies and half of the 2 South Lancashire Regiment to move up to the river loop, where they dug in near Le Bizet.
87. NA, CAB45/122.
88. NA, WO95/1765.
89. Birt was awarded a Bar to his Distinguished Service Order for his actions on 10 April, and Gent, who was commissioned in June 1918, a Distinguished Conduct Medal.
90. The Australian engineers had been under orders to prepare for the demolition of the Royal Engineers' storage dump at Steenwerck in the event of further enemy advance.
91. It is often quoted that this facility was large enough to hold two battalions. This is not likely to be the case. Engineers' drawings and reports suggest it may have housed 600 men.
92. NA, CAB45/123.
93. NA, CAB45/123.
94. Dougall, who is buried in Westouter British Cemetery, was awarded a posthumous Victoria Cross: 'Capt. Dougall maintained his guns in action from early morning throughout a heavy concentration of gas and high-explosive shell. Finding that he could not clear the crest owing to the withdrawal of our line, Captain Dougall ran his guns on to the top of the ridge to fire over open sights. By this time our infantry had been pressed back in line with the guns. Captain Dougall at once assumed command of the situation, rallied and organised the infantry, supplied them with Lewis guns, and armed as many gunners as he could spare with rifles. With these he formed a line in front of his battery, which during this period was harassing the advancing enemy with a rapid rate of fire. Although exposed to both rifle and machine-gun fire this officer fearlessly walked about as though on parade, calmly giving orders and encouraging everybody. He inspired the infantry with his assurance that "So long as you stick to your trenches, I will keep my guns here." This line was maintained throughout the day, thereby delaying the enemy's advance for over 12 hours. In the evening, having expended all ammunition, the battery received orders to withdraw. This was done by man-handling the guns over a distance of about 800 yards of

shell-cratered country, an almost impossible feat considering the ground and the intense machine-gun fire. Owing to Captain Dougall's personality and skilful leadership throughout this trying day, there is no doubt that a serious breach in our line was averted. This gallant officer was killed four days later whilst directing the fire of his battery.' *London Gazette*, 31 May 1918.

95. One company of the 9 Royal Welsh Fusiliers appears to have held its front at Denys Wood and not been attacked at all, while men to left and right were pushed back. The 7 Seaforth Highlanders reported that they only withdrew through the Seaforths' outpost line in the early hours of 11 April.

96. IWM, 86/9/1, private papers of W.G. Wallace.

97. NA, CAB45/123.

98. IWM, 88/56/1, private papers of H.W. House.

99. NA, CAB45/125. Robertson gives 'Dents Wood' but this is likely to be an error for Denys Wood.

100. The 7 Gordon Highlanders of 153 Brigade relieved the King Edward's Horse at Fosse at 5.30am.

101. This officer was made a Knight of the Military Max-Joseph Order, one of only 237 such awards made during the war, and became Paul Ritter von Hermberg as a result. The citation says: 'Obltn. Hermberg on his own initiative volunteered to provide artillery support for a night coup de main against the Lawe crossing. According to his own personal reconnaissance, effective intervention was only possible if a gun could be positioned in front of our pickets and only 250m away from the enemy strong-point, which was generously equipped with machine guns. Under the cover of darkness, this was achieved with great effort and caution. The sudden opening of fire from this gun so utterly surprised the enemy that the Stormtroops of 23 Bavarian Reserve Infantry lost not a single man.' He carried out a very similar action on 11 April. *Bayerns Goldenes Ehrenbuch, 1914–1918*, p. 28.

102. NA, CAB45/123. The poor artillery support mentioned by Dick-Cunyngham and in a number of war diaries conflicts with notes from the personal diary of Captain Frederick Jack, the reconnaissance officer of 51 Divisional artillery. He noted on 10 April that ammunition arrived in quantity during the morning, the enemy's guns were quiet and with quite a few targets to engage, he was kept busy. It is difficult to reconcile such differing views of the same action.

103. NA, CAB45/124. Morpeth was taken prisoner the next day.

104. Pont Levis appears to be a British mistranslation. The words mean 'lifting bridge'; the actual name was Pont d'Estaires, even though it was at that time well outside the town. Having no connection with the river of that name, 'La Meuse' at Estaires dates back to a fisherman's inn of bad repute seen on a map of 1550. Built in 1850, a lifting bridge with adjacent auberge 'A la Meuse' was on the site before the war but was destroyed in October 1914 and replaced with a wooden structure.

105. The water tower appears to have escaped destruction during the battle. The newspaper or parish bulletin *Voice of Exile*, published from Loudes in September 1918 for Estairois people who had fled and were now refugees, reported that 'Un soldat cantonné au Mont des Cats, dans les premiers jours de juin, a vu, à l'aide d'une lunette, le château d'eau encore intact'.

106. *London Gazette*, 28 June 1918. Poulter was discharged on 7 October 1918 as a result of his wounds.

107. IWM, sound recording, 19073.

108. NA, CAB45/122. The signals officer of 15 Brigade (5 Division) encountered large numbers of Portuguese troops 'still hurrying westwards' near Thiennes on 12 April. Thiennes is 14 miles from the front line of 9 April.
109. IWM, 92/19/1, private papers of Frank Parker. Frank was killed in action in the North Russia campaign on 22 March 1919.
110. IWM, 77/3/1–3, private papers of Walter Adolph Vignoles.
111. IWM, 80/14/1, private papers of Frank Glover.
112. Wace was killed on 14 April 1918.
113. Lieutenant-Colonels Sholto Ogilvie of the 1 Wiltshires, who had begun his army career as a ranker; Williams of the 10 Cheshires and Finch of the 4 South Staffordshires.
114. NA, CAB45/122. The officers concerned commanded all three brigades of 34 Division plus 88 and 147, attached.
115. Pacaut is given on modern maps as Pacault.
116. NA, CAB45/123. In the same letter this officer recalled how mustard gas droplets hung around in the leaves of trees in the Nieppe Forest, rendering latrines dangerous to use when the droplets fell on to them.
117. IWM, 74/7/1, private papers of Victor Fagence.
118. NA, WO95/18, one of many files to include a copy of this order.
119. On 16 April the Baroness, still in Paris, learned that the chateau had been pillaged. Two days later she received a letter from Beauvoir de Lisle, by then having replaced du Cane in command of XV Corps, to the effect that the chateau had been shelled but that he had sent his ADC to rescue some of her collection.
120. IWM, P457, private papers of Alfred Thomas.
121. IWM, sound recording, 12231.
122. IWM, 80/32/1, private papers of Geoffrey Christie-Miller.
123. The GHQ order defined La Motte as a point on this line and implied that the eastern edge of the Nieppe Forest would be given up.
124. Whenever the weather permitted, aerial activity and ground support remained important features of the battle. The RAF also continued to bomb the railways and roads well behind German lines.
125. The name derives from an oral legend of the burial-place of an Irish soldier, dating back to the Spanish Netherlands and the time of Louis XIV.
126. There is a curious inconsistency in the records with regard to the precise location of 152 Brigade HQ when it was captured. Dick-Cunyngham himself says Le Cornet Malo, as does his GSO2 Horatio Berney-Ficklin (both NA, CAB45/122); the brigade war diary says the western edge of Riez du Vinage, yet quotes a trench map reference on the eastern edge (Scot Farm). Frederick Bewsher, author of the divisional history, has it on the eastern outskirts of Riez. The Official Historian ignored the remarks from Dick-Cunyngham and Berney-Ficklin made when they reviewed a draft of the history in 1931. Riez du Vinage is over a mile and a half from the German start line. The fragmented nature of this fighting can be judged from the fact that Dick-Cunyngham (or was it Berney-Ficklin? They both claimed it) was on the phone to Lieutenant-Colonel J.W. Scott of the 1/5 Seaforths when he was captured. Scott was 400 yards to the east at this time, yet got away to safety.
127. Illidge was awarded the Distinguished Conduct Medal. His citation, published in the *London Gazette* on 3 September 1918, reads: 'When the enemy had broken through to the battery positions and had killed some of the teams by close-range rifle fire, he cut out the dead horses and got the guns away. Next day, under heavy shell fire, he carried two wounded men to the dressing station.

128. McFarlane lies in Vieille Chapelle Military Cemetery.
129. The intrepid Highmore finished the war having been awarded the Distinguished Conduct Medal and Bar, the Military Medal and Bar and a mention in despatches. His first DCM was for the Lys: 'For twenty-four hours he worked the regimental aid post and the front line, over roads under heavy fire, evacuating many wounded men. Was subsequently captured with a medical officer, but both escaped.' *London Gazette*, 3 September 1918. His second DCM was for his work near Cambrai in October 1918.
130. Not an easy spot for a battlefield walk, La Cornet aux Loups is now almost under the taxiway of Merville–Calonne airport.
131. IWM, 80/32/1, private papers of Geoffrey Christie-Miller.
132. Ibid.
133. IWM, P457, private papers of Alfred Thomas.
134. IWM, 83/12/1, private papers of James Wyatt.
135. The 5 Divisional artillery was still on the move, arriving in the area during the afternoon. The divisions of the Australian Corps and Canadian Corps, and the New Zealand Division, had not adopted the three-battalion brigade structure either.
136. Lieutenant-General Beauvoir de Lisle was placed in command of XV Corps at 9.00am, following the placement of John du Cane as liaison officer with Foch. Lyttelton, who was Brigade Major to 4 Guards Brigade, went to see him before going into action and described him as radiating 'courage, energy and decision, all conveyed in a rather overbearing manner'. Oliver Lyttelton, Viscount Chandos, *The memoirs of Lord Chandos*, p. 93.
137. The Guards' brigade and battalion diaries, and several books and papers, refer to Brigade HQ having been at Gars Brugghe with a Battalion HQ at Ferme Gombert. These names are disputed in a 1999 MPhil thesis (King's College, London) compiled by Geoffrey David Blades. The names may have been mixed up, with what is stated to be Gars Brugghe actually being Ferme Gombert, and Ferme Gombert being Ferme Bailleul. The point is also made that L'Epinette was a café at the end of the Arrewage lane rather than the moated farm 800 yards away.
138. IWM, 80/14/1, private papers of Frank Glover.
139. Bleu is shown on modern maps as La Bleu Tour.
140. Quoted in Captain Stair Gillon, *The Story of the 29th Division – a record of gallant deeds*, p. 189. The Victoria Cross citation appeared in the *London Gazette*, 22 May 1918.
141. Among them was Alfred Follows, who began the author's investigation into the battle.
142. IWM, 74/7/1, private papers of Victor Fagence. Second Lieutenant Frederick Russen was a former ranker, who had landed with the original contingent of 2 Queen's at Zeebrugge in October 1914. He was awarded the Military Cross for this action: 'When ordered to take a windmill with his platoon, he gained his objective with slight losses. He handled his platoon with skill and rapidity, inflicting heavy loss on the enemy, and greatly assisted his company to take the position allotted.' *London Gazette*, 16 September 1918.
143. La Belle Croix Farm lay on a lane (today an unnumbered road) that runs from Méteren to Outtersteene. Would-be battlefield tourists should not be confused by another lane, close by and of the same name, on the main D23 between Outtersteene and Bailleul.
144. Hutchinson writes graphically about swarms of men streaming down the roads in panic, and of men found dead drunk at an estaminet. His anger and outrage are apparent; whether, as he said, he struck officers who refused to turn about and stand fast, or went so far as to shoot men, as he implies, remains one of the mysteries of the Lys. Given the rest of his at-times-controversial life story, none of it would be a surprise.
145. IWM, 77/3/1-3, private papers of Walter Adolph Vignoles.

146. NA, WO158/91.
147. NA, WO161/97/68.
148. NA, WO161. This document, which records Horne's post-repatriation debriefing interview, gives his number as 206334. His medal index card gives 30661.
149. The author has identified these men as Privates 19428 George Astbury and 10459 William Savage. Both are buried in Cabaret Rouge British Cemetery, many miles away near Souchez. This cemetery was used by post-war search parties for the reinterment of bodies found scattered over a wide area of Northern France. Without names, it is not so straightforward to discover which of the 686 men of the army who died in France on 27 April are the fourteen known to have been killed by British shellfire. Only one man who died on that day lies in Cabaret Rouge. There are no military cemeteries in the village and few very close by. No identified burials of the right date are in any of them. It seems that either the fourteen were taken somewhere else or they remain to be found.
150. NA, CAB45/124, Captain John Kirkwood, D Company, 5/6 Scottish Rifles.
151. This part of the forest is also known as Aval Wood.
152. W.D. Joynt VC, *Saving the Channel Ports*, p. 78. William Joynt was awarded the Victoria Cross for his work at Plateau Wood in August 1918.
153. 1 Lancashire Fusiliers lost 9 out of 11 officers and more than 300 men on 11 April alone.
154. NA/CAB45/123, letter from Lieutenant-Colonel Gordon Gordon-Hall, GSO1 on 5 Division headquarters staff.
155. Joseph MacSwiney, who was awarded the Military Cross for his recapture of the keep, died of pneumonia on 2 November 1918.
156. NA, WO95/2929.
157. IWM, 80/32/1, private papers of Geoffrey Christie-Miller.
158. IWM, P457, private papers of Alfred Thomas.
159. From right to left the Australian battalions were nos 7, 8, 3 and 4. At dawn 6 Battalion was on its way up through the forest. The commanding officer Lieutenant-Colonel Clarence Daly was wounded by shellfire at around 5.00am and died of his injuries. He is buried in Hazebrouck Communal Cemetery.
160. On the division's extreme left, the 14 Royal Warwickshires, the old Birmingham City Battalion, had a difficult day, being attacked on several occasions.
161. IWM, 80/14/1, private papers of Frank Glover. The bedding he refers to was among material salved from an old Chinese Labour Corps camp in the forest.
162. Hocking, who was only 20 years of age, was among the many casualties suffered by his company. He is buried in Morbecque British Cemetery.
163. Harold Jacotine was born in Ceylon and had served in the Ceylon Defence Force. He has no known grave and is commemorated on the Ploegsteert Memorial. Private 16910 Eric Jacotine also served with the battalion; the author presumes them to be related.
164. *London Gazette*, 21 May 1918. Pryce, who had already won the Military Cross and Bar, has no known grave but is commemorated on the Ploegsteert Memorial. The author discovered that one of the few men to survive this action was Guardsman 24294 Allan Thornton. He was severely wounded by a bomb dropped by an RAF aeroplane shortly after being captured; one is forced to wonder whether Pryce was a victim of this same incident.
165. Maxwell Elderkin, who had already won the DCM and MM, has no known grave. He is commemorated on the Ploegsteert Memorial.
166. IWM, 74/7/1, private papers of Victor Fagence.
167. Ibid. John Dickinson was killed in action during the day. He is also commemorated on the Ploegsteert Memorial.

168. NA, CAB45/123.

169. An after-action narrative that is included with the battalion war diary (NA, WO95/2430) marks this on a sketch map as the Mairie, or town hall. Assuming that the location is accurately marked, it is not the town hall but the hospice, a large two-storey building that faces the village and sits on slightly higher ground. The town hall was in the village square facing the church, south of the Bailleul road, whereas the building shown is north of that road. The description of the building as the town hall is an error that has been perpetuated in many published works, including some that even show maps assuming the battalion's HQ was at the town hall in the square. It is perhaps possible that the hospice building was being used as a temporary town hall, thereby leading to the title given to it on the sketch map.

170. There are reports of some men of the Borderers having been in or near Neuve Eglise when the Worcestershires mounted their counter-attack.

171. Diaries and orders say Pewter Farm; maps say Feuter Farm.

172. General Gore is buried in Lijssenthoek Military Cemetery.

173. NA, WO158/60.

174. The post, held by Lance-Corporal 6142 John Schmidt, was part of Lieutenant Ivon Murdoch's platoon command. Schmidt was awarded the Military Medal for this action. Murdoch was a younger brother of Keith Murdoch, and uncle to the media mogul Rupert Murdoch.

175. Leutnant Wilhelm Lasch, *Geschichte des 3. Unterelsässischen Infanterie-Regiments Nr. 138, 1887–1919*, p. 291.

176. IWM, 74/7/1, private papers of Victor Fagence. Other records suggest the posts driven in on the left were not held by 5/6 Scottish Rifles but by the mixed XXII Corps Reinforcement Battalion.

177. IWM, 80/14/1, private papers of Frank Glover.

178. IWM, 80/32/1, private papers of Geoffrey Christie-Miller.

179. The memoirs of R.F. Ackerley, Great War Archive, University of Oxford, copyright John Ackerley (http://www.oucs.ox.ac.uk/ww1lit/gwa/document/9527). Tommy Rufus first arrived in France as a private of 21 Royal Fusiliers. Commissioned in August 1916, he was awarded a posthumous Military Cross for his action at Mont de Lille. 'His company was very heavily attacked, but the enemy were beaten off by fire. Subsequently, when out-flanked and ordered to retire, he rallied his men under a very severe machine-gun fire, displaying great coolness and a total disregard of danger, and it was entirely due to his splendid example that the enemy was held up in this vicinity for two hours.' *London Gazette*, 23 July 1918. Rufus has no known grave and is commemorated on the Ploegsteert Memorial. Second Lieutenants Norman Ward, who organised the counter-attack, and Richard Ackerley, who held on until all his platoon except one man had become casualties, were also recipients of the Military Cross for their actions on this day. Ackerley was also wounded on 16 April.

180. IWM, 77/3/1-3, private papers of Walter Adolph Vignoles. Captain Murray Patten PhD, MA, has no known grave and is commemorated on the Ploegsteert Memorial.

181. *London Gazette*, 3 October 1918. Hardman's first DCM was gazetted on 18 July 1917.

182. Anthony Johnson is buried in Kandahar Farm Cemetery near Wulverghem.

183. John Crowe was awarded the Victoria Cross for his voluntary leading of the break-out patrol that succeeded so brilliantly, *London Gazette*, 25 June 1918. Arnold Pointon was awarded the Military Cross and Gerald Stoney the Distinguished Service Order for their parts in the Worcesters' defence.

184. IWM, 88/52/1, private papers of Alexander J. Jamieson.
185. IWM, 88/56/1, private papers of H.W. House.
186. Harold Roffey is buried in Bailleul Communal Cemetery Extension. His brave and selfless act in 1911 rescued a soldier of the 2 Lancashire Fusiliers and two other men who were drowning in a 35-ft deep pool in the River Taff in Cardiff.
187. NA, CAB45/125. Sugden reported that on 16 April Sergeant 200453 Joseph Bancroft went out on patrol and recovered 56 watches from the bodies of Germans killed by fire from his battalion. Bancroft was killed in action on 4 May 1918.
188. Among the casualties was the author C.S. Lewis, then better known as Second Lieutenant Clive Staples Lewis of the 1 Somersets. He was struck by shell fragments that caused multiple wounds.
189. The rather ironic German codename for the operation was 'April Sun'.
190. Heaton Foster, 19, has no known grave and is commemorated on the Tyne Cot Memorial.
191. Fred Dawson was awarded the Military Cross for his part in the action and went on to win the DSO for his role in the tank attack in the Battle of Amiens, 8–9 August 1918 (*London Gazette*, 16 September 1918). His citation refers to 'another officer'. This was Second Lieutenant Percival Bayliss, who was not decorated. He was killed in action at Mannequin Hill on 3 October 1918.
192. AWM, item 23/1/33, Part 1.
193. *La Voix du Nord*, 10 November 1979, 'Les combats de 1918 à Méteren: un survivant témoigne'.
194. IWM, sound recording, 11581.
195. NA, CAB45/125.
196. Haig spent the day doing the rounds of his command, meeting De Lisle (who had recently taken over XV Corps from Du Cane) and Horne and finding both men quite confident, but late in the day he requested three more French divisions to relieve IX Corps.
197. South of the confluence with the Loobeek, the name of the Maartjevaart changes to St Jansbeek.
198. These attacks were undertaken by the German 214 and 35 Divisions, which soon after were taken out of the line for training. We have already seen how both were used in the earliest stages on the Lys.
199. With the new extra divisions, DAN would comprise 28, 34, 39, 133 and 154 Divisions and 2 Cavalry Corps.
200. Some miles of important railways had either been lost to the Germans or were now within shelling distance. Coal movement was also being affected by German fire on canals that had hitherto been out of range and by the inundations. On 18 April the British government offered to supply France's coal needs if local mining was halted to free the railways and release men for other work.
201. Both men were decorated, Reid with the Military Cross and Jeffrey with the Military Medal.
202. IWM, 77/3/1-3, private papers of Walter Adolph Vignoles.
203. Ibid.
204. NA, CAB45/123. The famished 1 Leicesters were pleased to find that there were enough chickens at Beaver Hall to provide one per man.
205. Adolphe Goutard, *Kemmel 1918*, p. 3.
206. James Adams is buried in Méteren Military Cemetery.
207. IWM, sound recording, 9424.
208. NA, WO95/2911. The trench-mortar teams of 55 Division had been relieved on 17 April.

209. NA, CAB45/123.
210. NA, CAB45/122.
211. John Hall was awarded the Military Cross for this action. *London Gazette*, 13 September 1918. It was one of 33 gallantry awards made to the battalion for its part in this action, including CSM Biddle.
212. Godfrey Hudson is buried in Gorre British and Indian Cemetery.
213. NA, WO95/1278.
214. Victor Batty is buried in Gonnehem British Cemetery. The register gives his name as Ernest Victor and his number, incorrectly, as 5814. He had already sustained a severe wound, ironically not so far from where he died, at Neuve Chapelle on 10 March 1915.
215. White was awarded the Distinguished Conduct Medal for his part in this action. His citation (*London Gazette*, 3 September 1918) noted his eagerness to make the attack. One wonders whether the fact that it was called White's Farm encouraged him. A machine gun taken from the enemy was presented to the city of Gloucester.
216. From private papers in the ownership of Archibald's daughter. The author has not been able to identify Second Lieutenant Ryan, whom Archibald describes as a Staff Learner. The officers who were killed by the explosion of a shell in a hut at the Scherpenberg were Lieutenant-Colonel Robert Horn (7 Seaforth Highlanders), Major Hugh Rose (RFA) and Captain Reginald Somers-Cocks (26 Brigade Major), all of whom are buried in Lijssenthoek Military Cemetery; the Reverend Charles Meister (Chaplain to 10 Argyll & Sutherland Highlanders) is buried in La Clytte Military Cemetery.
217. On 18 April Foch proposed to Haig that some British divisions could now be withdrawn from Flanders and replaced by French ones, if the British could go to quieter sectors such as the Chemin des Dames. Haig agreed but faced a War Office barrage complaining of the intermingling of formations and destruction of British army identity. So much for 'one continuous front' and the idea of a general strategic reserve, those innovative ideas of just a few weeks before.
218. NA, WO95/277.
219. Worthy of note but of no real consequence to the battle other than from a morale viewpoint was the Royal Navy's attack at Zeebrugge on 22/23 April 1918.
220. Paul Burgrave Farm was also known as Burgravehof and is on the lane that runs down from Kemmelberg in the direction of Brulooze and the Scherpenberg. It is just under a mile from the summit of Kemmelberg and a mile east of Locre. The Vijverbeek is a stream running north-east to the reservoir near Dickebusch. It is often referred to as the Kemmelbeek, by which it is fed from the south-west.
221. Peter Ingwerfen, '*Wie wir den Kemmel stuermten*', p. 28.
222. Adolphe Goutard, *Kemmel 1918*.
223. Quoted in Adolphe Goutard, *Kemmel 1918*, p. 75. *Thalweg* is an unusual term, presumably derived from the German and meaning small valley, watercourse or creek.
224. Ibid.
225. NA, CAB45/124. 'My General, Kemmel is lost.' 'My General, it is an accident, but it is not – not an accident – very grave.' It is hard to conceive of what, in this area, might be a more grave loss of ground.
226. The South African Brigade had by now been reduced to a composite battalion.
227. James Coles has no known grave but is commemorated on the Tyne Cot Memorial. He had first arrived in France in September 1914. The three officers to escape were two second lieutenants of D Company (Stanley Howard and A.D. Robinson) and the medical officer, Captain Reginald Raine RAMC.

228. Macgregor was awarded the Military Cross for his work on this day. The citation reads: 'During severe fighting, this officer with a few linesmen constantly patrolled under an intense artillery barrage and concentrated machine-gun fire, the whole length of his cable and kept up communication between brigade headquarters and the advanced report centre. Eventually, finding that the enemy had almost succeeded in isolating this place, he returned there and withdrew his men, removing such instruments, etc as could be carried and destroying the remainder. By his very gallant conduct and his devotion to duty he enabled his brigade commander to keep in touch with the rapidly changing situation, and make successful dispositions accordingly.' *London Gazette*, 13 September 1918.

229. NA, CAB45/124.

230. NA, CAB45/123. Major C. Jennings was with 25 Division HQ.

231. Quoted in Robert Blake (ed.), *The private papers of Douglas Haig 1914–1919*, p. 305.

232. Maurice Walker was awarded the Military Cross. His citation (*London Gazette*, 16 September 1918), reads: 'He assumed command of his company and men from other units, and fought his way right through the village into the open country beyond and occupied an old, dilapidated strong-point. He held this for over an hour against large numbers of the enemy, on whom he inflicted heavy casualties, and then withdrew to the remainder of the attacking force. His good leadership and coolness set a fine example to all ranks.' Walker served with the artillery in the Second World War.

233. Two of the commanding officers were killed. Lieutenant-Colonel Arthur Cade of the 1 Wiltshires has no known grave and is commemorated on the Tyne Cot Memorial; the same is true of John Stewart of the 4 South Staffords. His place was taken by Lieutenant Albert Miller, a former ranker of the Motor Machine Gun Service, who was awarded the Distinguished Service Order for his organisation and leadership on assuming command (*London Gazette*, 16 September 1918). Colonel A. Reade of the 10 Cheshires was wounded.

234. The Bluff is a man-made feature of no great height but in the very flat ground south-east of Ypres it affords good observation across to the town and over much of the salient. It had been the scene of bitter fighting in previous years; the Germans had in effect captured a graveyard.

235. 75 Brigade was supplemented by 8 Border Regiment, 105 and 106 Field Companies RE and other details, and was known as the La Clytte Defence Force.

236. Quoted in Malcolm Brown, *1918: the year of victory*, p. 95.

Sources and Bibliography

The research for this book referred to many British unit and formation war diaries, reports and correspondence principally in the WO95, WO158 and CAB45 document series held at the National Archives, and for Australian equivalents at the Australian War Memorial. Other primary sources used are referred to in the Notes. The list below outlines the core of secondary works that were consulted and found valuable.

Australian
Bean, C.E.W., *Official History of Australia in the War of 1914–1918. Volume V: The Australian Imperial Force during the main German offensive, 1918* (Sydney: Angus and Robertson, 1937)
Joynt VC, W.D., *Saving the Channel Ports: 1918 after the breach of 5th Army* (North Blackburn: Wren, 1995)

Belgian
Baert, Koen, *Kemmel 1918: hoe Ieper uit de greep van de Duitsers bleef* (Brugge: Uitgeverij de Klaproos, 2008)
Tasnier, Colonel-d'Etat-Major and van Overstraeten, Major d'Artillerie brevete d'Etat-Major, *La Belgique at la Geurre, Tome III – les Operations Militaires* (Brussels: Henri Bertels, 1926)
Verbruggen, J.F., *La bataille de Merkem* (Brussels: Musee Royale de l'Armee, 1977)

British
Addison, G.H., *Work of the Royal Engineers in the European war 1914–1919, Miscellaneous* (Chatham: W. & J. Mackay & Co., 1926)
Amery, L.S., the Rt Hon., *My political life*. Volume 2: *War and Peace 1914–1929* (London: Hutchinson, 1953)
Bewsher, F.W., *The history of the Fifty First (Highland) Division 1914–1918* (Edinburgh: Blackwood, 1921)
Brown, M., *1918: the year of victory* (London: Sidgwick & Jackson, 1998)
Buchan, John, *The history of the South African forces in France* (London: Thomas Nelson & Sons, 1920)
Edmonds, Sir James, *History of the Great War based on official documents – Military Operations France and Belgium 1918, March–April: continuation of the German offensive* (London: Macmillan, 1937)
Falls, Cyril, *The history of the 36th (Ulster) Division* (Belfast: McCaw, Stevenson & Orr, 1922)
Garwood, John M., *Chorley Pals: a short history of the Company in the Great War 1914–1919* (Manchester: Neil Richardson, 1989)
Gillon, Stair, *The story of the 29th Division* (London: T. Nelson, 1925)
Griffith, Paddy, *Battle tactics of the Western Front* (London: Yale University Press, 1994)
Griffith, Paddy (ed.), *British fighting methods in the Great War* (London: Frank Cass, 1996)

Hankey, Lord, *The Supreme Command 1914–1918, Volume 2* (London: George Allen & Unwin, 1961)

Harington, Sir Charles, *Plumer of Messines* (London: John Murray, 1935)

Jones, H.A., *History of the Great War based on official documents by direction of the Historical Section of the Committee of Imperial Defence. The War in the Air: being the story of the part played in the Great War by the Royal Air Force. Vol. IV* (Oxford: Clarendon Press, 1934)

Lyttelton, Oliver, Viscount Chandos, *The memoirs of Lord Chandos* (London: Bodley Head, 1962)

Rorie, David, *A medico's luck in the war* (Aberdeen: Milne & Hutchison, 1929)

Seton Hutchinson, Graham, *The Thirty-Third Division in France and Flanders 1915–1919* (London: Waterlow & Sons, 1921)

Seton Hutchinson, Graham, *Warrior* (London: Hutchinson & Co., 1932)

Shakespear, J., *The Thirty-Fourth Division 1915–1919* (London: Witherby, 1921)

Sheffield, Gary and Bourne, John (eds), *Douglas Haig: war diaries and letters 1914–1918* (London: Weidenfeld & Nicolson, 2005)

Whitton, F.E., *History of the 40th Division* (Aldershot: Gale & Polden, 1926)

Wyrall, Everard, *The History of the Fiftieth Division 1914–1919* (London: Percy Lund Humphries, 1939)

Zabecki, David T., *The German offensives 1918: a case study on the operational level of war* (Abingdon: Routledge, 2006)

French

Goutard, Adolphe, *Kemmel 1918* (Paris: Charles-Lavauzelle, 1930)

Grange, Baroness Ernest de la, *Open house in Flanders 1914–1918 Chateau de la Motte au Bois* (London: John Murray, 1929)

Mott, Colonel T. Bentley (transl.), *The memoirs of Marshal Foch* (London: William Heinemann, 1931)

Roquerol, Jean Gabriel Marie, *Le Kemmel, 1918* (Paris: Payot, 1936)

German

Anonymous, *Kriegsberichte aus dem Grossen Hauptquartier, No. 31 Die Schlacht von Armentières, Die Eroberung des Kemmel* (Stuttgart and Berlin: Deutsche Verlags-Anstalt, 1918)

Fehr, Otto, *Die Marzoffensive 1918 an der Westfront* (Leipzig: Kohler, nd)

Goes, Gustav, *Sturm und Sterben um einen Berg* (Berlin: Kolk, 1932)

Ingwersen, Peter, *Wie wir den Kemmel sturmten* (Langensalza: Beltz, 1937)

Jochim, Theodor, *Die vorbereitung des deutschen Heeres fur die grosse Schlacht in Frankreich in Fruhjahr 1918* (Berlin: 1927–30)

Kabish, Ernest, *Um Lys und Kemmel* (Berlin: Vorhut-Verlag, 1936)

Kuhl, Hermann von, *Der deutsche Generalstab in Vorbereitung und Durchfuhrung des Weltkrieges* (Berlin: Deutsche Verlag, 1920)

Ludendorff, Erich, *My war memories 1914–1918, Volume 2* (London: Hutchinson & Co., 1919)

Ludendorff, Erich, *The nation at war* (London: Hutchinson & Co., 1936)

Reichsarchiv, *Der Weltkrieg 1914–1918: Die militarischen Operationen zu Lande: Vierzehnter Band: Die Kriegführung an der Westfront im Jahre 1918* (Berlin: E.S. Mittler und Sohn, 1944)

Sempf, Adolf, *Der Tod am Kemmel* (Leipzig: Kurt Vieweg Verlag, 1927)

Zimmermann, Bodo, *Der Sturm bricht los!* (Berlin: Verlag v. Karl Siegismund, 1918)

Zimmermann, Bodo, *Schlag auf Schlag! Von Armentières bis zum Kemmel* (Berlin: 1918)

Newfoundland
Parsons, W. David, *Pilgrimage: a guide to the Royal Newfoundland Regiment in World War One* (St John's: Creative, 1994)

New Zealand
Officers of the New Zealand Cyclist Corps, *New Zealand Cyclist Corps in the Great War 1914–1918* (Auckland: Whitcome & Tombs, 1922)

Portuguese
Carvalho, Vasco de A., *2a Divisao Portuguesa na batalha do Lys, 9 de Abril de 1918* (Lisbon: Lusitania Editoria, 1924)
Costa, Gomes da, *O Corpo Exercito Portugues na Grande Guerra: a batalha do Lys; 9 de Abril de 1918* (Porto: Renascenca Portuguesa, 1920)
Fraga, Luís Alves, *Guerra e marginalidade* (Lisbon: Prefácio, 2003)
Henriques, Mendo Castro and Leitao, Antonio Rosas, *La Lys 1918: Os Soldados Desconhecidos* (Lisbon: Prefacia – Edicao de Livros e Resvistas, Lda, 2001)

United States
American Expeditionary Forces General Staff, G-2, *Histories of Two Hundred and Fifty One Divisions of the German Army which participated in the war* (Washington: GPO, 1920)

Index

Infantry Units: MarineKorps Flandern, 150, 152; 2 Bavarian Jaeger Reserve, 172–3; 3 Lieb Regt, 172; 10 Bavarian Jaeger, 172; 31 Landwehr, 152; 68 Regt, 100; 78 Regt, 174; 84 Landwehr, 152; 88 Regt, 171, 174; 96 Regt, 146; 103 Regt, 152; 106 Regt, 152; 138 Regt, 131; 141 Regt, 131; 360 Regt, 37, 41; 362 Regt, 37; 370 Regt, 56

Portuguese Army Forces: CAPI, 26; CEP, 26, 29, 32, 34; 2 Div., 27, 46, 84; 3 Bde, 28, 29, 53; 4 (do Minho) Bde, 28, 34, 46, 47, 48; 5 Bde, 28, 34; 6 Bde, 28, 34; 1 Bn, 34; 2 Bn, 34; 3 Bn, 34; 4 Bn, 32; 8 Bn, 34; 10 Bn, 32; 11 Bn, 34; 13 Bn, 32, 53; 15 Bn, 53; 17 Bn, 34; 20 Bn, 34; 29 Bn, 34; 2 Group Artillery, 34; 6 Group Artillery, 34